Water Carried Uphill:

A Sense of Place and Past

Carol Mallman Raynor

2007

Water Carried Uphill:
A Sense of Place and Past

Cover Design by Roseanne Huck
Edited by Jane Bartlett and Mary Lou Porter

Credit Notes

ISBN 978-1-59872-914-6

Published in the U.S. by Instantpublisher.com

Dedicated to the congregation of
First United Methodist Church
Past, Present and Future
225 East Arrow
Marshall, Missouri

Contents

Assorted Memories

Foreword

Twenty years as a psychiatric nurse therapist have left me with an addiction to listening to stories of people's lives. When Ed Richards began collecting material for a history of Marshall First United Methodist Church, it was my job to talk with long-time members. Very few had grown up in the church; however, everyone with whom I talked shared fascinating accounts of their youth, other communities and times past.

Over the next eighteen months, I began to collect stories by first contacting church members who were eighty and older. Some declined the opportunity. A few contributions are from friends or companions of church members in the same care facility. Additional names were added at the suggestion of others.

The more than one hundred interviews herein are predominantly of people born before 1940. Each interview takes its own unique direction even though the same questions were asked. Names of children and grandchildren have generally been omitted unless they entered directly into the story. In a second session, the person interviewed reviewed what was written; and finally, the edited material was mailed to the participants for their approval.

The word "ladies" at the present time appears to denote rigid gender roles; however, the women interviewed here were raised with a philosophy of grace and gentility implied by "being a lady." Substituting any other word for "lady" would seem to be a lack of respect for this generation.

I was inspired for the project by the book, *If I Live to be a Hundred* by Neena Ellis, who interviewed a series of centenarians for National Public Radio. In addition, sections of *The Fountain of Age*, a 1993 book by Betty Friedan, sparked my interest in conveying the hearts and souls of our older church members. Friedan, founder of the Feminist Movement, pointed out that patronizing attitudes toward the aged rob them of their individuality, just as gender ideology locks women into roles.

Before Friedan's death in 2006, she was working on issues of the elderly and theorized that one reason for the decline and despair that can occur at the last of life is because older people are not taken seriously by those around them.

Midway through the venture, I read *The Greatest Generation.* Tom Brokaw showed enormous respect for those born in the first decades of the century who lived through the chaos of the Great Depression and World War II. Likewise, I felt a sense of awe when I heard similar accounts.

In the final stages of the editing process, I happened to see Bill Tammeus' weekly column in *The Kansas City Star* February 24, 2007, "A Familiar Place for Hungry Hearts." Over and over again, the people whom I interviewed spoke of places—one-room country schools, small towns that no longer exist, childhood churches—anchors of strength and faith as Tammeus suggests. These stories are a monument to communities which have been major influences in lives for decades.

I have laughed and I have grieved with these individuals whom I have come to regard as close friends. Their resilience springs, I believe, from their personal faith. The boundaries of my life have expanded; and at moments, it seemed I could reach out and touch the history of Mid-Missouri and the reality of the first half of the twentieth century.

I am deeply appreciative for being allowed to share pieces of the persons' lives recorded here. I hope readers will agree with Mary Lou Porter who said after editing many interviews, "I will never again look at these people in the same way."

Just as I have been inspired by the writing of Neenah Ellis, I hope others will be inspired by the stories included here.

Asking questions and listening thoughtfully elicits history, shares wisdom and spurs new relationships among generations. Churches, families and other groups could enhance life for older people by initiating a collection of similar stories.

Special thanks to Jane Bartlett who has spent countless hours poring over the manuscript. Roseanne Huck gave me invaluable advice as well as designing the cover and helping with photographs. Without the support and encouragement of Mary Lou, Jane and Roseanne, I would have foundered. Also thanks to Joyce Garrison, Melissa Spitzig and Betty Stone for assistance.

To my daughters Kitty, Carrie, Sarah and Susanne and to their husbands--thank you for your continuing interest in the project and for your computer advice, and always—my appreciation to my loyal husband, Richard.

Carol Raynor

c.raynor@sbcglobal.net

Great Dogs and Goose Liver!
Paul Ahrens   November 2005

Along with his parents, Mary Golden Phelps Ahrens and Carl Otto Ahrens, Paul Ahrens attended two or three different churches in Bland and Bell when growing up in South Missouri. He remembers a group of teen-agers from the congregation would gather for picnics on Sunday afternoons. One family had five boys who could play anything with strings and everyone would sing.

Paul moved to Mid-Missouri when he was 18, and most of his life work has centered around farming. Planting and harvesting with horses and mules that he had often broken himself, he was thrown a few times but never seriously injured. His favorite horse, Dawn, was so gentle that he could catch her without any trouble in a 100 acre pasture.

Paul and his first wife, May Wright Ahrens, lived in the Miami, Missouri, area and attended Mount Carmel Methodist Church. Their thirty-year marriage ended with May's death, and three years later he married Virginia Fox. Paul has always had a special feeling for Reverend Chris Oetting who performed their wedding ceremony. As a member of the church, Paul's contribution for many years was to oversee the general maintenance of the church van.

In the late sixties, Dr. Bill Hayden, a local veterinarian asked Paul if he could build a rock retaining wall behind his A-frame house near the public golf course. "Doc couldn't find anyone who would tackle the job. Nobody knew how—and didn't want to learn how either." Paul said. "I just lathered on the mortar and put it together like a puzzle." Dr. Hayden was so pleased with the results that he paid Paul more than promised for the work. . . eight dollars an hour as he recalls.

Paul's sense of humor emerges as we visit. As he was born in 1917, I asked why he thinks he has lived so long. When he did not respond, I said, "Some people say 'just good, clean living.' Do you think you have just lived right?"

"Part of the time," he said with a quiet laugh.

Paul said he sits every day with five men in the dining room at Mar-Saline Manor. "Sometimes they have a good laugh over some of the expressions I use like, "Great dogs and goose liver!" Paul thinks it would be hard to live a long life without a good sense of humor.

You Won't Know If You Can Do It, If You Don't Try
Virginia Ahrens   May 2006

Virginia Ahrens was born in Flint, Michigan, in 1923. She was the oldest of five children in a fun-loving household. Her dad, Uel Chasteen, would lie on the floor and shout, "Pile sacks," and all the children would stack themselves on him, and he would throw them off to their delight. She remembers her dad spending a lot of time with the children.

Uel Chasteen went to Flint to work in the first Buick plant when his parents would not let him enlist for World War I. Unlike farmers who worked from sun-up to sun-down, Virginia's father got home about 5:30 p.m. and spent the evenings playing with his kids. Likewise, her mother, Hazel Burns Chasteen, was deeply involved with the children.

In the summer, they all went swimming at Long Lake. The family had about two dozen apple trees; they picked apples together and sold them.   The Chasteen children thought this was great fun, too.

Virginia started first grade in Fenton, Michigan, in a modern school with separate grades for each class. She remembers the Maypole Dance in the spring. Every child held a ribbon and marched to music, weaving the ribbons in and out until they covered the pole.

Imagine Virginia's shock when after the fourth grade, she transferred to Blackjack School in South Missouri with all eight grades in one room. She walked one and a half miles each direction. Her 27 year old teacher, Miss Hardwood, had her hands full with these pupils; one eighth grader was 16 years old.

"There was lots of monkey business," says Virginia. "Outdoor toilets and a water pail in back of the room. One boy was assigned to keep the pail full from the well. We all drank from the same dipper!"

With the onset of the Great Depression, the Buick plant in Flint closed; consequently, the family moved to the farm near Dora, Missouri. Originally from South Missouri, her father took his savings, bought 165 acres of farmland complete with a house, furnishings and livestock for the Chasteen famiy. "However, I was a happy kid—I have had a happy life, some bumps in the road...but mostly a happy life." said Virginia.

Virginia's mother was a fine seamstress and a good manager, making everything for her four daughters. Her sons had overalls made from Mr. Chasteen's old ones. An aunt sent boxes of her old clothes to the children. "It was like Christmas. My mother could make over anything to fit us, and we were thrilled." Flour sacks and feed sacks were material for underwear and night clothes. Virginia made her first dress in 4-H at age ten, taught by her mother.

Virginia rode a bus 16 miles to the high school in Dora, Missouri. The school had four classrooms. The superintendent of schools, R.O. Edmonds, was one of the teachers, and his wife was the principal. The high school had recesses which provided physical education; the students played baseball and basketball.

Virginia married her high school sweetheart, J. Leslie Fox, in 1941. They were married at 6:00 p.m. in the Chasteen farmhouse and drove to Springfield to a one-room apartment so that Leslie could go to summer school at Southeast Missouri State College in order to teach school the next fall. The apartment had two chairs, a table and a two-burner hot plate.

"I didn't know a hot plate from a hole in the ground," she says. "The first meal I cooked was fried potatoes, and I burned them!" Rent for the summer was $60. The summer education prepared Leslie for a job teaching in a one room school with 20 pupils near West Plains, Missouri.

Virginia learned to do laundry in the washtub on the back porch, and manage a three room household with an outhouse.

During the war, Leslie worked in a defense plant in St. Louis for two years; defense plant operations were secret, and people did not talk about what kind of work was done.

After nine years of teaching, Leslie decided to go into the ministry. He went to Missouri Valley College, and to Garret Theological Seminary in Evanston, Illinois. "Being a pastor's wife was interesting, not at all boring." Virginia said.

"Didn't congregations expect you to do many different jobs just because you were the preacher's wife?" I asked.

"I never resented it," she replied, "I got to do things and learn things that I might not have otherwise." For five generations in her family, someone has been a Methodist minister, and it seemed natural to her for her husband to go into the ministry.

"I don't remember ever not going to church; I can remember my dad carrying me around in church." She started singing vocal solos at age eight and continued throughout her adult life.

Virginia appreciated the sewing lessons of her youth; her four children wore many home-sewn garments. "I could make a pair of boxer shorts in 45 minutes. All my life, I have mended, shortened and lengthened garments. Once I made a sealskin cape for myself." Virginia always wears stylish tailored suits and nice hats on Sundays. "I was taught that you dress your best for church," she said.

Leslie and Virginia Fox were assigned to Miami and Mount Carmel Methodist Churches in Saline County. She remembers singing vocal solos accompanied by Helen Louise Weber, the church pianist. "I would go to her house to practice—Helen Louise just felt like kin folks!"

Virginia and Leslie were good friends with Paul and Mae Ahrens, and their families often made homemade ice cream and played cards on Saturday night. "Leslie and Paul pitched horseshoes, and the children enjoyed playing together."

9

Methodist ministers move on. Virginia enjoyed moving and meeting new people. "If you care about others, and if you are really interested, you are going to absorb quite a bit from every experience that you have. I loved the experience of a mission trip to Anchorage, Alaska, with a group of 23 people, primarily high school students."

Virginia loved learning and did a lot of reading and occasionally took a college course. "Every church is a challenge, completely different, a different atmosphere, a different feeling about each one."

The time came when Leslie and Virginia went their separate ways. If Virginia gave out advice, she would say: "Sometimes life is a rocky road. Bad things happen. If you don't turn it loose, you can't live a good healthy, normal life." For several years Virginia was in charge of housekeeping at Bethany Retirement Home, a United Methodist facility. "Living in Chicago was interesting," she said.

Years passed. Her daughter, Lydia Gober, had a new baby, and sent a birth announcement to Richie Ahrens Carson who showed it to her father, Paul Ahrens, who was widowed at this point. When he found out she was in Chicago, Paul called her and said, "Guess who this is?" Paul and Virginia have now been married for 30 years. She recently joined him at Mar-Saline Manor, and it is obvious that they appreciate being together.

Virginia has written about her life for her family. She has painted portraits of family members. "I could get started with oil and canvas and paint until 3:00 a.m.," she said.

I remarked that she has tackled a variety of things with confidence. "Well, I guess my motto would be 'You won't know if you can do it, if you don't try.'"

Many Brothers and Sisters

Bonnie and Bill Boedeker   December 2006

Rays of sunshine bounce off snowdrifts, and warmth radiates through the windows of the sunroom of the Boedeker home. Bill, Bonnie and I visit beside the wrapped presents and the Christmas tree. Between the two of them, they have an enormous number of Mid-Missouri relatives.

Bonnie Chevalier Plattner Boedeker is the next to youngest of nine children reared in the Malta Bend bottoms between the Missouri River and Van Meter State Park. Bill is next to oldest of nine boys and a girl born to Fred and Freda Starkey Boedeker near the borders of Lafayette and Saline Counties. Bill's mother once received a certificate for having the most children to graduate from Malta Bend High School.

Four of Bonnie's brothers were in World War II; one was missing in action, a prisoner of war, but all returned safely. Six Boedeker men are veterans, and two others served in the National Guard. Bonnie and Bill speak of the pleasure of having so many brothers, sisters, nieces and nephews.

Bonnie, born in 1935, went to Van Meter Grade School. "We walked to school; the roads in the isolated area where we lived were gumbo, a silty soil of the Missouri River bottoms that makes sticky mud balls on your feet. My brother and I often carried kindling with us as we walked, because we were the ones who got the coal fires burning to warm the school. After school we stayed to sweep and dust.

"When I went to Malta Bend High School, the bus would pick us up on Weaver Hill, where Jim and Joyce Weaver live now—it was six or seven miles from our home. If the weather got bad, I stayed with friends in town because the roads were impassable."

Bonnie and her family went to church in Van Meter School on Sundays, a Baptist congregation. She was baptized as a member of her rural congregation in the baptismal font of First Baptist Church in Marshall. "My mother told stories of baptisms held in the Missouri River," she said. When she was older, she went to the Malta Bend Methodist Church and was a member of the youth group there.

Bonnie's great-grandfather, Francois Chevalier, came from France to Missouri through the port of New Orleans. He described wearing his overcoat the entire eight day journey on ship. Francois made several trips to the States before settling in Saline County. Missourians pronounced his name "shiv-ah-leer" instead of the French "she-val-yay." Bonnie's many relatives retain that pronunciation.

As a young married woman, Bonnie bought a retail business from Marie Barnhill and opened a children's store, Bonnie's Town Shop, on the east side of the Marshall Square at 76 North Jefferson. Later she acquired Gilkey's Children's Clothing Store and moved her women's and children's clothing store to the north side of the square near the present Wood and Huston Bank building. Coachlight, as it was renamed, operated at that site for a number of years before Bonnie sold it to C.W. Flowers, a department store from Sedalia.

"I loved retail. I remember my first buying trip in 1961 to Chicago. I went with my aunt who was an experienced buyer of women's hats. We got on the train at Carrollton and went to a huge market at the Palmer Hotel. I was stocking bell-bottom pants and mini-skirts. On our return trip, the train hit a truck at a crossing. No one was hurt, but it was an exciting trip."

Ten years later, when she was divorced, she and her three daughters lived away from Marshall for a time. Bonnie operated restaurants in the food service business.

In 1974, she moved back to Marshall and renewed her acquaintance with Bill Boedeker, a widower who lived in her apartment building. She had known Bill and his first wife, Mary Hayslip Boedeker. Bill and Bonnie were later married.

Bill was born in 1922; the Boedeker family lived at several locations near the Lafayette-Saline County border. He recalls his parents would give $1.50 to him and his brother, Fred, when they were in high school; and they could buy gas, drive to Marshall, eat 15 cent hamburgers at The Spot, a restaurant on North Street, and go to the movies with the money.

The Boedekers were members of the Salem United Church of Christ. His baptism certificate from the Evangelical Church is written in German as there were many families of German heritage in the community at that time.

When Bill was a senior in high school, he was cutting fence posts in a hedgerow, and a metal piece of the sledgehammer broke loose and flew into his left eye. He was rushed to the hospital in Boonville for treatment, but he lost the eye.

"Hasn't that been a big handicap to you, only having one eye?" I asked.

"It probably saved my life. I was 2B during World War II instead of 1A, so I did not serve in a combat area." Bill was in an artillery unit, nevertheless. "I was shipped out to Pusan, Korea, and when we stopped for a lay-over in Hawaii, I unexpectedly ran into my brother, Fred. Bill spent 12 months in the Asiatic-Pacific Theater. "A lot more of us would have been killed if President Truman had not dropped the atomic bomb on Japan," he said.

After the war, Bill farmed with his father until he started working with Dekalb Seeds in Marshall. He had been married for 24 years when his wife died with cancer in 1971. He and Mary raised a niece, Becky Hayslip Hudson, whose mother died while her father was in the Navy overseas.

13

For many years, Bill spent six months of each year in Homestead, Florida, as production manager for the seed corn raised there for Dekalb. It was his responsibility to see that it was planted right, that the pollination process went well and that it was harvested, sorted and returned to Missouri.

In April 2006, Bill and Bonnie were in a major car accident on I-70. "It is a miracle we survived," said Bonnie who suffered serious injuries. "When we hit that semi-truck trailer, God must have taken hold of the wheel and saved us." Their adult children and extended family and their faith have helped them regain their health.

Both speak of the sadness of losing brothers and sisters. "Even the youngest is not young anymore," said Bonnie. "Life goes by so fast; it is important to find something that you really enjoy doing and make the most of every moment."

Memories of Mount Carmel
Martha Parks Brown   February 2006

Martha Parks Brown lives in a room near her sister, Mary Ruth Hanna, at Westport Estates. She does not have a good memory for many things and depends on Mary Ruth to keep her straight about details. However, she spoke fondly of memories of her parents, George and Lena Parks.

"They would stand in the door of the porch back of the kitchen and look out over their farm. We never heard them fuss," she recalled, "and they never talked about money in our presence, so we never knew when times were hard."

Martha and her husband, Edwin, lived in the Miami community and raised their children, George and Ann, in Mount Carmel Methodist Church. She and Mary Ruth have fond memories of that congregation: I.G. and Nina Dyer and their sons, Anna Mary and Harold Harvey and their sons, Louis and Helen Louise Weber and their son.

We laughed as we talked about Helen Louise and the way she entertained groups wearing formal dresses and singing, "Frankie and Johnnie", and "Won't You Come Home, Bill Bailey?" Martha said, "Helen Louise was a lot of fun." Mary Ruth said that Nelson Weber bought the Parks' farm when it was sold, and he takes care of the farm business on the Hanna and Brown properties for them at the present time.

Martha and Mary Ruth are ladies with style and taste; one never sees them when they are not nicely dressed and well groomed. It is heartwarming to see two sisters whose bonds have remained in their older years.

It is an Honor

Ann Adair Burge   February 2006

Ann Adair Burge, a member of First Christian Church in Marshall, lives on the corridor with several of her Methodist friends at Westport Estates assisted living facility. Born in 1911, Ann grew up in a large family on a country road east of Hardeman, Missouri, known as "Stringtown Road."

Edgar Lee Fenwick and Lena Mallman Fenwick, her parents, had ten children, seven girls and three boys. Ann was one of the middle children, and is the only one surviving. The three Fenwick sons died in mid-life from heart problems, but the seven sisters lived long lives and remained close friends throughout their lives.

As I enter her neat and tidy room, filled with some of her lifetime treasures, I catch a waft of perfume. Ann seems to always be stylishly dressed and well groomed. As her first cousin, Josephine Wiegers, says, "Those Fenwick girls were always 'fixy'."

"Our aunt and uncle, William and Lou Mallman, lived right across the field from us," Ann said. "We played with my four first cousins, and there were enough of us to play baseball! We also loved to play croquet. A creek ran between the two farms; sometimes the water would be high, and we would make our horses swim across it.

"Aunt Lou would drive us to the Hardeman Community Church as our mother didn't drive. We always had a car; I remember a Hudson that had the gears on the outside!

"Devere Gregory was our Sunday School teacher and he would take us on trips just to go out for drives. I remember several cars of kids went to Sedalia once, and we stopped to eat along the way. Devere said to us when we went into the café, 'Move along now, don't string out like a bunch of green beans.'"

Ann and her brothers and sisters went to Hardeman School which had two years of high school; then their dad paid tuition for them to go to Napton High School. "I hated horseback riding, but that's how we got to school," she said. Three of the Fenwick children went to Marshall High School; when the roads improved, school buses picked up kids to take them into town.

"It must have been hard for your father to come up with the money for tuition for so many children," I commented.

"I expect so, my parents never talked about money. We always had what we needed." Ten kids made for a full house. She recalls they had folding beds set up at night in the dining room and kitchen. The living room had nice furniture and was used as a sitting room only.

The Fenwicks milked cows, butchered hogs and had a big garden. Like many farm families, they never butchered beef as it was worth much more sold on the market. Ann remembers her mother baking bread for the family, and on the back porch was an ice box which held 100 pounds of ice to keep food cold.

Ann recalls that as a young man, one of her brothers, Bill, and his cousin, Leeper Mallman, decided to drive a Model T Ford to North Dakota to get jobs harvesting the wheat. Roads were dirt and poorly marked; they did not have good directions, and they got lost on the way. After camping out for several days, they reached their destination and worked for a dollar a day, good wages for the times.

After graduating from high school, Ann went to Boonville, Missouri, and managed a Wards order office there. She married Roy Adair who was a mechanic. Eventually they bought a farm near Blackwater and saved enough to get machinery; they moved to Blackwater and became full time farmers. Ann was 42 years old when her daughter Karen was born. Now at age 95, she enjoys having a college age grandson.

18

Ann remembers that during the Depression years, trucks would come by in the rural areas selling food, watermelon and cantaloupe from the Miami bottoms and fish caught from the Missouri River. Also the "Watkins man" went house to house selling vanilla and spices from his truck. Most rural families raised everything they needed in order to have to purchase as little as possible.

Roy and Ann were part of the Blackwater community for many years, belonging to the Blackwater Federated Church. When Roy died, he and Ann had been married 40 years. She was a widow for many years and then married Paul Burge, also a widower, since the death of his wife, Edith Burge. Ann and Paul attended the United Church of Christ in Arrow Rock. Before his death six years ago, the Burges had been married for ten years.

Ann says when she looks back, she has great respect for her parents. "They raised seven daughters who finished school, married well and lived good lives. It is an honor to raise seven girls and three sons and have them turn out well. Then, too, the Fenwick great-grandchildren and great-great grandchildren are successful adults, many of them business and professional people...it is an honor."

Each Day is a Gift

Evelyn and Arnold Burns   January 2007

"I wanted to be a minister when I was six years old and in the first grade," Reverend Arnold Burns said with a smile. "I was a farm boy, and the most educated people I ever saw were in the pulpit on Sunday morning."

Arnold, 97, and his wife, Evelyn, 92, sit together holding hands on the sofa in their suite of rooms at Shirkey Leisure Acres care facility in Richmond, Missouri.

Arnold was born in the country southwest of Cowgill, Missouri, in Caldwell County, "in the middle of three sisters." In the years following his birth in 1910, William T. Burns and Hattie Richardson Burns, his parents, lived in a four-room house. "The girls had one bedroom, my parents had the other, and I slept on the sofa.

"Mostly, as a kid, I remember working. We did play horseshoes now and then. My sister, Maude, was 14 months younger, and she and I were the garden team! We hoed down one row and up the other. I was not very old when I started driving the team of horses to harrow the ground before planting corn. I was in charge of re-planting the rows where corn did not come up—by hand, using a garden hoe.

"Another job for a kid was working on the hay wagon. My dad would pitch the loose hay up on the wagon, and I would put plenty of hay in the middle of the load. The hay lapped over the edges of the wagon-bed, and it was tied to take it to the barn. A harpoon fork, powered by horses, lifted the loose hay up into the loft for storage."

Arnold was kept at home until Maude was old enough to start school; he was six years old and she was five. The two went through twelve years of school together.

"She was competition, too; she was a good student! She was chubby; I was skinny and short, we were a pair. We walked one and one-fourth miles to grade school, and we rode horses five miles to Cowgill High School. I rode "Old Blackie" without a saddle, and we slid around in the mud! Sometimes we took a horse and buggy to school.

"When I was 12 or 13, my dad got a used Model T Ford. Dad learned to drive, but I knew lots more about that car than he did, and I had to show him how to do things!"

Arnold entered oratorical contests in high school. He had to learn how to speak because he intended to be a minister; he never thought of doing anything else.

Arnold worked his way through Central Methodist College in Fayette by mowing lawns. "I ran the wheels off those lawnmowers! I was the motor, of course." Quite literally, he ran the wheels off because the bolts would come loose, and the wheels would have to be repaired.

"I came up the hard way," Arnold said. "I didn't go to seminary. I took a conference course of study. It took me eight years to complete the four-year correspondence course. I didn't have a typewriter, and all the work was handwritten."

After dating Mildred Jones for four years and a marriage of four years, Mildred died from complications of childbirth when their son, Ralph, was born. "I just took things as they came. You put it all in the Lord's hands," Arnold said. Mildred's parents, John and Belle Jones, cared for the baby; Arnold's older sister, Grace May Burns, moved in with him and kept house for him while he served his circuit of four churches.

Little Ralph was three years old when Arnold married Evelyn Huffine, a first grade teacher at Sweet Springs, Missouri. They had been acquainted at Central Methodist. "A friend told me about Evelyn," Arnold said. "I knew she was a fine girl and a P.K., "Preacher's Kid," so she would know what the life is like."

"It about broke his grandparents' hearts when we took Ralph to live with us," interjected Evelyn.

Evelyn was the youngest of seven children born to Reverend Herman D. Huffine and Virginia Collins Huffine. When she was in the eighth grade in Warsaw, Missouri, Reverend Huffine had a stroke and died at age 48. Her mother was left with five teenagers at home.

"My dad died in January, and the congregation let us stay in the parsonage until school was out," she said.

The Huffines moved to Fayette; it was the dream of the parents to send each of the children to Central Methodist for two years, then they could get jobs to finish their college education. Reverend Huffine left a $5000 bond for their education, and their dream was fulfilled.

"I loved being a P.K.," said Evelyn, "People were so nice to us, and I loved church activities." Evelyn graduated from Fayette High School in 1933, attended Central Methodist for two years, and then started teaching school. She went to summer sessions for eight years at Central Missouri State Teachers College, now Central Missouri University, and finished her degree in education.

The Burns family moved often as Methodists ministers do. A daughter, Elaine, was born. Arnold worked up to having one church instead of having a circuit of churches, miles apart. "My longest charge was 15 years at White Avenue United Methodist Church in Kansas City. When I retired, I was Minister of Visitation for a few years at the Marshall Church."

"Honey, it was 15 years. . .1976 to 1991." said Evelyn, consulting a written record on the table.

"That's right, 15 years—100 calls a month. I loved those people, shut-ins who couldn't get out." Arnold reminisced, "Evelyn has been a good preacher's wife, a good cook, just a good girl. We moved and moved, and she never griped about it."

"That is nice to hear," said Evelyn. "It has been a long time since you have said something like that."

Evelyn enjoyed the Marshall years as her sister, Helen Weeks, and her family lived in the community, and they had good times together. Both Arnold and Evelyn express pride in their niece, Kathy Weeks Thompson, who is now one of the parish visitors to the elderly for First United Methodist Church.

Arnold and Evelyn Burns have lived a life close to the Lord. A plaque hanging on their wall sums it up, "Each Day is a Gift from God."

An Angel on My Shoulder
Evelyn Woirhaye Campbell   May 2006

I sat at the kitchen table with Evelyn Campbell while two black cats, "Sissy" and "Blackie" watched us closely. "They miss Ervin," Evelyn said. Within the last month her husband has moved to Highland Court Residential Home because of increasing forgetfulness and confusion. While it is hard for Evelyn to get used to living alone on Briarwood Street after more than 65 years of marriage, she firmly believes she can adjust.

"I always say that I have a little angel on my shoulder, and the Good Man Upstairs takes care of me." She has had multiple health problems herself over the years, but at present she is "holding her own."

Evelyn was born in 1922 at home on the farm near Lucas, Missouri. This attractive gray-haired lady speaks with a soft, Southern Missouri accent, and I sometimes have to ask her to spell a word because it seems to me to have more syllables than usual.

Her parents, James and Elsie Ewing Woirhaye, worked hard to make a living. Most of her childhood was during the Depression years. "I suppose my sister and I did play together, but mostly I remember work. I was Daddy's boy doing the farm work and she helped in the house."

Evelyn remembers beginning to work driving the team of workhorses when she was nine years old and weighed not more than 80 pounds. One day she was harrowing when she saw a black snake and turned too quickly. The harrow flipped up on the horses! "I got it down before I went to tell my dad!" she said.

24

"I was raised poor, but we were not alone. In the thirties, no one had much. We always had enough to eat. If we ran short, we had fish from Big Creek near our home."

Mr. Woirhaye was a strict father, but he believed you should learn from your mistakes. Because Evelyn was such a young farm helper, she made a few. She was 11 or 12 when her father got their first tractor, and she ran it into the corner of the house trying to learn to drive it.

"We always had a car, some old wreck," she said. "The roads were terribly muddy. One day I was driving, and the ruts must have been a foot deep. The car jumped a rut, and I ditched it! Daddy got it out with the tractor, and then he just said, 'You get it home.'"

The Christian Church has always been an important part of Evelyn's life. She loved going to church in Urich, Missouri. But the roads were often so bad that the Woirhaye family could not get there. She remembers picnics in the summer and basket dinners.

Evelyn walked the half mile between her home and the one room Cornett School. She remembers math contests in which the pupils stood at the blackboard and were given a problem. The one who solved it the fastest was the winner, and it was often Evelyn. She changed schools when the Woirhayes moved to a different farm.

Evelyn attended Urich High School walking three and a half miles each direction by herself her freshman year. During the rest of her high school years, her father drove a school bus, and she could ride.

When she was a sophomore, Ervin Campbell asked her to the junior-senior prom. "Ervin would tell you that I had to milk eight cows before I could go out on a date," she said. After graduation, she wanted to go to beauty school, but there was no money for any further education.

Evelyn and Ervin were married on her birthday, December 4, 1940, in Deepwater, Missouri. Her father said, "You will always be in deep water."

"And I guess it is so," she said with a smile. They moved to Clinton. Ervin got a job trucking fruits and vegetables from farmers' markets. For sometime he hauled coal to Kansas City; sometimes Evelyn helped him drive. Then he got a job with the MK & T Railroad.

Ervin was drafted and left Clinton along with five busloads of men. Some had families with five kids, and Evelyn was pregnant. Their daughter, Carolyn Diehm, was born in Fort Leavenworth where he was stationed for 14 months. When Carolyn was nine months old, Ervin was shipped out to the Philippines and Japan from Tacoma, Washington.

Evelyn and her baby daughter went back to stay with her parents on the farm. The day that Ervin left, his father died. He did not learn of his father's death for three months. Ervin was a non-commissioned officer in charge of a medical unit by the end of the war.

After the war, Ervin went back to Clinton to work for MK&T Railroad again; eventually the family moved to El Dorado Springs where they lived for 37 years. Evelyn always had a job in a restaurant or a factory, but after Carolyn graduated from high school, Evelyn fulfilled her earlier dream, and went to beauty school in Springfield.

For twenty years she had her own shop and when she retired, she had three employees. In 1961, the railroad disbanded, and Ervin worked until retirement for KAMO Electric Company.

The Campbells enjoyed many retirement years. They took care of their elderly parents but were able to travel extensively in their recreational vehicle, wintering in Brownsville, Texas. The two of them worked together on woodworking projects which they took to craft fairs.

Evelyn and Ervin made a wooden rocking horse for their grandchildren, which stands two and one half feet high with a realistic mane, tail and saddle. Another heirloom toy made by the Campbells is a large Noah's Ark with pairs of wooden animals.

Evelyn and Ervin have been regular in attendance at First United Methodist Church since they moved to Marshall in 1988. For the past four years, they have stayed close to home because of health concerns.

Evelyn says, "Every night I pray to God to see me through the next day. If you give up, you won't make it. God helps your mind prevail over your body."

Master Sergeant Ervin Campbell,
Evelyn Woirhaye Campbell, and
Carolyn, one month old in 1942.

Not Your Regular Grandma

Amy Carey   February 2007

Amy Carey, a member of Macon United Methodist Church, has been a frequent visitor to First United Methodist since 1949 when she and her family would come to Marshall to visit old friends, Margaret and Ronald Hackler. Suzann Carey and Richard Hackler would find teen-age activities while the Careys waited for Hackler's Shoe Store to close at 8:00 p.m. on Saturday night.

Little Mary Lou would amuse herself by looking at her feet in the store x-ray machine which magically showed where the bones of the toes were in relation to the shoes. After closing, the two families would have hamburgers at the Hackler home, and they would attend First United Methodist Church on Sunday morning.

Years later, Mary Lou Carey Porter attended Missouri Valley College, and she and Ronnie Porter became permanent Marshall residents and members of the church. Thus, Amy has been a friend and associate of the church for almost 58 years.

After a broken hip and wrist from a fall before Thanksgiving, Amy has found it increasingly difficult to get around. In January, she moved into Westport Estates in order for Mary Lou to have closer contact with her. "I believe it has been one of the hardest things I have ever had to do," she said. "Leaving my lovely home and all my friends in Macon."

Amy, petite and attractive, wears a stylish bead necklace, a gift to her from her friends at a special luncheon in her honor in Macon last week.   The chest of drawers is covered with greeting cards with handwritten messages mailed to her from friends and neighbors since her move. Amy played cards with three bridge clubs and maintained an active life.

The "Anti-Rust" club was one of Amy's activities in Macon. Organized in the 1880s, Anti-Rust is the oldest non-federated women's group west of the Mississippi. Determined to keep their minds from getting stale, group members choose a theme for each year and have speakers, programs and entertainments. One year, the theme was "Missouri Authors," and Amy's daughter, Mary Lou, an English teacher, presented an overview of Mark Twain's work.

Amy's father, Guy Norton, would have been especially pleased to know that his granddaughter was a Mark Twain fan. Amy remembers bringing home a copy of *Huckleberry Finn* when she was in grade school. "Dad loved to read and when he got hold of that book, none of the rest of us had a chance at it. He read it aloud dramatically."

Amy rode Topsy, her pony, to Centerville School. She regretted that the library had few books. "We maybe got one new book a year. I remember *Little Women* and *The Five Little Peppers and How They Grew*. I loved to read. I got so desperate for books to read that once I read the stories of ancient gods and goddesses." In later years when she was traveling in Greece, she remembered the mythology book.

Before she finished at Centerville School, the teachers began to combine teaching two grades in one year, three, five, and seven one year and four, six, and eight the next. Born in 1914, she was able to master eighth grade work, so she was ready for high school at age 12. Her strict mother, Belle Morris Norton, did not want her little girl to start Macon High School early, but Amy really wanted to move on.

"More books at the high school library," she said; her father supported her promotion. As the Nortons lived ten miles from town, it meant that Amy boarded in the home of Miss Nanny Butler with three other girls.

In high school she was introduced to the works of Charles Dickens; she loves novels to this day. She had parts in school plays, such as *Blue Moon,* an operetta. She met George Carey, her future husband, at Macon High School.

"Was he the only boy friend you ever had?" I asked.

"Oh, no!" she said with a twinkle in her eyes.

After high school, Amy went to Central Methodist College in Fayette. She would have liked to finish four years at Central, but her father had other ideas. Mr. Norton felt one year of college was enough education, and her parents both wanted her to live at home and teach school. Amy received her teaching certificate and taught one year at Hazel Grove School north of Macon, riding her horse three miles each way.

"Did you like teaching?" I inquired.

"Not really," she replied. George Carey was always in the picture. "I remember there was a blizzard; it must have been 20 below zero, and I had to stay with neighbors close to the school. I was in a northwest bedroom for three nights, with quilts piled high on top of me. They did not have wool blankets like we did at home. I slept with all my clothes on; I was so cold that I almost froze. As I lay there, I began to think that getting married wasn't such a bad idea!"

George and Amy began housekeeping "at the junction," in a house across from his parents near the intersection of Highways 36 and 63 in Macon. George Carey, born in 1910, ran his father's service station.

Eventually George became a Shell Oil jobber and had service stations of his own. When he was growing up, his mother, Iva Wheeler Carey, ran the farm with her five sons, and Mr. Carey was a mail clerk on the railroad.

George went to the University of Missouri, Columbia, for two years and was on the wrestling team. When he came home for visits, he hitchhiked back and forth to Macon. George and Amy had been married for almost 71 years when he died. For 25 years before his death, they spent winters in

Scottsdale, Arizona; the two traveled to Hawaii, Turkey, Norway, Sweden, Ireland and Greece.

Looking back at her childhood, Amy remembers attending Bloomington Methodist Church. Her father drove a team of mules, pulling a sled in the winter. Leather straps with sleigh bells hung around their necks; when Mr. Norton left the team, he tied the sleigh bells around their feet so that no one would try to steal the bells.

Amy and her brother liked to go to the Valencia Theater in Macon, a lovely brand new auditorium with tiers of seats on the upper level. Mrs. Sanders played the piano for silent movies. Amy remembers Rudolph Valentino, the movie star.

"After all the special effects and drama in today's movies, it is hard to imagine what silent movies were like," I said.

"They were very exciting to us," said Amy.

During the Depression, she recalls the extreme heat that caused the dust storms. "People would go out to sleep beside the Macon Lake because it was cooler. No one had any money, but we always had the basic things we needed.

"During the depression and during World War II, we couldn't get nice stockings, so we painted our legs with make-up and carefully made a seam up the back of our leg so it looked like we had on hose!"

The Anti-Rust Club has fulfilled its purpose—the wheels in Amy Carey's mind are functioning quite well after all these years. She has enjoyed attending the athletic events of her great-grandsons, Jared and Collin Porter. At her ninety-first birthday celebration, Jared was heard to explain to one of his friends, "She is not your regular grandma!"

Eastwood Memories

Dorothy Reid Baughman Carter   April 2006

Childhood memories for Dorothy Reid Baughman Carter, who was born in 1913, center around the Reid home at 534 East Eastwood, the present home of Tony and Sharon Day. Next door lived a lady who loved children and did not have any of her own, Mrs. Docia Cooney.

The neighborhood children spent a lot of time at Mrs. Cooney's house. Judge and Mrs. Cooney had traveled all over the world; Mrs. Cooney had a trunk full of treasures she had brought back from her travels, and she told the children stories about them. She hid wrapped stick candy in the back yard for the kids to hunt.

Mrs. Cooney grew up in Glasgow during the Civil War. She had a housekeeper who lived with them; Dorothy thinks this servant, Annie, also lived during the War and may have been part of a slave family. Some of the large homes on Eastwood had back stairways and living quarters for servants upstairs, but Annie lived in one of two little log houses in back.

Sometimes on the front porch at 526 East Eastwood, Mrs. Cooney would gather the children together, and they would stage a "wedding" complete with an old lace curtain for the bride's veil, a pretend ceremony, flowers, and attendants. Dorothy was often the bride, and she was "married" several times to Joe Burrus, a boy who lived across the street.

In the Cooney back yard, now owned by Bob and Jean Blalock, was a platform with a railing between two huge maple trees that had been built for programs and entertainments. The day the Reids were moving in next door, Mrs. Cooney was hosting the local chapter of the Daughters of the American Revolution.

Dorothy says, "At this time, there was a distinct upper class in Marshall, and this was a group of very proper ladies. We had been playing outdoors, and our dresses were not very clean, and Mother told us to stay out of the back yard so as not to bother the meeting next door. My sisters and I went just as close to our property line as possible so we could see what was going on. Mrs. Cooney saw us and invited us into her yard."

Of course, the little girls were glad to oblige, and Mrs. Cooney asked them if they knew a song they could sing for the ladies. They went up on the stage and sang to the tune of "The Star Spangled Banner," "O Say Can You See any bedbugs on me? If you can, pick them off, for they make a good stew. . ." Mrs. Cooney laughed and laughed.

Soon the girls heard their mother calling, "Dorothy, Maxine, Janice, you get home right this minute!" Dorothy recalls they got a "licking" over that incident.

Dorothy regrets that little girls today grow up so fast—wearing make-up and acting older than their ages. She and her sisters had such fun together playing outdoors and making up their own pastimes including building houses out of fallen leaves in the fall.

Ice for home iceboxes was delivered in 100 pound chunks to the houses on Eastwood by horse and wagon. Dorothy and her sisters liked to hop on the back of the wagon with their feet hanging down, and ride to the end of the street where the wagon turned around and came back to deliver on the other side of the street. Her brother, Van, the oldest, got a job washing dishes when he was 15, working at the Green Mill on the east side of the square, a candy store that served soft drinks.

Before Indian Foothills Park was established, there was a campground at the end of Eastwood in a wooded area. In the summer, gypsy families would camp there; they drove big open touring cars. Parents warned, "The gypsies are in town—they steal children!" As long as they were camped, the kids all had to play in their back yards.

George William Reid and Pansy Aker Reid, Dorothy's parents, owned G.W. Reid Jewelry Store on the north side of the square. Her brother, Van, continued the business until his retirement.

The Reid family was very active in the First Baptist Church. Mrs. Reid played the piano for the opening assembly for Sunday School, and Mr. Reid led the singing. Dorothy went to the Baptist Youth group. She especially remembers summer picnics at Sulphur Springs campground. All the kids sat in the back of a truck with high sideboards and rode out to the country where they had games, sack races, and relay races carrying a potato in a spoon held in the mouth.

Dorothy and her siblings walked to Eastwood School, then a two-story building. There was no playground, but they spent happy hours playing and sliding down the hill into the ravine beside the school. Dorothy had the lead in several musicals at Marshall High School. After graduation, she attended Missouri Valley College for three years where she was chosen Harvest Queen one fall.

While visiting in Kansas City, she met Frank Baughman whom she later married. During the war, Frank worked for U.S. Cold Storage in Chicago. The company had contracts to provide dried eggs for the army. Dorothy remembers traveling to Chicago to join her husband; she was alone with baggage and baby supplies and a basket carrying her baby, little Frank.

Trains carried soldiers from all points west through Union Station in Kansas City to be shipped out from the East Coast. Not a seat was available, but a soldier gave up his place to her. Union Station was crowded with people and many good-byes were said "under the dome." A popular song had a line that said, "Meet you under the dome," referring to the train station in Kansas City where so many sweethearts had parted from each other.

In 1945, Frank and Dorothy purchased a business in Marshall, String's Bakery, renamed Baughman's Bakery, and located in the building that is now the Cable Television office, 117 East Arrow. Little housing was available when they moved to town, but eventually they lived in the big red brick house between the Methodist and Baptist churches on Arrow Street. This house was torn down for the new Baptist church extension.

Dorothy became a Methodist when she got married because Frank was Methodist. She says denominations mean little to her because it is all the same God. She counts many good friends from the Keystone class, Clara Walker, Dorothy Meyer and Margaret Hackler. They spent hours in the kitchen cooking and serving meals for community events.

Prayer has been a source of strength for her during difficult times. "You may not always get what you ask for, but God always gives you strength and sees you through."

After 33 years of marriage, Frank Baughman died leaving Dorothy a widow for nine years. She then married a friend of Frank's from Arkansas, Leland Carter. She and Leland were married for 14 years before his death.

Dorothy is an engaging storyteller with an infectious laugh. Planters of spring flowers sit on the porch of her home on South English welcoming grandchildren and great-grandchildren who are frequent visitors. In spite of hearing problems, two knee replacements and arthritis pain, Dorothy continues to exude a zest for life.

See page 334, photograph of the balcony belonging to Docia Cooney.

Just Pretend to Sing

Annette Claycomb   January 2006

Born in 1918, Annette Claycomb had lived at 995 South Redman since she was 3 years old until she moved to Mar-Saline Manor this fall.   Annette's father, James Earl Claycomb, helped to build the house.

Annette is a lifetime member of First United Methodist Church in Marshall. Mrs. Gladys Haynes was a Sunday School teacher whom she remembers well. At one time Mrs. Haynes arranged for a group of children to go to Kansas City to a place that took care of poor children, a Methodist organization, possibly Della C. Lamb.   Annette saw how these children lived; she thinks that all kids should know that there are poor children who do not have as much as most of us do.

One of her favorite ministers was Rev. Cecil Swockhammer. She sang in both the children's choir and the adult choir; although she modestly says she does not sing well. "Sometimes you have to just open your mouth and pretend!" The choirs always wore black robes.

Annette took piano lessons from Mrs. Ethel Davis and Sister Mary Elizabeth and learned to play some of her favorite hymns, "Softly and Tenderly," "Rock of Ages," "In the Sweet Bye and Bye," "Jesus Calls Us" and "In the Garden."

The Keystone adult class hosted an annual ice cream social in the summer, and Annette remembers helping the class cook a big Thanksgiving dinner for the entire church on a Sunday in November. Even now, she is president of her church circle, continuing to attend from the nursing home.

Annette has always been shorter in stature than everyone else. "It is a great inconvenience because a short person just cannot reach things." She feels the best things in her life have been having a strong family. Her mother, Gwendolene

36

Walker Claycomb, taught her how to behave and to have good manners. Her mother taught her to overlook disparaging remarks about her height. Her Aunt Blanche, Aunt Bess, Aunt Louise and Aunt Gladys gave her lots of affection, and she has "cousins everywhere!"

Annette seems glad to have people around after living alone for a long time. Residents and staff at Mar-Saline Manor appear to have a special feeling for her. Several stop to talk, smile and wave to her as we are talking in the dining room. There is an air of contentment surrounding this lady which is not always present in the lives of older people.

A Catholic-Methodist Heritage

Mary Frances Coad   January 2006

I chatted with Mary Frances Coad one winter afternoon in her neatly arranged duplex on South Lafayette. Her personal warmth when talking to people makes her seem much younger than her 94 years.

Mary Frances McDonough Coad was named for and influenced by two very strong grandmothers. Matilda Frances Mosier Crank, her maternal grandmother, was Methodist from the word "Go" while Mary Brisbois McDonough, her paternal grandmother, was Catholic through and through.

Mary Frances' mother, Nellie Jane, one of three daughters of Frances and Douglas Crank, lived on a farm on Highway 20; the Core Slab Structures business is located on their former property. The Crank grandparents lived in a big farmhouse which sat on the site of the present day Marshall Lodge. Mary and Thomas E. McDonough lived in Marshall.

When Nellie and Edward McDonough were married, he was no longer able to be a practicing member of the Catholic Church according to the traditions at that time. Before his death at age 88, he was able to return to the church which was a great comfort to him.

Mary Frances went to grades one to twelve at the Sion Academy, a girls' school run by the Sisters of Sion in a beautiful old brick building on the site of the present St. Peter's elementary school. Her parents drove her to school. Although Sion Academy later admitted boys, her younger brothers* attended the neighborhood country school, Elm Grove.

When Mary Frances was in the seventh grade, the Sisters of Mercy took over the school, and it became Mercy Academy. She remembers wearing navy skirts and white blouses in the spring and fall, and blue serge pleated dresses with a detachable white collar in the winter. A few girls boarded at the school, living on the second floor of the building. In the basement, the nuns cooked meals for the boarding students.

The nuns' residence was on the third floor, a mysterious area to the students who wondered what the nuns looked like when they were not wearing their long, flowing, black habits. Also on the third floor were cells where the nuns gave piano lessons. Sister Mary Elizabeth resided there for decades, teaching piano. On the second floor were classrooms. The nuns were custodians for the building as well.

"In the front hall was a beautiful staircase," Mary Frances recalls. "The floors shone—everything was spotless." A monthly assembly was held, and the students with honors wore sashes over their uniforms for the next four weeks.

On Sundays, Mary Frances attended First United Methodist Church. She remembers Mrs. McClure and Mrs. Plattner, Sunday School teachers of whom she was very fond. She learned the books of the Bible, Bible verses, and read from the Bible each week. Kitty Sue Thompson, Martha Emerson, Ruthie Barron and Bob Gibson were in her class.

She remembers Reverend J.E. Alexander among other ministers. Mary Frances has never been a member of any other church. She was a member of an adult class that served banquets in the church dining hall for fund-raising. At that time there were not many facilities for banquets in the community.

"The Marshall High School boys used to drive around and around the block of Mercy Academy over the noon hour," she said. "It used to make Father McCardle so mad." Bill Coad was one of those high school boys, and they were married in 1932.

She and Bill moved to a farm just north of Marshall. For her entire life, she lived within a mile or so of town. Their daughter, Sarah Jane, also known as Sadie, was named for her two grandmothers just as Mary Frances had been.

Mary Frances was a 4-H leader and a member of a county extension club for many years. Her mother-in law, Sarah Coad, was a beautiful seamstress and taught her to sew; her sewing talents led to a vocation for her in later years.

The Coads' daughter, Sarah Jane, went to the University of Missouri and then married Robert Baxter, moving to another state; it was a great time of transition for Bill and Mary Frances as they had been very close to their only daughter. Mary Frances made clothes for her grandchildren, sending them by mail.

In 1969 Bill had a serious heart attack and was in the local hospital for 10 weeks. One year later at the age of 56, he died; Mary Frances was left a widow after 36 years of marriage.

Mary Frances was approached by Berniece McVeigh, county extension agent, at an extension club meeting about the possibility of working part-time for a new fabric store. Jules and Minnie Bange had opened a shop on East Arrow just off the Marshall square.

Mary Frances began to work for them temporarily and stayed for 20 years. Her work filled many empty hours and helped with changes after the death of her husband.

I asked her how she has coped with the bad times in her life. "I had two strong grandmothers, and I saw them cope with major problems," she said. "I knew I could do whatever I had to do." In the 1918 influenza epidemic, the McDonoughs son-in-law died, and her grandmother helped her daughter, Margaret McDonough Hayob, with the care of her three pre-school children, Leo, Ray, and Anna Margaret Hayob, first cousins to Mary Frances. Mary Frances' Catholic-Methodist heritage has shaped her life.

*Bob McDonough, her brother, is interviewed elsewhere in the book.

A Career in the Kitchen

Helen Cross   January 2006

Helen Reid Cross spent her early years in Elsberry, Missouri, south of St. Louis. Helen was the only child in her family; with no children living nearby, she remembers entertaining herself. Her parents, Thomas Samuel Reid and Margaret Susan Davis Reid, subscribed to *The Pictorial Review* whose pages included paper dolls and their clothes with which Helen played. She learned to sew and enjoyed embroidery and fancy work.

Helen spent most of her school years in Hannibal where her family moved. She walked to school, but occasionally she rode on the back of a donkey with a neighbor boy. The donkey was tied out to graze during the school day.

Helen remembers the hard years of the Depression; she and her mother were alone and struggled to make ends meet. Mrs. Reid never owned a car, and she managed with very little. Helen learned to drive as an adult. The sewing and cooking skills she learned from her mother have served her well throughout her life.

As a child, she attended the Christian church and Sunday School. Helen, born in 1914, moved to Marshall as a young woman, and she joined First United Methodist Church. Rev. Chris Oetting, a pastor during the sixties, stands out in her memory. She was a member of the Keystone Class and the Wesleyan Circle.

Helen's vocation was cooking, and she was head cook at the Marshall Habilitation Center for 34 years. She made use of this talent as a church member. The United Methodist Women cooked meals for banquets in the community for many years to make money for missions, and Helen helped with food preparation and serving. She remembers the late Kathryn Bagnell who organized these events and whose cinnamon rolls were a featured part of the menu.

41

Helen was married to William Warren Cross for 21 years before his death in 1963. He was the meat cutter and butcher at the Habilitation Center. They lived and farmed his father's farm near Marshall.

In her retirement, Helen went to the Marshall Senior Center every day. A quiet lady by nature, Helen said, "I made friends at the center, played cards and worked at the reception desk. The Senior Center made my retirement years a happy time." Helen has always enjoyed listening to ball games and working jigsaw puzzles. She is a member of Eastern Star and the White Shrine of Jerusalem.

Helen lives now at Highland Home on Highland Court in Marshall. She said, "Prayer helps when you are all alone".

Water Carried Uphill

Elda and Farris Day May 2006

May, 2006, marked the 73rd wedding anniversary for Elda and Farris Day. I talked with them in their comfortable home on Mar Drive with their daughters, Rhonda Wickam and Rita Bristow, who joined into the conversation from time to time.

Elda, born in 1911 to Frank and Floy Mansfield Matlock in Randolph County, grew up in Thomas Hill, Missouri, the oldest of eight children with six sisters and one brother. "I was the second mother," she said.

Her home was the central telephone exchange for the Thomas Hill area. Twenty-four hours a day, her mother or one of the older children responded to switchboard calls, plugging the cords into the right receptacles to connect callers.

A call from another community went to the central exchange to be connected to the person in that area—no direct distance dialing at that time. Her mother's most exciting experience was helping to connect a serviceman in Rome, Italy, with his wife in Thomas Hill during World War II.

To say it was a busy household is an understatement. I asked Elda if she walked the half-mile to school. "Ran," she said, "After we packed lunches, carried the day's water supply up the hill from the pump, got everyone ready for school and washed the breakfast dishes, it was a rush to get to school!"

Her mother had asthma and hay fever and did not always feel well. But she loved having extra people in and out of the house and cooking for visitors; she would often invite people to her home from church for Sunday dinner.

Elda and her siblings had lots of fun in the midst of all the work. They played checkers, tiddlywinks, a card game called Flinch and Hide the Thimble. "Not with Mother's good thimble though, with an old one!" Her mother did much sewing for her flock of children, and she did not want to risk the permanent loss of her good silver thimble. Elda and her siblings invented a game with old calendar pages and buttons that they called Fox and Goose.

Elda's grandfather was a minister in the Church of God (Holiness) church. When the congregation finally disbanded, the Matlock family attended the Thomas Hill Baptist Church. "When the church doors opened, we were there."

Elda went from the first grade through high school graduation in the same school in Thomas Hill. The town had two grocery stores and a blacksmith shop in addition to the church and school. After she graduated from high school, she continued to stay at home to provide the family with much-needed help. In 1933, she married Farris Day with whom she had gone to high school.

Farris was born in a farmhouse near the boundary line between Macon County and Randolph County. Farris describes himself as an outdoor person; he has always loved the rural life. He worked as a miner, broke and trained horses and belonged to the painters union among his many vocations.

It was necessary for him to ride the seven miles from his home to the high school. To earn money to buy his own horse, Farris rode horses belonging to others to break and train them.

One day a prankster secretly put a burr under the saddle of a new Western horse that he was riding. He was thrown off so badly that he got dirt ground into his mouth, and he had to walk the seven miles leading the horse.

Later he found the burr and was relieved to know the source of the problem. He was afraid the horse was "an educated bucker." Elda interjects that his mother had said Farris was rather a daredevil, and sometimes he did tricks on horseback.

Farris and his family attended a country Presbyterian church called Mount Carmel. His love of the outdoors is reflected in his favorite hymns, "In the Garden," and "Sunrise with Jesus." The Days went to church in their buggy, pulling the curtains around it if the weather was bad.

The buggy was kept in the barn when not in use, and one Sunday they got to church and discovered a hen setting on a nest of eggs in the rear of the buggy. The hen sat there patiently all during church and rode back home again without stirring.

Both Elda and Farris recall camp meetings in their part of the country. Elda's grandfather, the Reverend George Matlock, would preach, and her grandmother, Maggie, cooked for many of the people. Preachers came from all around for a 10 day period delivering "fire and brimstone" sermons.

Some families pitched tents and stayed for the entire event; others would come and go for the services. Farris said it was a great place for young people to have a good time, and they would meet for a reunion of friends every year.

After Farris graduated from high school, "things got kind of dull" at his family farm. His brother was there to help with the milking of the 20 dairy cows, so Farris left for Long Beach, California, in 1929. He got a good job working as a painter for the city schools; he painted classrooms, flagpoles and anything else that needed painting.

Unfortunately, in October, 1929, came the great stock market crash. He remembers people coming to work who did not eat at noon because they had no money for food. Houses were built and abandoned with only the framework; no walls or roofs were added. His job "dried up," and he worked at shipyards and wherever he could find a job. Eventually he returned to the family farm. His dad bought 20 more cows, and the family pulled together to make it through hard times.

In 1933 when the Days married, the economy was not improving. The young couple moved in with his parents and his brother. "If I had it to do over," said Farris, "I wouldn't have done that. It was hard on Elda."

"It was hard on your mother, too," said Elda, "but we made it work."

Farris remembers, "Farmers would drive three miles to the cornfield, work all day shucking 35 or 40 bushels of corn from an acre, then take it to the neighbors to sell to them to feed their livestock for 17 cents a bushel. Hogs sold for four cents a pound. It was hard to make a living."

Elda added, "Fabric was five cents a yard. But we always had clothes and we were never hungry." As time went on, Farris' brother married Elda's sister, and they all lived together with one joint bank account. According to Elda, they never had an argument and got along really well. Part of that time Farris' parents lived with them, too. Her sister's baby did not know which one of them was her mother.

Elda and Farris joined First United Methodist Church almost 50 years ago. They thought it was quite a large church after the congregations where they had belonged previously. Eleanor Dubois, a member of the Marshall church, especially wanted them to join because Farris was her first cousin. Elda was very active in the Sewing Circle which made hundreds of quilts from fabric scraps and gave them away to needy families and to people who had lost their homes in fires.

Farris, born in 1909, is house-bound these days and reads a great deal. He misses hunting which he gave up when he was 92. "I got my deer that year, though!" He and his daughter Rita bantered about which gun he had used to shoot it.

Warm family feelings prevail in this household. I asked the couple for some words of wisdom about a long marriage. "Nobody ever accused me of having wisdom," joked Farris.

"We have just enjoyed each other's company," said Elda.

"I guess really, it is our devotion to one another," Farris said quite seriously. A sense of humor seems to be a part of their relationship as well. Several years ago, Farris was seriously injured falling out of the back of a truck. "A nurse in the hospital said to me, 'You are durn-near dead, and you are still cracking jokes!'"

Elda reflects, "I think part of the reason Farris and I are contented after so many years is because we appreciate what we have. We started out at 'the bottom of the pole.'

"I never turn on the faucet and watch the water go down the drain without remembering carrying buckets of water up the hill from the pump. Life is better now!"

Epiphany in Korea
Frank Duggins   June 2006

Marshall, Missouri, was always home base for Frank Hall Duggins, Jr., even though he moved frequently as a child and lived all over the world as an adult. Fitzgibbon Hospital was a new structure at 868 South Brunswick when Frank was born there December 7, 1928, to Frank Hall and Camille Wilson Duggins. His father was in the restaurant and food service business; at the time of Frank's birth, his father operated the Duggin's Café at 157 W. North.

The Duggins family moved on to Denver, Colorado, when his mother was diagnosed with tuberculosis, and the climate seemed to be more favorable for her health. Later they moved to Wichita, Kansas, where his father managed the Allis Hotel, an 18 story building in which the family had an apartment. He thinks his father's salary was $200 a month.

"The Allis Hotel, since torn down, was ultramodern for the times; each room boasted ice water piped in, a ceiling fan with retractable blades and a central radio system; and restaurants were air-conditioned." Living in a hotel was a different sort of existence for a child; Frank recalls having a sandbox on the roof. His brother was nine years younger so Frank was raised as an only child for his first several years.

For his ninth or tenth birthday, Frank remembers receiving a 22 rifle as a present, and he used it to shoot jackrabbits. "It was a time when people in Kansas were throwing sticks of dynamite up into trees where crows were roosted to get rid of them as a nuisance. One of the local service clubs had a 'crow breakfast' as a stunt to make money. You could 'eat crow,' but they had other food as well."

Frank's mother was a school teacher; and as she wanted the best education for her son, she switched him from school to school based on which she felt was the best. He remembers a kindergarten in which French was taught. "I never went to the same school two years in a row," he said. "My fifth grade year we lived in Marshall, and I went to Eastwood School."

For a time Frank Sr., worked for Trans World Airlines in Kansas City, designing kitchen services for their new transoceanic passenger planes. When Frank Jr., was 14 years old, his mother died of cancer. His most stable school experience was Kemper Military Academy in which he was enrolled after her death. Holidays and vacations he was with family in Marshall; grandparents, aunts, uncles and cousins lived in neighboring houses on East Arrow Street.

"Mother switched churches according to whether she liked the minister. I think we attended churches of every denomination except a Jewish Synagogue or an Eastern Orthodox. I went to the Catholic Church with a friend when I was at Kemper." Still, Frank has only been a member of First United Methodist Church in Marshall. "When I was 11 or 12, I was inspired to read the entire Bible. The 'begats' were a terrible chore."

Frank was happily enrolled as a freshman in Engineering School at the University of Missouri at Columbia when his father called one day and asked if he would like to go to West Point. As Frank tells the story with his touches of ironic humor, he was not very enthusiastic; but he wanted to please his father. Frank Sr. was managing a country club in Kansas City at this point, and he had contacts with a senator who could make appointments. To Frank Jr.'s dismay, he was accepted.

"I never wanted to be in the Army. I was told I had an aptitude for languages, and they enrolled me in a Russian language class. Math was my strong subject, Russian was terrible. I signed up for horseback lessons. But riding on the banks of the Hudson River wearing a wool uniform on hot, humid days was not really much fun."

After graduation, Frank was sent to Ft. Riley, Kansas, for training. Soon the Korean War heated up, and 2nd Lt. Duggins was sent with the Fifth Calvary to Pyongyang, Korea, for "on the job training" with live ammunition. In his regiment, 1500 of 3000 men died in 30 days. Frank felt disillusioned with the Army and with war.

He remembers one day when he was out alone ahead of his platoon, scouting for trouble in the combat zone; he came upon a Korean school with a thatched roof, mud walls and rice paper windows. He stepped inside and on the blackboards were childish drawings with a universal quality. "I had an epiphany about war and people...these kids didn't deserve to be in the middle of a war. They could have been children anywhere in the world."

After his stint in Korea, he went back to Ft. Carson, Colorado. The officer in charge knew Frank's father and his dad's line of work, and he asked Frank if he would be manager of the officer's club. "It was frowned upon to put a combat-trained graduate of West Point in charge of the officer's club, but I did it," said Frank.

After a time, he became an aide to General George Kaiser, "who became like a second father to me; he was very important to me." When Frank's tour of duty was completed, he seriously considered leaving the Army, but General Kaiser convinced him that he could make a difference if he stayed in; and consequently, Frank did stay in the military until retirement.

Next he went to Europe, Austria and Italy where the U.S., Britain, and France were engaged in the "Cold War" with Russia. Frank's unit was in the western half of Austria under joint control of the three nations. Eventually Austria became neutral, and his unit was in charge during the last 90 days of Allied control.

"It was chaos. The situation made the television series, 'Mash' look like Shakespeare," said Frank. Often he spoke of trying to keep up the morale of the men who served under him.   They moved on to Italy, and Frank recalls his impressions of the land, the architecture and the culture.

Later on a blind date in New Orleans while he was finishing his studies in aeronautical engineering, Frank met Margaret "Maggie" Duggins.   "We met on Memorial Day and were married on Labor Day."

While Frank went to Vietnam as advisor to the Military Province Chief of the Southern Province in the Mekong River Delta, Maggie returned to New Orleans.   Following Vietnam, he became Commandant of the West Point Prep School outside of Washington, D.C.

Both of the Duggins daughters were born while they were at Fort Belvoir, Virginia.   Kathleen was christened at West Point, and Molly at Christ Church in Alexandria where George Washington attended.   The family attended non-denominational services on bases usually, but Frank says most were conducted by Episcopalian priests.

Frank's career next led to research and development in the behavioral sciences within the Army, administrating research programs on how to train individual soldiers better in working with military equipment.   In 1974, he went back to Vietnam at the conclusion of the war, and he was on one of the last planes out of the country.

Back in St. Louis, Missouri, Colonel Duggins was assigned to work on the transition into the new all-volunteer Army. Repeatedly in our visit, he acknowledged the excellent people with whom he worked who developed solutions to problems. Frank designed a computer system for the National Guard to match recruits with potential assignments in 600 various job descriptions at posts all over the country.

Frank and Maggie retired to Marshall, Missouri, to live in his great-grandfather's home, 534 Arrow Street, which they restored.   He served on the board of Kemper Military Academy for 25 years, acting as president for one full academic year while conducting the search for a new president.

From 1980 to 1983 Frank served as mayor of Marshall. He recalls the Missouri Valley College television station had a weekly news program which was really quite first rate, and they staged a challenging debate between Frank and his opposing candidate. During his term of office, a murder occurred near Ridge Park Cemetery, and Frank pushed hard on the ensuing investigation and solving of the crime.

Another scandal emerged during his term as mayor when the Ash, Trash and Garbage Department employees were discovered to be repackaging and selling discarded freezer burned food. They did not seem to be breaking any laws, but pressure was applied to stop this practice.

In 2003 after 39 years of marriage, Maggie Duggins died after several months of battling pancreatic cancer. Frank admits to extreme loneliness. He get tears in his eyes as he says, "Sheer determination is what keeps me going."

Maggie was active in community organizations: Daughters of the American Revolution, United Daughters of the Confederacy, Monday Club, PEO and the Fitzgibbon Hospital Auxiliary.

She and Frank shared an interest in antiques and history. She worked for Betty Sue Odell Simonson for several years in her business of designing specialty clothing and patterns for quilts.

Frank and Maggie shared a passion for restoring the old family home at 534 East Arrow. They also shared a zany sense of humor that they seem to have passed on to their daughters.

Frank said he learned considerably from moving around as much as he did. "Whatever your situation is in life, wherever you are, you need to try to make it better than you found it," he said. He said, "I think people are terribly arrogant when they think they know everything about God. God is so much bigger than ordinary human beings."

Frank Duggins. 1939.

Missouri Mules

Emmet Dyer   May 2006

"I'm supposed to go blind, but I haven't gone yet," said Emmet Dyer when I asked him about the open newspapers lying on his bed at Mar-Saline Manor. I hardly expected anyone to joke about macular degeneration, but Emmet is a man with an unusual sense of humor. Emmet sits at the dining room with Paul Ahrens, whose interview appears earlier in this book. I had several conversations with Emmet over the months and decided to include his memories.

Emmet, who is 90 years old, mostly remembers work as a kid. By age eight, he was driving a team of mules raking hay in 40 acres of clover on his dad's farm near Malta Bend, Missouri. One day he drove over a bees' nest which stung the mules and caused them to run away with the hay rake.

"The 12 foot long rake ended up sideways, higher than the team when they stopped at a hollow. The mule colts in the field were biting and kicking because they got stung, too."

Emmet was the youngest of four children born to John Dyer and Ione Smitherman Dyer. The boys did have a good time riding "Old Jack" who was one of the work mules. Every year his dad raised one or two mule colts to sell.

Emmet rode his horse to Union School, three miles from his home, where one teacher had 44 kids in eight grades in the one room school. One of his favorite teachers was Miss Pattie Norvelle; he remembers she had a thick hickory stick to keep order. "She used it, too! I just got a whacking once in school from Miss Marie White for talking. But I had on a thick coat because it was cold that day, so it didn't hurt much."

The Dyer family attended Saline Presbyterian and Union Baptist Church at one time or another. John Dyer was Presbyterian, and his wife was Baptist.

"I spent a lot of hours on horse-back going back and forth to school. Malta Bend High School was quite a step-up from little Union School. I think tuition was $50 a year, but small school districts got a discount if they had several kids enrolled. It was six miles each way on the horse to get to high school.

"I regretted that I never took typing in school. But you had to bring your own typewriter—the school didn't own any, and I didn't have one.

"I well remember my last day of high school. Four of us boys skipped school and took our sack lunches to Van Meter, what is now the state park. I had the family car, a two door Chevrolet. On the way, a bridge was out and someone had just thrown some boards over the creek to cross it...I went over that at 30 miles an hour!

"We took another route home. I remember unsuccessfully trying to run over a duck on the road with the car on the way back. We got back to school before classes dismissed; they were having a last-day-of-school picnic outdoors, and we joined the others. I don't think anyone knew we had skipped school that day."

The fun of high school adventures ended quickly. Emmet's father was killed in an automobile accident in 1931, and Emmet had to quit school to work on the farm. "Mother and I moved to Sweet Springs to an 80 acre farm. I was the last child at home, so I had to work."

Emmet recalled that during the Depression they bought 200 pigs for 50 cents each. When they weighed 250 pounds, the pigs were sold in St. Louis for $2.80 per 100 pounds. Unfortunately, the grain they fed the pigs cost twice as much as the selling price.

"I never went hungry, but I delayed a lot of meals," said Emmet with his droll sense of humor. "I count myself fortunate. We had hams in the smokehouse, and we raised

55

chickens. We had lots of fried chicken. Mother raised two flocks a year. I went out and caught the chicken, wrung its neck and plunged it into boiling water to loosen the feathers. Then we plucked it clean, gutted it and plunged it in cold water to cool it off before it was cut up to fry. Nothing beats the taste of fresh fried chicken!" Without refrigerators or freezers, the dressing process preceded every fried chicken dinner.

During World War II, the government set a ceiling on the price of farm equipment because of shortages. "For example, a farmer could not sell a used John Deere tractor for more than $700. But buyers were willing to pay much more.

"I went to an auction where they sold the tractor for $700, and then auctioned a bale of hay to go with it for as high as the bidders would go. Of course, no one got the tractor without paying for the bale of hay that went with it."

In 1942, Emmet moved to Marshall. For 24 years, he operated the Mobile Oil bulk gasoline station on Miami Street. Emmet, his wife, the late Reba Montgomery Dyer, and their daughter were members of Odell Avenue Presbyterian Church, now Covenant Presbyterian Church.

"Do you want to hear a good yarn?" Emmet relishes a mule story told to him by an old-timer when he was young. A farmer near Malta Bend raised mules in the 1880's. A mule trader, well-known to him, said, "I can buy your 100 mules, take them to St. Louis, and get $10,000 in gold. I'll be back in two weeks."

The farmer agreed, and the trader took the mules to swim them across the Missouri River and drive them all the way to St. Louis.

The farmer's wife was irritated with him for putting so much trust in the trader. Two weeks went by and nothing was heard. The farmer thought he had lost his money, for sure, and his wife was furious. Ten days later, the mule trader showed up with gold in hand. It seems the river was out of its banks from flooding; the trader could not get across to make it by the agreed upon time. The farmer said to his wife, "Kill some chickens; he is staying for dinner!"

Emmet is a great storyteller who has an anecdote for any subject that arises. Storytelling is a tradition in the Dyer family; his brother I.G. was known for his humorous tales. "We were all good talkers," Emmet said with a smile.

An Ease With People

Elmer Fisher   September 2005

Blessed is the man that walketh not in the counsel of the ungodly, nor standeth in the way of sinners, nor sitteth in the seat of the scornful.

But his delight is in the law of the Lord; and in his law doth he meditate day and night.   And he shall be like a tree planted by the rivers of water, that bringeth forth his fruit in his season; his leaf also shall not wither; and whatsoever he doeth shall prosper. Psalms 1:1- 3 KJV

Elmer Fisher recited the first chapter of Psalms from memory without faltering when I visited with him at Hartland Residential Care Home. In the eighth grade at the Lutheran Church in Blackburn, Missouri, he memorized this selection, printed on his confirmation certificate, March 28, 1926. It was the first confirmation class to be conducted in English; most of the community spoke a "flat Dutch," low German, and church services were in German.

A few weeks before Elmer and I met to visit, Elmer had talked to the children at First United Methodist Church during the children's sermon. Because I missed hearing what he had said that Sunday, I went to Hartland Care Center to ask him about it. His response stimulated my thoughts, and soon I launched into the series of interviews I have conducted for this book.

"These are words to live by," Elmer said.

"What exactly do you mean?" I asked.

Elmer indicated that if you try to keep close to the Lord, go to church and stay away from wicked people, God will help you to be successful and make a good living. Then he added, "You know, be at ease with people."

Knowing Elmer, as I have for several decades, "being at ease with people" certainly describes him. When I was a child, the

Skelly truck came to our farm to deliver 300 gallons of gasoline into the tank used for the farm tractors. Elmer would bring the ticket for the amount into the house after pumping the gas. "With tax included, 21.5 cents a gallon or $63 a tank," he recalls.

My mother always had a cup of coffee ready; my grandfather would join them, and often my dad would stop work to come to sit at the kitchen table with Elmer. I liked to listen because Elmer always had stories to tell. Jovial and good-natured, he asked questions, listened and paid attention to everyone with great respect.

As he and I talked, he recalled that when he made his rounds in the country, people would talk to him about problems with their adult children and their concerns. On his next visit, he would inquire about the subject, and people were glad to tell him about their lives.

Elmer, born in 1912 to Marte Jaster Fisher and Otto Fisher, was known as "Fisher" to his wife, the late Frances "Fanny" Fisher; and henceforth, to all his friends and the next generation of family, he remains "Fisher." Fanny and Elmer became active members of First United Methodist Church when their two children were young. Elmer has held many leadership positions in the congregation.

"Why are you interested in what I had to say in church that Sunday?" he asked.

"Many people in our church think you are a wise man, Elmer," I replied.

He chuckled, "Me? I am just as common as an old shoe. Why, I didn't even finish high school." He recalled that the elders of the Lutheran church had come to him and suggested that he go to school to become a Lutheran minister. "They even offered to pay for my education. But my family needed for me to stay at home and help them," he said. "Those were the depression years, and it was difficult for people to just get by.

"My dad worked on the railroad, had a butcher shop for awhile and then became the bulk agent at Blackburn for the Fajen Oil Company, later Skelly Oil Company." Elmer eventually followed in his footsteps, adding the Grand Pass area and then Marshall. "When I started in the gasoline business, gas was 14.5 cents a gallon."

We laughed; the price at the pump that day was $2.47.

I understand why the Lutheran Church at Blackburn wanted to recruit Elmer for the ministry. In a way, he has had his "ministry" on his delivery rounds—bringing pleasure, comfort and peace to his customers with his visits. Certainly he has been prosperous as the Scripture says, and God has given him "an ease with people."

Born on the Missouri River

Jewel Rae Fox   December 2005

Jewel Rae Fox and I visited on the sun porch at the Blosser Home for Women while she told me a little about her family history. Her grandparents immigrated to the United States from France.

Jewel Rae, born in 1919, and her parents, Lucinda Maxwell Veche and Arthur Charles Veche, lived on Dodd's Island on the Missouri River near Bonnot's Mill, Missouri, not far from Jefferson City. The family transportation was a motor boat. She recalls going to church every Sunday to a little white church across the river; and sometimes the minister, the Reverend Barton, came back with them in the boat to have Sunday dinner. It was the custom, especially in rural churches, for the pastor to go home with one of the member families for dinner after the service. During the time she lived on Dodd's Island, Jewel Rae remembers a trip by boat to Jefferson City to attend the dedication of the Missouri State Capitol.

The Veche family moved to Miami, Missouri, and Jewel Rae spent most of her growing-up years in the country. She rode a horse to school on a big hill in Miami overlooking the Missouri River, and she graduated from Miami High School.

Church has always been an important part of Jewel Rae's life. She has had many good friends in the Keystone Class and Circle Five of United Methodist Women. Her faith became even more important to her when she lost a son and a grandson when they were young.

"I don't know how I survived it. I am pretty close to my Lord. I could not sleep at night without praying first." Believing in an afterlife is a comfort for her. "Nobody gets through this world without trouble. You have to just throw it off and keep going."

Jewel Rae walks with a fashionably colored cloisonné cane, and she maintains her sense of style. As I left, she and the other members of the Blosser community gathered in the formal living room to relax and listen to a staff member play the grand piano.

Workshop, Art Studio, Home for Two Generations
Helen and Merle Griener   April 2006

Helen Long Griener was born in Pilot Grove, Missouri, in 1932. She was the only child of Mabel Rothgeb Long and William David Long. "My dad was my hero," she said, "He could fix anything; he operated Long's Garage in Pilot Grove."

She remembers walking and roller-skating all over Pilot Grove. Helen was sent to the grocery to buy bread for eight cents a loaf. A restaurant in town had a dance floor; adults and children, too, danced to the juke box.

At age five, she took piano lessons, but her mother said that she was more concerned with arranging her pretty dress on the piano bench than she was at playing a duet with her teacher at a recital.

The family moved to Rolla when Helen was in grade school. She went to a very small rural school with eight students between Rolla and Salem, Missouri. The district could not decide on which road the school should be built, so they put it between the two roads with a long lane leading to it.

In order for Helen to get to school she had to walk alone through woods to reach the lane, an adventure because the path also led through a pasture with a resident bull. In winter at recess, the children skated on a little stream near the school.

The farm home in Rolla was also a continuous adventure. Helen had to outwit a goat that chased her in order to get to the chicken house. It was her task to clean the chicken house which engendered a dislike of chickens to this day.

Her parents bought her a treadle Singer sewing machine, and she happily sewed away, developing skills in 4-H. Sewing has been a life-long pastime because she is too small to buy ready-made sizes, and she has made her own clothes.

63

Helen and her family were Presbyterian. On Sundays the Longs visited her grandparents and attended the church of her mother's youth, New Lebanon Presbyterian. Eventually the church no longer had a minister, and only Sunday School was held. The entire service sometimes took place around the wood stove to keep everyone warm in the winter. Later, after the family move to Granite City, Illinois, her closest friends were from her church.

The Granite City Church sponsored dance parties with round and square dancing for the community. The high school students served as candle lighters and sang in the choir. Helen remembers memorizing the catechism when she joined the Presbyterian church as a child. This large church offered singing lessons for young people, and she continued to sing in choirs as an adult.

Granite City was in the Mississippi River floodplain; when the river flooded, the high school closed so teen-agers could help with the job of sandbagging the levees. Once the river came within a block of the Long home. Mr. Long had a motorboat, and he was a volunteer for the Corps of Engineers rescuing cows and other animals that were stranded by the waters.

After graduating from Granite City High School, Helen went to Jewish Hospital School of Nursing in St. Louis, Missouri. Helen worked mostly in hospital medical-surgical units, but she had experience in obstetrics, the operating room and the emergency room. Toward the end of her career, she was engaged in home care and psychiatric nursing.

In St. Louis, she met Merle Griener on a blind date. She and a nurse friend had an arranged date; upon arrival, they decided who went with whom based on the tallest and the shortest. She began her relationship with Merle because she was the right height. In December, 2005, they celebrated 50 years of marriage.

Merle, who was born in St. Louis, Missouri, in 1927, is retired from a career as a wood pattern maker; he created patterns for industrial design needs such as fire hydrants, train wheels and plane parts. At one point, he worked with engineers' blueprints to prepare a part for the space shuttle. There were only a few hundred pattern makers then, and almost none at present, as patterns today are done by computer.

Merle's career required artistic ability as well as advanced math skills. His teachers recognized early that he had a special aptitude, and it was proposed that he go into advanced art classes. However, when he got into trouble for shooting spit-wads, he did not get the privilege. Merle was active in Sea Scouts, and the boys went sailing on the Mississippi River. He and his brother and sister were raised by their grandmother.

Merle volunteered in World War II at age 17 with family permission; he was a carpenter in Japan. Joining the Army Reserves after the war, he was called up during the Korean War and served as a cook. Asia made a lasting impression on him.

The Grieners lived in Pekin, Illinois, for a number of years before moving to Quincy. Helen was very active in the Presbyterian church, serving as an elder and a member of the session, teaching Sunday School, Bible School and singing in the choir.

Merle took an art class at the YMCA and began painting with oils and watercolor. He has received Best of Show awards in both the Illinois and Missouri State Fairs for a watercolor painting, "Moments from Japan."

Helen and Merle became Methodist in Quincy, Illinois. They moved to Marshall to be closer to their daughter, Jeanne Snoddy. When they visited First United Methodist, they were impressed with the friendliness.

When asked what has helped her through difficult times, Helen said without hesitation, "Faith in God." It is impossible to convey the depth of feeling in those three words. Helen and Merle lost a son when he was a teenager and a son-in-law in an automobile accident.

Every inch of space in the house at 1129 Fairlawn is utilized. Helen's mother, Mabel Long, has the living room, a bedroom and a bathroom. The garage is organized into a workshop for Merle's projects. Another bedroom is Helen's sewing room. Downstairs is the art studio and an area for framing.

Art by Merle on the walls includes landscapes, animals and birds, still life and realistic portraits—several of their grandson, Daniel, on the Snoddy farm. Everywhere their interests are reflected, and it is a wonderful environment for an aging parent.

Keeping Busy

Caroline Hahn   December 2005

When I asked Caroline Hahn what year she was born, she said, with a twinkle in her eyes, "1914. . .I think that makes me 110." She was shelling cracked pecans in a large box as she sat in her room at the Blosser Home. "I like to keep busy."

Caroline Dehm Hahn was born on a farm north of Slater. The family moved to another farm southeast of Marshall when she was 4 years old, and she and her sisters and brothers went to Thorp School, a quarter of a mile from their home; at noon, they walked home for lunch. The family went to Smith Chapel United Methodist Church; the roads were mostly dirt, and weather often kept them from attending.

I asked her what the children in her family used to do for fun. She paused. "Fun? I don't remember much fun. We just worked. Milked cows, dressed chicken, canned and cooked!"

Caroline attended Marshall High School, staying in town with her older sisters, but when they moved out of town, she had to go back to the farm. Traveling on muddy roads was often impossible. On the farm, she helped keep everything going, driving the team of workhorses, helping with planting and shucking corn as well.

She married the next door neighbor, Otto Hahn, who was a widower, and she helped to raise his 12 year old son on their farm near Blackwater. Today, she is close to great grandchildren whose family home is on Eastwood near the Blosser Home where she resides.

She joined First United Methodist Church in Marshall when they retired. "When Franklin D. made Social Security for farmers, my husband could quit!" Caroline was a great admirer of Eleanor Roosevelt. "She would attempt anything and she could do it."

Caroline's husband, Otto, was drafted to serve in World War I. It was entirely possible that he was fighting German relatives because his family had immigrated to Missouri from Germany. Caroline's grandmother was also a native of Germany.

Caroline has lost count of how many quilts she has made, a skill she learned from her mother. A colorful quilt covers her bed, and a hand-made crocheted afghan is thrown over the back of her chair. She has always kept busy and worked hard.

"Emptying the dishwasher does not seem like much of a daily chore for children these days, but it is the way they help out the family. It looks easy for young people today, but maybe it only looks that way...they probably have it hard in other ways than we did." Hard work and "the will to keep going" have seen Caroline through many years.

Southern Roots

Sarah Hains   November 2006

Sarah Martha Hains came to Marshall, Missouri, as a bride, a transplant from the South. Born in Cuthbert, Georgia, in 1916, to Lena Belle Grimes Tittle and James Arthur Tittle, she lived in Vidalia, Savannah and Memphis, Tennessee, before moving to Houston, Texas, during grade school.

Her father was in the cotton business, operating a compress—a process that reduced cotton bales to half their size to facilitate shipping. Sarah had a sister four years older, Evelyn Grimes Tittle Dunlap, with whom she forged a life-long bond. Separated by many miles as an adult when Evelyn lived in Houston, the two of them managed to see each other two or three times a year plus holiday visits.

"When I was very young, my father had a touring car, a Cole 8, which seated seven passengers. One day when it was at the garage to be fixed, it burned up. Our next car was a Chandler. There were no windows in cars at that time. Eisenglass on rods were put into holes in the door to protect you from the rain, and cars did not have windshield wipers."

Sarah experienced the "roaring twenties" when she was six years old. She remembers learning to do the "Charleston," dancing to the Victrola to the music of "Yes sir...that's my baby...No sir, don't mean maybe...Yes sir, that's my baby, now."

Sarah said, "We moved to Houston, a city of 300,000, in 1927 for my dad to go to work for the Anderson Clayton Cotton Company. I have fond memories of good times in Houston. I went to San Jacinto High School."

Sarah laments that teen-age relationships have become so serious these days. "It wasn't the thing to 'go steady'—you just went out with lots of different people, and you never settled down to date just one person. The high school had a dance every Friday night. The girls wore long dresses, and the boys wore white linen suits that cost 50 cents to have dry-cleaned. My mother made my dresses; she could look at a picture in Vogue magazine and copy it.

"Walter Cronkite lived two blocks from my house. We roller-skated together on our quiet street, and he took me to the Senior Prom. He was an immaculate person; he drove an old Dodge sedan touring car. Walter said I was never ready when it was time to go!" Sarah said with a smile.

In high school, Sarah and her friends went to Sunday night youth meetings at different churches. Groups would have parties in their homes and dance to the Victrola. "My daddy was President of the Men's Sunday School Class at the Baptist Church. My Grandfather Tittle had been a Baptist minister, and I was dunked! I was Baptist until I married Randall."

"In the summer, dances were held on the roof of the Rice Hotel with big name bands, Jimmy Dorsey, Guy Lombardo, Jan Garber—you name it, they all came to play at the Rice. My friends and I went several times a week. Afterward we would go to the 'Pig 'n Whistle' drive-in for hamburgers, or we would go to an eating place called 'One's a Meal' and get scrambled eggs, raisin toast, and milk. We had to be home by 11:30 p.m. There was no drinking of alcohol—kids just had fun!"

Sarah remembers going to the Sylvan Beach Dance Pavillion. "It was not a honky-tonk place, I once saw Dorothy Lamour sing with a band there." At Ellington Field, Sarah had the experience of going up in an open cockpit airplane, riding behind the pilot.

After graduating from high school, Sarah went to the Rice Institute, now Rice University. Languages were a big part of the curriculum. In high school, she studied Latin for three years and French for two years. At Rice she had three years of French and one year of Spanish. After graduating, she went to work in the stenography department of Gulf Oil

Company, also serving as a tour guide of Houston for company visitors.

"Aristide Joncas, a Canadian widower who owned six oil companies, would take my sister and me out to dinner, to symphonies, concerts, boxing matches and movies. He would buy us orchid corsages for big events; sometimes he would come to our house for dinner," Sarah remembers.

"Along came the War and everything changed," Sarah said. Gas was rationed. All the young men were drafted. Many were stationed far from home, and it was patriotic to entertain the soldiers. Gulf Oil Company sponsored a Christmas dance for the officers at Ellington Field, and Sarah was in charge of the arrangements. As she knew there were four Naval officers in the building near the Gulf offices, she took invitations to them.

"I remember what I was wearing that day," she said. "A gray pin-striped suit with a white blouse, a gray felt hat with a turned-up brim, white gloves of course—we always wore gloves—and I was carrying a red lizard purse that matched my shoes." One of these Naval officers was Randall Hains who figured prominently in her future.

"Randall just sort of took over my social life," Sarah said. "In four months, he left on a cargo ship taking fuel from New York to Africa. Later when he had leave in New Orleans, I met him there." Before the war was over, Randall was captain in charge of a Landing Ship Tank (LST) at the Battle of Okinawa. The back of his ship opened down and troops exited to storm the island. His ship was hit once, but no one on board was injured. A year after his return from the war, Randall and Sarah were married.

Randall, born in 1913, was the son of Edna Lawless Hains and Rosier Hains of Marshall, owners of the *Marshall Democrat News*. Randall attended Missouri Valley College and then transferred to the University of Missouri at Columbia,

71

majoring in journalism. Knowing that he was going to be drafted, he joined the Navy immediately after graduation.

After the war, Sarah and Randall moved to Marshall, and Randall began working with his father, Rosier Hains, at the newspaper. Sarah, a city girl, found quite a different life when she moved from Houston to Marshall, but she made the necessary adjustments to living in a small town.

"When I was president of Monday Club, we performed a musical to make money for charitable community projects. *The Best of Musical Comedies* was presented in the high school auditorium, and it was so popular that the one dollar tickets sold out, and a second night was scheduled. I was director, and Mary Louise Miller was pianist. Randall helped with casting, and we made the sets.

In the show, Joan Lewis and Leo Hayob sang 'Annie Get Your Gun;' Donna Huston appeared as Dolly in 'Hello Dolly,' Dorothy Potter and I did the Charleston in a dance number, and Jean Blalock shampooed her hair during every rehearsal singing 'I'm Going to Wash That Man Right Outta My Hair' from *South Pacific.*"

Sarah played Bloody Mary in the "Bali Hai" number and she was also Eliza Doolittle, *My Fair Lady*, singing "Wouldn't It be Loverly?" As a finale to the show, nine-year-old Arthur Hains sang "With a Little Bit of Luck," and "Get Me to the Church on Time."

In the aftermath of the production, Monday Club received a letter from a New York law firm telling them that they had no permission to use this material. Sarah asked her lawyer, Lamkin James, to write an explanatory letter in response. Nothing further was heard about the matter.

Later, Sarah played the part of Madame Ernestine Von Liebedich, her favorite role, in an Arrow Rock production of *Little Mary Sunshine.*

In 1957, fire destroyed the *Marshall Democrat-News*. The Haines family worked quickly to continue publication of the paper. Issues were initially printed in Slater and Sedalia in off-hours from newspapers there. Then equipment was rented.

Sarah said, "Our employees worked day and night to keep things going. Type was set by hand then and required lots of time. The Kays Engineering building behind the Auditorium Theatre, 118 East North, was unoccupied, and it had the necessary pit for employees to work under the press. Eventually a new building was built with up-to-date equipment, but it was a very bad time for the Marshall paper."

Years later, the Hains family sold the newspaper to Stouffer Publications; Randall continued to work for the new company. After he retired at age 65, Sarah learned that three employees were hired to replace him. Unfortunately, Randall died with a heart attack at age 67. He and Sarah had been married 33 years.

Sarah Hains has lived life with pizzazz, possessing a dramatic flair and dressing with style. At age 90, she still maintains a zest for life. "I am not one to get bored," she said. "I have my routine at home, and I am not a worrier. I really depended on my sister, Evelyn, and I do miss her. My son, Arthur Randall, his wife Lisa, and my grandchildren, Christopher Randall and Kathleen Sarah, in Springfield are always here if I need them; family is very important to me."

Building Highway 41—about 1930

Watching Highway 41
Mary Ruth Hanna

One would never know when meeting Mary Ruth Hanna that she has a serious vision problem due to macular degeneration. On her desk in her room at Westport Estates sits a reading machine with the *Kansas City Star* in place. Her computer is near-by; she prints out e-mails and puts them under the viewer to enlarge so she can read them. Her room is furnished with family heirlooms and lovely pictures from her travels. She says her favorite travel adventures were to the Far East: Singapore, Hong Kong, Thailand and Japan.

Mary Ruth, born in 1914, grew up on a farm north of Marshall on Highway 41. She and her sister, Martha, two years younger, used to love to swing in the porch swing on the front porch of their big old-fashioned country home and watch the road in front of the house. "You would just hope some cars would drive by," she laughed. "Usually a car or two would come down the road for our entertainment."

Highway 41 was a dirt road when they were girls. People regularly got stuck in the mud and would come to their door asking her father, George Parks, to pull them out with his team of horses. Later he would use his tractor. Even in the middle of the night, travelers would be stranded and want his help.

She remembers that the Fourth of July was an especially big event. They would buy sparklers in town, and neighbors, George and Ruth Klinger and their daughter, Billy Jose Klinger Conrad, would come over after dark. They would enjoy a simple fireworks display, no firecrackers or cherry bombs.

Mary Ruth started school in Marshall at age six. Her mother, Lena Veatch Parks, was artistic, and she loved nice things. She wanted her daughters to appreciate the finer things; she thought that perhaps school in Marshall might be better than the country school near them. Therefore, Mary Ruth moved into town with her widowed grandmother, Annie Gower Parks, and her Aunt Minnie Parks who lived on South Odell. She started first grade at Eastwood School. She was miserable, homesick and lonesome for her family. She can still remember the clock on the mantle at her grandmother's house that ticked ever so slowly and time seemed to drag. After about four months, her grandmother and aunt moved to California, and Mary Ruth happily returned home to go to Robert Leigh School.

The teacher at Robert Leigh was also the janitor and kept the building clean and kept the fire going in the pot-bellied stove in the corner. Mary Ruth remembers two rows of desks joined on a wood runner at the bottom; the desktop lifted up for books; the seat was attached to the desk behind. All eight grades were taught in the one room by Miss Lettie Nevelle at first, then Mrs. Lucille Cott from Gilliam.

Spelling bees required all pupils to stand in a line in front; as soon as a word was misspelled, the student sat down. Box suppers were school fundraisers; every girl and woman filled a shoebox with food and decorated it, and the box was auctioned off to the men. More money could be raised if someone was bidding on his girlfriend's box; everyone knew he wanted it, so they would keep raising the bid.

When Mary Ruth was 12, her family moved their membership from Mount Carmel Methodist Church to First United Methodist Church in Marshall. Her mother wanted her to meet some girls her age as she would be going to Marshall High School. She recalls good times in the Epworth League which met every Sunday night for a program and fun together.

Several carloads of young people went to a conference at Cottey College in Nevada, Missouri, among them Bob Gibson, Margaret Gore, Elizabeth Winn and Nell Marshall Barnhill. Mary Ruth traveled in a convertible with a "rumble seat" that pulled up to seat two people.

Mary Ruth learned to drive on the farm when she was twelve, and she would drive the family to church in Marshall in their Chevrolet touring car. By the time she was in high school, her dad was driving her to school because new laws had cracked down on young drivers.

After graduating from Marshall High School, Mary Ruth went to Missouri Valley College for two years before she got married. Mary Bell Ingram, who taught school at Robert Leigh School, was boarding with the Parks family at the time and introduced Mary Ruth to Audsley Hanna. Mary Ruth and Audsley had a blind date to a card party in Marshall.

After they were married in 1934, they lived in Kansas City for 33 years. Audsley had a good job as supervisor of Kansas City registered mail. At first they rented an apartment for $32 a month, later buying a home at 55th and Woodland, a nice residential area that has since become part of the inner city.

Before they moved back to Saline County in 1967, the Hannas were residing in the Red Bridge area of Kansas City. When they came back to take over the family farm, Mary Ruth was very happy as she loves the community, and the countryside here in Mid-Missouri. Audsley died in 1972 leaving Mary Ruth a widow after 38 years of marriage.

I asked Mary Ruth how she has coped with the bad times in her life. "There have been some," she said thoughtfully. It has been especially hard for her to see her younger sister's health deteriorate; they are together in the assisted living facility. "I am not one to wear my religion on my sleeve," she said. "But on the inside, I am very religious."

Mary Ruth Parks Hannah holding parasol, George Parks holding Martha Parks Brown others, unknown - 1919 or 1920.

A Gentleman With Dignity
Elmer Hare   October 2006

For twelve years, Elmer Hare and his wife Lucille Davis Hare were in the food service business, the Estes Coffee Shop in the Estes Hotel in Warrensburg, Missouri. "It was hard work," he said, "We worked from 5:00 a.m. to 8:00 p.m. six days a week. Lucille would come in at noon.

"There weren't motels back then, so hotels were busy. Central Missouri State University, now University of Central Missouri, only had 9000 to 12,000 students at the time. Half lived in private rooms in town, and many of them ate their meals at our coffee shop." In 1949 Elmer and Lucille decided it was time for a change and sold the coffee shop.

Elmer was considering a job as supervisor at a local uniform factory when one of the partners in Jerry Tally Motors, a Ford dealer, offered him a job as a salesman. "No pay, just commissions. But they would provide me with a car. When they showed me that nice Ford car, I would've worked for nothing just to have it. I thought surely I could make $50 a week in commissions which is what the other job would've paid me!

"After a year or so, I remember the boss calling us in and saying, 'Boys, you are going to have to work a little harder this year; Ford has raised the price $17 a car.'" He progressed to the sales manager position with a salary; and in 1958, he purchased the franchise on the Ford dealership in Marshall.

Elmer Hare, the middle child of seven, was born in Lincoln, Missouri, in 1918, to Clara Kelb Hare and Clayton Hare. His father was a rural mail carrier for most of his life. Lincoln had a population of 400 with grocery stores, hardware stores and doctors. The railroad ran one passenger car between Sedalia and Warsaw, and it was possible to travel back and forth between towns along the way. Farmers shipped their cattle and grain by train.

The Hare family attended Sunday School every Sunday at the Christian Church in Lincoln; once a month the church had "preaching." Elmer recalls, "We took one or two pennies for the collection each week. When I got older, I was in charge of firing the coal furnace. The church had one big heat register. I had to get up before 6:00 a.m. in order to get the building warm enough."

Elmer went to grade school and high school in Lincoln, and married his high school sweetheart, Fern Lucille Davis. The young couple moved to the then small town of San Diego, California, where Elmer had a job with Consolidated Aircraft Corporation as an assembler and sheet metal worker. At first, he started working on the two engine PVY2 aircraft which landed on water. Later he became lead man of a crew that fitted the fuselage to the wing of the B-24 bomber known as "The Liberator."

Because of his job, Elmer was deferred until 1944; he joined the infantry, but transferred to the Air Force. From Portland, Oregon, Elmer was transferred to Greensboro, North Carolina; Lucille and Baby Gayle returned to Lincoln. He thought he would be shipped out for the occupation of Germany; but as he had 19 months of service he finished out his time in the military police in Greensboro, after which he joined his family back in Missouri. Elmer's brother in Lincoln owned a service station, garage and café on Highway 65, and Elmer worked with him until the purchase of the coffee shop in Warrensburg.

Elmer's son, Phillip, and Elmer's daughter, Gayle Bradshaw, have both worked in Elmer's Ford business; it continues to be a family operation today. Elmer and Lucile retired in 1984 and enjoyed traveling and golfing, spending several winters in Harlingen, Texas, in the Rio Grande Valley.

In 1995, Lucille had a severe stroke which changed the course of their lives. Elmer remodeled their home on South Redman and hired help so that she could remain at home in spite of her handicaps. He drove a van with a wheelchair lift in order to be able to take Lucille to visit their lake home. When she died in 2000, the Hares had been married almost 63 years.

A red lamp over the altar in First United Methodist Church sanctuary, representing the Eternal Flame, was given in Lucille's memory by her family. Elmer also arranged to have a shelter house with restrooms constructed on the back nine of the new municipal golf course at Indian Foothills Park. A stone marker in Lucille's memory is near-by. "She loved golfing and held the Ladies Championship for two or three years," Elmer recalled.

Elmer is a gentleman with dignity who accepts gracefully that he can no longer live alone. He continues to spend part of every afternoon at the Ford agency. He said, "Westport Estates is a good place to be if you can't live at home."

A Young Scholar
Anna Mary Harvey   March 2006

Anna Mary Wilhelm Harvey was sitting in her room at Westport Estates reading *Guideposts* devotional magazine when I came to visit. She had just returned from having lunch with a friend.

Bosworth was the birthplace of Anna Mary in 1926. She was the only child of Bunn and Jean Craig Wilhelm. When she was four years old, her mother's sister died, leaving seven orphan children. Her parents took Robert Dooley, who was eight months older than Anna Mary, and raised him as her brother. Later Robert's older sister lived with them to finish high school. Hubert Dooley, another member of this family, worked for her father and was also very close to the Wilhelms. Hubert was drafted into World War II, and his experiences made the war quite real to Anna Mary.

Hubert's fleet was shipped to Ireland and on the voyage, the soldiers got scarlet fever. One-half of these troops died with the disease. Sulfa was the miracle drug at that time, and instructions to the sick were to take as much of the medicine as they could. Hubert always wondered if some boys died from an overdose of sulfa. He survived the trip to Europe, and afterwards he held the Irish people in high regard; they took American soldiers into their homes on weekends and shared their rations of coffee, tea, and sugar. Ireland was a welcoming place for homesick soldiers. In 1944 Hubert took part in the Battle of the Bulge, one of five who survived in his unit. Anna Mary heard the news from him; and as a teen-ager, she became aware of the horrors of war.

Anna Mary remembers the steam thrashing machines and cooking for thrashers. A crew of about 35 men would be at the farm for the noon meal, eating in three shifts. Her mother, her aunts and a neighbor would produce huge quantities of food for the working men, sometimes fried chicken, sometimes enormous cuts of beef purchased in Bosworth. "Cooking for thrashers" came to be a term used in the Midwest whenever large quantities of food were served.

Bundles of wheat were thrown into the machine which separated the grain from the stems and chaff. Straw and chaff were stacked for the livestock to eat. It was necessary to keep an eye on the cattle as they ate the stack; if they ate too far into the bottom layers, the top of the stack could fall in on them.

Robert, of course, started school first; Anna Mary played school at home with her mother who had been a school teacher. Toward the end of Robert's first year at Linden, a country school nearby, Anna Mary went with him to school to visit for a day. She joined in the schoolwork with the rest of the first graders.

The teacher was impressed with her knowledge and made arrangements for her to recite for the county school superintendent. She was given permission to start second grade the next fall when she was only five years old.

Robert and Anna Mary had a pony named Queen who provided them with great fun at home, but they walked to the country school. Linden had outdoor toilets and a wood stove, and the teacher did all the tasks of daily upkeep.

The Wilhelms attended the Christian church in Bosworth. Anna Mary took piano lessons; she practiced hymns and learned to play for Sunday School and sometimes for church. She loved her Sunday School teacher, Miss Floy Stewart, a wonderful person who sometimes had parties for the children. Anna Mary said she learned the Twenty-third Psalm sitting on her father's knee which has made this scripture very special to her.

The area roads were graveled by the time she started high school in Bosworth so a bus picked up the rural students.

Anna Mary was 16 going on 17 when she graduated from Bosworth High School, the valedictorian of her class. She says she was small for her age, and people always thought she was much younger than her actual age.

Anna Mary went to Stephens College in Columbia for two years, and then lived with two cousins in Kansas City, working in an insurance office. She was promoted to treasurer of the office, but the boss came to her a few days later and told her that the bonding company would not bond anyone who was just 19 years old.

Anna Mary decided to go back to school at the University of Missouri in Columbia to major in accounting. She entered the University in 1945 along with the hundreds of returning veterans who were getting tuition paid under the GI bill. GI stands for "government issue" and may have originally stood for "general inductee" or the common soldier.

Temporary buildings were everywhere at the University. "The housing situation was pitiful," Anna Mary said, "Some of the veterans lived in garages with dirt floors and ate oatmeal three times a day. I had to get a room in the upstairs of a house with no cooking privileges. Two girls from Rocheport boarded there, too; they could not commute because gas and tires were not available. Sometimes I went home with them for week-ends." Classes were huge. Anna Mary remembers one class had 350 students; there were only nine girls in the business school at that time.

Having to eat meals out ended up being a bonus, however, because at the cafeteria in downtown Columbia, she met a college boy named Harold Harvey who dispensed salads. He asked her to a dance at the Farmhouse fraternity and gave her a beautiful corsage of Talisman roses.

Poor Harold then had some bad luck.   One day he got a parking ticket while he was at work. When his boss found out, he said, "You can afford a car? You don't need a job here! I am going to hire a veteran who needs the work worse than you do!" He was fired. Harold was not old enough for the draft, so he could not compete with the many veterans who needed work in Columbia.

Harold and Anna Mary dated for two years, then married and moved to a farm at Triplett, Missouri, for five years before moving to the family property near Stanhope. Stanhope, near Miami, Missouri, was a thriving community with houses and a grocery as well as holding pens for cattle which were shipped at the railroad stop.

Harold's ancestor, Thomas Harvey, always referred to as "the Major" was Superintendent of Indian Affairs and had dealings with the Sac and Fox Indian tribes in the Miami area in the 1840's. Out of respect for Major Harvey, he tribe performed a death dance when he died.

The Harveys raised Angus cattle, corn, soybeans and wheat. Both Harold and Anna Mary were very active in the community. Anna Mary is a former president of the Missouri Cattlewomen's Association, an organization promoting the use of beef. Every year at the Missouri State Fair, Anna Mary and other members staffed a booth sharing information and beef recipes.

Harold and Anna May raised their four sons in Mount Carmel Methodist church. "I remember that Helen Louise Weber played the piano. She was a dear friend of mine. We went to Beta Sigma Phi sorority meetings in Marshall together for 25 years. She was a one-of-a-kind person who loved to sing and dance and entertain people with her talents."

Many families in the Miami community had sons; and on Sunday afternoons in the summer, the Harvey yard was filled with boys playing ball. "We lost a window or two regularly. But we never minded because we knew where the boys were and who they were with. It was all worth the trouble."

"My faith in Jesus Christ and in God has helped me through bad times. I talk with God every day," Anna Mary said. "The past year has been especially hard."

Harold died after 55 years of marriage; and shortly afterwards, Anna Mary fell and broke her leg. After hospitalization and rehabilitation, she recently had to leave her country home and move to Westport Estates.

Anna Mary is optimistic and upbeat and knows that she can make the necessary adjustments. Tables in her room hold books and magazines, evidence of the active mind that showed early promise and enabled Anna Mary to start second grade at age five.

Education by Horseback

Bertha Heffron   May 2006

"I got the biggest part of my education riding back and forth on a horse," said Bertha Heffron. She was the youngest of seven children born to Joseph Porter and Mary Edna McMillan Cunningham on the family farm eight miles north of Tishomingo, Oklahoma. A few months before Bertha's birth in 1919, an older sister died at age four, probably from the 1918 flu epidemic.

Bertha started to school in Rolf, Oklahoma, four miles from her home; her seventh and eighth grade years were in a bigger school with two rooms, and later she graduated from Wagoner High School. Bertha's brothers had Indian ponies, and they all rode horses for fun as well as for transportation. During her sophomore and junior years, she stayed with her sisters who lived in Ada, Oklahoma. For a time, she attended East Central Oklahoma College.

Bertha set aside her *New York Times* crossword puzzle in the *Kansas City Star* when I arrived to visit with her. I expressed my admiration for her ability. "I have to have my dictionary handy," she said. A few months ago she moved into her spacious room at the Blosser Home for Women.

Bertha's father died of cancer when she was 11 years old and an older brother who had been teaching returned home to help. Bertha grew up driving the workhorses and mules and helping with putting up hay. Another chore was milking her share of the 11 cows before she went to school in the morning. The milk was picked up by truck and taken to the cheese factory in Muskogee. Cream was separated from the milk for the Cunninghams to sell to the neighbors.

Bertha worked for the Tulsa Board of Education, distributing food orders for the school lunch programs in the city. A friend who had worked in the same building moved to Bogard, Missouri, and Bertha took the train to visit her one

Thanksgiving. It was in Bogard that she met Lowell Sutton who worked for the Missouri Farmers Association Seed Division. He had just returned from military experience in India and Burma during World War II.

Lowell and Bertha were married in 1947. They moved to Marshall because of his job with the M.F.A. Seed Division; soon Lowell became in charge of maintenance at the Red Comb Pioneer Feed Mill. First United Methodist Church in Marshall was quite different from the little rural church in Roth, Oklahoma, where Bertha grew up. "People were not as friendly as they were in the South." But the Suttons made good friends in Marshall, especially Alma and Willard Heffron. Lowell Sutton died about the same time in the early eighties. About three years after the death of their spouses, Willard and Bertha were married.

Bertha became a widow a second time when Willard died after 19 years of marriage. "Willard's children have been good to me," she said. "I watched them grow up." Being alone again has been a big adjustment. Bertha feels, over all, she has had a good life and good times.

"I am thankful that I grew up when I did, even though it was hard work on the farm. I feel sorry for kids today. They have more things, but I don't know if it is good for them. There are many more things to hinder them. It is important to learn how to work hard and get by."

Using the Mind Enriches Life

Libby and Harry Heinemann   May and July 2006

The military career of Harry Heinemann during World War II would make a good plot line for a situation comedy. Harry graduated from Paseo High School in Kansas City, went to Iowa State University for a semester and then enlisted in a program for cadets to become Navy pilots.

He studied navigation and aeronautics at William Jewell College and then went to Washburn University to flying school. In a Taylorcraft plane with dual controls, the would-be pilots were learning how to do "spins" and "stalls".

"The plane must never touch the ground. Our instructor decided to demonstrate 'what not to do' so he began 'hedge-hopping' over fence rows, and the plane hit the ground and conked out!" After this introduction to piloting, the candidates moved on to Iowa University for preflight training. Halfway through, it was announced that the Navy had too many pilots. So Harry went back to Kansas City to the Army Air Corps.

He was told that Army pilots were being chosen in ways as scientific as standing in a line and counting "one...two...one...two" and eliminating the "twos". Harry transferred to Navigator School in San Marcos, Texas. There were three cadet positions in each plane, one was copilot, one navigated by the map and one was positioned by a drift meter in the back of the plane used to "dead reckon" their position.

"Guess what?" said Harry with self-deprecating humor. "I got airsick with all the updrafts and down drafts in Texas." But they told him this would not be a problem in the large planes that he would be navigating so Harry continued his training. Thirty days before graduation, the announcement was made that the school had too many navigators. Harry went to Scott Field, Belleville, Illinois, to radio school. Graduates had to be able to type 25 words a minute—code words—that is,   not English words. The bad news is that Harry could only get to 20 words a minute; the good news is that the civilian typing instructor was a tall, pretty, dark-haired, young woman from Minnesota, named Marie Lee.

Harry moved on to officer candidate school in Ft. Sill, Oklahoma. When he completed the course in 1945, he and Marie were married. The atomic bomb was dropped while Harry was stationed at Fort Sill. "When President Truman decided to drop the atomic bomb, he probably saved the lives of the boys in my field artillery unit because we were headed for Japan," Harry said.

His unit went to the southern tip of Hokkaido, Japan. Experienced soldiers went home, and the new unit took over. Harry was made battery commander because he had been in the Reserve Officer Training Corps (ROTC) at Iowa State University. McArthur had taken over the occupation of Japan. Harry and 12 enlisted men were sent as the military police in a town of 300,000; they collected weapons at police stations. In Harry's experience, the Japanese people were cooperative and friendly.

McArthur ruled that houses of prostitution were off-limits to U.S. military. Harry became a "geisha house" inspector. He would talk to the Mama-San in charge to see if any GI's were customers, and she would say "No", and offer him a cup of tea. These inspections occupied his time until he finished his tour of duty. Harry has remained active in the Retired Officers Association and the Veterans of Foreign Wars, and he is a lifetime member of the American Legion.

Harry was born in St. Louis in 1922 to Olive Hanson Heinemann and Harry B. Heinemann, Sr. but moved to Kansas City when he was three years old. He was the youngest of four children. His father was manager of a dairy and creamery equipment supply company in the West Bottoms.

He remembers seeing poor people marching in the Kansas City streets during the thirties.

"I worked as an office boy for 15 cents an hour. When Roosevelt raised the minimum wage to 25 cents an hour I was happy. If I worked on Saturdays, I could buy a hamburger for 25 cents and a coke for a nickel." His siblings remember that Harry always had money to loan, but he wanted it paid back promptly.

He went to Frances Willard Elementary School two blocks from home, then to Paseo High School. Grade school in Kansas City ended after seventh grade, and students went on to four years of high school. Because Harry was 16 when he officially graduated, his parents arranged for him to have an extra year post graduate. Josephine Baity was the teacher who supervised his extra year.

Harry must have been a very responsible 16 year old because Miss Baity would let him take her Ford convertible during study hall to get gas and wash it for her. Miss Baity's father was Reverend George Baity, minister of Westport Presbyterian Church and the president of Missouri Valley College; Baity Hall is named for Reverend Baity. Miss Baity encouraged Harry to consider attending Valley.

Harry and Marie moved to Marshall because Missouri Valley College offered married student housing for veterans on the GI bill. When they arrived, the housing was not finished, and they moved into a one-room apartment with a shared bathroom and refrigerator until the seven barracks with 28 apartments were finished. "We thought it was heaven; everything was new!"

Marie also took more college courses in education. The GI bill paid $90 a month for living expenses, and Harry worked part time for I.G. Dyer, State Farm Insurance agent, to supplement his stipend. He asked Valley to review all of his military training to try to get some credit hours for the military coursework he had done. They excused him from physical education and from health and hygiene.

When I.G. Dyer became district manager for State Farm in addition to his farming and auctioneering businesses, Harry became the local State Farm Insurance agent. His office was on North Street across from Silverthorn's Gambles store, a block of buildings torn down when it was purchased by First Christian Church. Harry began to get involved in city government; he ran for City Council and was elected. "No one else was running," he said modestly.

In 1954 he became the youngest Mayor of Marshall at age 31. He recalls a great controversy during his tour of office; ash, trash and garbage pick-up was started at a cost of one dollar a month. The city council chambers were packed with people who objected. One man said, "I don't have any trash, why should I pay a dollar a month?" Objections were over-ruled, and the service became permanent.

Sadness engulfed the Heinemann household. Their first child died of a congenital heart problem at age two; a house fire destroyed almost everything they owned at their home on South Redman. They rebuilt the house.

Later Marie and Harry built a lovely home on East Mission purchasing the lot from Wayne Elsea who developed the pasture of his farm near the south edge of Marshall. A large barn was torn down on the site of the Heinemann lot; bricks from the Slater railroad roundhouse were used to build a central fireplace. A daughter and a son joined the family.

But dark clouds continued to gather. In 1969 Marie died after a battle with cancer; Harry was left with two small children. "It could have been worse, but I don't know how," said Harry, in what seems to be a huge understatement. There is an unspoken determination, strength and strong will about Harry Heinemann.

How did he avoid becoming deeply depressed and bitter in the face of his grief and loss? "I had no choice; I had two little children to take care of," he said. He found a dependable housekeeper and babysitter, Mamie Wilkes, who helped him keep his home going.

Harry has been a member of First United Methodist Church for over 50 years, served on the board of trustees several times and was treasurer of the church for 24 years. He remembers that Alma Heffron, the church secretary and bookkeeper for many years, would bring the checks down to his office on North Street for him to co-sign.

Harry facetiously said that it would not be necessary for me to interview Libby because she is not a Methodist and never has been. But I told him that it was obvious to me that he has only had half a life without Libby to whom he has been married for 37 years; the picture is not complete without her.

Libby was married to Bill Seelen for 27 years when he appeared to have the flu one Christmas and died from lung cancer the following March at age 50. Her daughter, Susan, was married six weeks later as she had planned to be. Within one year of his death, both of Libby's parents died. Her youngest daughter, Sarah, was in college, and Libby moved to Marshall and coped with overwhelming grief by pouring her energy into teaching English at Missouri Valley College.

As Harry and Libby drove to Sedalia for dinner the first evening they got together, each told their story of devastating grief from losing spouses to cancer, and they both cried. Sometime later, Libby assumed responsibility for raising a second family, Jayne, age 15, and David, age 7.

Her parents, Lenox Berry Hanley and Charles Leslie Hanley, had a daughter, 17 years old, and a son, 12 years old, when Lenox became pregnant at age 42 with Hannah Elizabeth "Libby" Hanley. "Mother wouldn't go out of the house because she was so embarrassed about having another baby at that point in her life.

"My brother, David Byrd Hanley had to babysit me and he hated me. I even went along on dates with him. I was not shy and quiet. Only boys lived in our neighborhood at 16th and Beacon in Sedalia. I would join in their ball games, and they threw terrible pitches to put me out."

Mr. Hanley was Cashier of Third National Bank in Sedalia. The Hanleys owned a Ford, a "tin lizzie" as Libby calls it, and she remembers her brother cranking it while her father twisted the wheel and stomped on the floor. "It would be so wonderful when it started up!" she said.

Libby walked to Horace Mann Grade School except on snowy days when a neighbor boy had a sled which was pulled by a large dog, and she got to ride with him.

One of her favorite teachers, Laura Margaret Mellotte, saw Libby's aptitude for reading and literature in the sixth grade and gave her an extra reading list of classics and advanced her one half year in school. Thus began an insatiable quest for learning which has been a hallmark of Libby Heinemann's life.

Libby has a childhood memory of hearing the phone ring one night about 9:00 p.m.—her father answered, and it was the Dean of Students at Central Methodist College in Fayette where her brother was a student. She heard her father say, "What? He did what? I will come to pick him up first thing in the morning. He has some work to do first, you say. Right, I'll be there to get him around 10:00 a.m." It seems that her brother along with some other boys had pulled a cow up three flights of stairs into the chapel, and Central Methodist kicked him out. Of course the boys had to clean the chapel first.

Libby remembers going with her mother and seeing the Brinks armored trucks with money for Third National Bank and people standing in lines outside to get their money out during the bank runs of 1929. "My father said, 'We are not closing,' and our bank did not close. I think my father had something to do with it staying open during these hard times."

While attending Christian College, Libby and her friends met a young woman from Denver who had a pilot's license. A group of co-eds decided to hitchhike to find an airport that would rent a plane to their friend so they could take a flight together. It is no surprise that they were unable to find an available plane. A stranger boarding a bus said to her, "Aren't you Libby Hanley from Sedalia?"

For young people, hitchhiking was an acceptable way to travel in those days but not with Libby's father. The word got back to her family; he was not pleased, and she got into trouble the next week-end when she went home.

Following Christian, she got a degree in education from the University of Missouri and returned to Sedalia to teach third grade to children with severe learning problems. The class came from homes with poverty, and one child came to school bare-footed. She worked with them to learn to read, but only taught one year before she and Bill Seelen were married; married teachers could not hold a teaching position. Libby and Bill had met at Smith Cotton High School when she was president of her class, and he was president of his class.

As Libby remembers, sermons at the church attended by her family in Sedalia every Sunday focused on wickedness and evil, and how death would be disastrous if you did not change your ways. She loved the Episcopal Church, which she attended with Bill, with its emphasis on living in the present and songs of praise and thanksgiving. Libby especially loved midnight mass at the Episcopal Church at Christmas. She attends First United Methodist Church with Harry because her church, Trinity Episcopal, is not handicapped accessible.

Bill and Libby started their married life in Columbia, Missouri, but moved to New York City for him to pursue a Ph.D. at Columbia University. Libby worked as receptionist giving information and directions on the main floor of one of the buildings of the Rockefeller Center. One day, a beautiful woman in a long ermine coat and high heels entered the building.

The men who operated the elevators usually were slouched around their posts waiting for people wanting to go up, but they suddenly stood up erect and payed attention. Gypsy Rose Lee, the famous stripper, was headed to an upper floor for an appointment with the editors of the company that published her autobiography, *Gypsy*.

Living in New York City was interesting for Bill and Libby. They left their car, which they had purchased for $300, in New Jersey and used public transportation to get around. One day, while riding on a double-decker bus, Libby saw police taking handcuffed Japanese diplomats from the Japanese Embassy just after Pearl Harbor. Sometime later, the Seelens drove their car, a Chevrolet with a rumble seat in back, back to Missouri and sold it for $900 because cars were scarce and sold for premium prices.

Bill, whose health prevented his participation in World War II, was never able to finish his doctoral thesis because the five faculty on his committee were drafted and sent to various parts of the country without approving his work before they departed. For a time, he taught at Dartmouth; but then the boys were all drafted, and faculty was no longer needed. The Seelens returned to Columbia, Missouri, and Bill taught public speaking at the University of Missouri.

Bill had an opportunity to go into business with George Bagby, brother of his step-father, Julian Bagby, in the chick hatchery business in Marshall. At first, Bill was at the hatchery in Kansas City but later moved to Marshall to work with George. Libby and Bill lived on North Brunswick Street, and their two daughters started school at Eastwood School.

After several years, Bill decided to go to law school, and he was hired as assistant dean of students at the University of Missouri in Columbia. He rented an apartment in Columbia, and Libby stayed at their home in Marshall as she was teaching at Missouri Valley College. In his last year in law school, the family moved in with him in the small apartment, and Libby taught freshman English at the University of Missouri while she got her master's degree in English.

The Columbia apartment was rented from Ruth Rollins of the Rollins Road and Rollins Fieldhouse family. Mrs. Rollins had a lovely garden in front of her house which featured an attractive urn. One day Libby noticed the urn was missing and asked about it. Mrs. Rollins replied that it held her husband's ashes, and she had moved it inside for the winter months. Bill became ill shortly after the Seelen family had joined him in Columbia.

Libby can only walk a few steps when she is not in her wheelchair, and Harry has trouble getting around as well. They are able to stay in their home because of loyal and efficient helpers. The people who work for them help maintain a normal lifestyle. Harry, a member of Lion's Club for 57 years, still attends weekly meetings; Libby takes duplicate bridge classes and plays bridge with friends regularly. With the assistance of her home-helpers, Libby audits a class each semester at Missouri Valley College; she does the homework assignments faithfully.

She has been able to pursue her special interest in the literature of Medieval England, and she speaks highly of her professor, Dr. Mark Adderly. "People in Marshall don't know what they have in Missouri Valley College. I have learned as much in my classes here as I learned in my master's degree program at the University of Missouri," she said. Harry, a board member for 20 years, shares her pride in Missouri Valley.

From their chairs in the family room, Libby and Harry can look out over the back lawn which looks like a lush green park. Stacks of books are all around Libby's chair, and Harry has a two-drawer file cabinet with his resources handy. As we talked, he stopped and found a paper listing the terms of

96

former mayors of Marshall. Although Harry and Libby have found their physical health has deteriorated, their minds are sharp and active. One can only wish more older people could lead the kind of lives that Harry and Libby do with their capable and dependable assistants. Libby sums it up, "If you sit in ashes, you sit alone." Harry and Libby demonstrate that using the mind enriches life at any age.

Japan 1945

One Day at a Time

Margaret Hackler Hill   November 2005

As I entered Margaret Hackler Hill's room at the Blosser Home for Women, I was interested in a photo of a gray-haired man with a long beard and four children. "My grandfather, John Collett," she said. "He homesteaded a poor farm up in Macon County coming from Virginia.

"My father, George Austin Collett, was three months old when his mother died. John never remarried and raised the boy with the help of his unmarried sister and brother, Jenny and Joseph Collett." She laughed and said that one genetic trait her father passed on from generation to generation was that of red hair and early baldness; her grandson Mason enjoys this genetic gift.

Margaret Collett, born in 1907, was raised in the Methodist church in Macon. She recalls her dad at one end of the pew and her mother at the other. The Primary Class was taught by Miss Mary, and everyone loved her. Margaret had a spiritual foundation that has endured. "I never go to bed at night without thinking of all the wonderful blessings in my life.

The Collett family lived on a city block in Macon that was 150 feet deep. There were trees to climb and a barn with a hayloft in which they played. The barn was essential as her father was a rural mail carrier; at first, he rode on horseback to deliver the mail. Later he got a closed-in rig which was a great improvement. Finally, he got a car. But the roads on his route were so bad that he often had to rely on the horse to deliver the mail.

Margaret went to first grade through high school graduation in one big school in Macon. She took teachers' training classes the last two years of high school. After taking a county test, she taught in rural schools, going to college in Kirksville in the summers. Her husband, Ronald, also taught school. Later he went into the retail shoe business. Margaret quit teaching school when her son, Richard, was born.

A severe teacher shortage existed during World War II, and one day the school superintendent showed up on her doorstep begging her to come back to teaching. She taught in a rural school 11 miles from Macon. She rode to her school in the mornings with the school bus that drove out to pick up high school students in the country.

Then she got off at a farmhouse a mile from the school, borrowed a horse and rode the rest of the way; she repeated the whole process in the afternoon. At that time rural schools were teaching first through fourth, fifth and seventh grade curriculum one year, and second, fourth, sixth and eighth grade curriculum the next year.

In 1949, the Hackler family moved to Marshall to open a shoe store. They immediately joined First United Methodist Church, an extremely friendly church as Margaret remembers. The Hacklers joined the Keystone class when it was just starting, and Margaret suggested the name "Keystone" because she had attended a class in Macon by that name. Pat Reid was the class president. Sally Sherwood invited them to dinner within the first six weeks after they arrived.

Margaret served in many leadership positions in the church. She taught the Keystone class, along with other members who rotated as teacher, and she taught the high school Sunday School. Margaret was vice-president of United Methodist Women when she was 91. One of her favorite church activities was the Business Women's Circle.

Margaret has appreciated all the ministers she has met as a Methodist, but she and her family especially enjoyed the service Dave Huck presided over last fall when she celebrated her birthday. The theme was "Who is the church?" and involved the children's choir and included every age group.

Margaret has been blessed with the gift of positive thinking and the ability to overcome adversity. She has been no stranger to sorrow. Widowed twice—she was married for several years to Dr. Hobart Hill, a retired professor at Missouri Valley College—she also lost her only son. When talking about her life, she said that her favorite hymn is "One Day at a Time, Sweet Jesus."

"That says it all," she said. "I have lived it."

World War II Bomber Pilot
Jean Klein Horman and Elmer Horman   June 2006

Over the sofa in the comfortable family room at 215 East Mission hangs a dramatic oil painting of a P51 fighter plane painted by aeronautical artist, Dave Galloway. A gift from his son, Steve, the painting is a reminder for Elmer, a World War II pilot.

From October, 1944, to May, 1945, Elmer was part of the 364th Fighter Group escorting bombers over Germany from Honnington Air Base, Bury St. Edmonds, England. Escort planes flew in shifts to accompany the bombers, protecting them from German fighter attack. "We lost some men," said Elmer quietly. Before the war was over, Elmer had flown 45 missions.

Elmer Horman was born on a farm southeast of Alma, Missouri, in 1922 to Flora Roehrs Horman and August Henry Horman. When he was five, the Horman family moved to Marshall where Elmer's father was in the grocery business, first with A&P, Atlantic and Pacific Tea Company, then Krogers and later Associated Grocers. In 1930 Mr. Horman became a distributor with the Sites Meat Company out of St. Joseph, eventually opening the Horman Meat Company in Marshall.

"I worked on Saturdays, taking orders on the phone and delivering. At that time there were dozens of little grocery stores and cafes in Marshall. Hamburger stands were the forerunners of the fast food business. On the south side of the square, Lubensky's Meat Market still made deliveries to homes using an enclosed wagon pulled by horses," Elmer said.

The Lutheran Church was important to the Horman family, and they rarely missed Sunday School or church services. Elmer remembers catechism classes taught by the minister every Saturday morning at the parsonage for a year before confirmation.

Athletics was Elmer's first love, and he played every sport offered. After Northwest Grade School, he went out for football, basketball and track at Marshall High School. He remembers the annual Pig Roast, a celebration of football achievements in the fall. "Coach Bill Lyon was the coach for all three sports plus he taught physical education and driver's education. I think he had one assistant. Sometimes I wonder if coaches today really need so many assistants."

Elmer lettered in all three sports and then played football for Missouri Valley College. "We only lost two football games in the four years that I was in college." Coach Volney Ashford had an outstanding football team for a number of years, and Elmer believes that at one time the Vikings had the longest winning streak of any college team in the nation.

College for Elmer was interrupted by World War II. Recruiters were coming to campus, and Elmer decided to enlist in 1942. "Boot camp at Jefferson Barracks, St. Louis, on the banks of the Mississippi, was called 'Pneumonia Gulch'. We stayed in huts made of boards with canvas on top. In the morning we would wake up with ice on top of the water buckets!"

Living conditions improved as the future pilots moved to other parts of the country for more training. In San Antonio, at the Classification Center they underwent tests and tests, classes in codes and identifying ships and aircraft. Elmer chose to be a single engine pilot because he did not think he wanted the responsibility of having a crew aboard. At Cimmaron Air Field in El Reno, Oklahoma, he flew in an open cockpit with an instructor behind him.

Later bigger planes had closed cockpits, and he soloed cross country and had instrument training. To his surprise, one of his final flight check instructors was a familiar face from Marshall, Missouri, Eddie Brandecker, who passed him on for advanced training.

102

Soloing cross-country at night was especially challenging, but at last he got his commission and wings; and as a Second Lieutenant, he took gunnery training off the Gulf Coast of Texas, Matagorda Island. Women's Air Force pilots pulled 12 by 50 foot targets on 50 feet cables behind their planes and the student fighter pilots shot live ammunition through their propellers. The painted bullets made a print on the canvas so accuracy could be determined.

Eventually, Elmer and his company embarked from Camp Kilmer, New Jersey, on the British ship, Mauritania, destined for England. "We ate fish for every meal. The Mauritania was unescorted; and to avoid detection by the enemy, it zigzagged back and forth across the ocean on its way to Liverpool, England." Escorting bombers over enemy territory began when he reached Honnington Air Base.

When the war was over, Elmer returned to Marshall to work in his father's business, and he met Grace Ann Dyer, an aircraft communicator and meteorologist from Mason City, Iowa, who was stationed at the Marshall Airport by the Civil Aeronautics Authority. Grace Ann was boarding with Ruth and Werner Hermmerding, and Grace Ann and Elmer met at the Lutheran Church. They were married while Elmer was finishing college at Missouri Valley.

Elmer worked at Horman Meat Company until the family sold it in 1974, after which he was with Wilson Foods for 11 years. Grace Ann had been a member of the Congregational Church; she and Elmer visited several churches before deciding to join First United Methodist. The Hormans were very active in church matters; their sons, Bruce and Steve, were part of the youth programs, and Elmer helped with finances and served on the Board of Trustees. Grace Ann taught in Marshall Public Schools for 17 years.

After retirement, Elmer and Grace Ann had eight years of traveling and enjoying life together before her health failed.

Elmer and Grace Ann had been married 48 years when she died following a long illness.

Elmer found being a widower difficult. "I did not like being alone," he said. Jean Klein was a friend of his sister Irma Horman Whitlock, and he invited her out for dinner. They discovered they had much in common, and the two have been married for ten years.

Jean Klein Horman says she does not qualify as a Methodist because she has been an Episcopalian since age 18. But she did have a five year period, in Mexico, Missouri, when she was Methodist because there was no Episcopal Church. However, during these Methodist years, she joined Bob and Mary Napton Searfoss, former Marshall residents, in helping to organize the Mexico Episcopal Church.

Born in 1928 in Hannibal to Bess Mason Hafner Hulse and Fred Berkley Hulse, she was the youngest of three children. "Things were getting bad economically in 1928, and they had a boy and a girl. I was not wanted," she says with a smile. She remembers good times playing jacks, hide and seek, stringing a "telephone" between two trees with cans and a string connecting them and having a continuously running Monopoly game at her house. Talkative and friendly then as now, her deportment reports in grade school were not good, because she visited with others during class time.

Jean has a special memory from Hannibal in 1934 at the dedication of a new bridge between Hannibal and Quincy, Illinois. Her father was city attorney and sat on the platform during the opening ceremony with President Franklin D. Roosevelt. Jean was in the front row, "So close I could've reached out and touched the President." When President Roosevelt had his heart attack a decade later, her father sat by the radio for three days, overcome by grief, just as the next generation gathered around their televisions for three days when President John F. Kennedy was assassinated.

The Hulse family moved to Sedalia, and Jean went to Smith-Cotton High School. She and her friends played tennis, dressed in football uniforms and played touch football. Occasionally they came to Marshall to swim in the modern pool at Indian Foothills Park, a pleasant change from swimming in farm ponds in the Sedalia area.

Jean was editor of the high school year book, beginning a lifetime interest in writing; presently she is a member of the Marshall Writers Guild. At Christian College she studied with Mary Paxton Keely, a well-known Columbia journalist, but she decided to major in teaching when she went to the University of Missouri.

Jean married Milton Klein who worked for the Equitable Life Assurance Society as a farm loan appraiser. The Kleins and their two sons moved several times in Missouri when Milton promoted to regional director. The East Coast became home when Milton became Equitable's vice-president in charge of agricultural loans in the United States.

Jean's outgoing personality and adaptability carried her from small town to metropolitan area. "If you are going to be a part of a community, you have to give of yourself. You can't just sit in a chair," she said. The Kleins retired to Marshall and Jean has been a volunteer at Fitzgibbon Hospital and a member of P.E.O. among other activities.

Milton had been in a coma for four weeks before he died; he and Jean had been married for 43 years. "When you love somebody, you don't want them to suffer. You have to give them permission to die." Jean says. The Twenty-third Psalm was a comfort to her during those dark days. Both Elmer and Jean talk freely about their long and satisfying first marriages; still they are glad to be enjoying these years together.

Fun in the Backyard
Lucille Humphreys November 2005

Martha Lucille Humphrey, age 101, grew up in Grand Pass, Missouri.   When she attended the Blackburn Methodist Church, her parents, Leland Watkins Suggett and Minnie Bell Strader Sugget, expected the children in her family to "sit up in church and act right."   Lucille had a twin sister, Mary Louise. Seven children were born to the Suggetts; two died as infants. Lucille is the only surviving member of her family.

Now living at Mar-Saline Manor, Lucille remembers good times in her country home. Mr. Suggett put little Lucille on the back of the workhorse when he plowed the garden. "My father tried hard to create fun for the family at home because he wanted us to be happy and not go out running around to other places.

"Dad hung a hammock made from the staves of a barrel between trees in the yard. We also had a trolley between trees, a wire with a wheel attached. We climbed a tree, hung on and swung across to another tree and back again. Visiting children always enjoyed the trolley as much as we did!"

In November of 1926 Lucille married Roy Andrew Humphreys. The Humphreys farmed near Blackburn, Missouri. After Roy's death, Lucille moved to Marshall and joined First United Methodist Church.

One of the worst times in Lucille's long life was when her son, Roy Leland Humphreys, was critically injured in a tractor accident; he survived after a long recovery. The death of her daughter, Minnie Berniece Liemkuehler, was another difficult time.

Lucille remembers hearing her father, sing "Rock of Ages," her favorite hymn. Mr. Suggett sang at funerals and her son, Roy Leland, inherited his vocal talents, also singing publicly.

Lucille's grandson, Kenneth Leimkuehler of Sunrise Beach, Missouri, recalls her famous Denver biscuits; the dough was kept in the refrigerator, and portions were brought out for baking in the wood-burning stove. "My grandmother loved to fish in the farm ponds for catfish, and she often took us fishing."

Sometimes Lucille's memory is better than at others, but she clearly remembers the closeness of family

Generation to Generation in Saline County
Virginia and Alfred Hupp   February 2006

Alfred Rector Hupp grew up with one brother and one sister at 104 North Brunswick in Marshall, the present home of Fred and Jane Hartley. Born in 1918, Alfred remembers that his maternal grandfather, for whom he was named, came to live with his daughter, Docia Rector Hupp, and her family after his grandfather was widowed.

A.F. Rector was a significant person in the history of First United Methodist church. Apparently he was a very good-natured man, as Alfred and his brother Wilbur must have tried his patience greatly. Mr. Rector loved gardening and had a special pair of boots that he used. The boys poured water into the boots to surprise him when he put them on. They also mixed all his seeds together.

The Hupp children raised rabbits for a time, but there became so many of them that it was a tiresome task; and one day they turned them all loose in the woods behind their home.

A stained glass window with a shining star on the east wall of the sanctuary is in memory of Alfred Frost Rector; a family connection exists with the poet Robert Frost. Mr. Rector taught a men's Sunday School class for many years; it was known as the Rector Class until it combined with the Philathea women's class in 1989 or 1990.

Alfred remembers coming to First United Methodist Church Sunday School with his grandfather; he and his brother, Wilbur, participated in the children's Sunday School program while their grandfather taught the men's class. The Hupp family was Baptist, and at times during his childhood, he attended First Baptist.

Mr. Rector and his wife, Susan Docia Venable whom he married in 1877, lived on Arrow Street. They never owned a car. His law office was on the square; he got up very early and went to the office to open it and start the day. Many of the merchants and professional people on the square kept this daily routine. Then he would go to the grocery and buy fresh meat to take home for a big breakfast before he returned for the day's work.

On Sundays, Mr. Rector and the Hupp boys would catch the "jitney," a truck with bench seats. After Sunday School, they would go to the Marshall depot and board the train to Slater where they would eat dinner and visit with friends and relatives, returning on the 5:00 p.m. train back to Marshall.

The Portrait and Bigraphical Record—Lafayette and Saline Counties 1893 states that A.F. Rector's father, William, was a Confederate Captain in the Civil War who was injured at the battle of Kernstown, Virginia, and died in 1862 leaving a widow and eight children. By the age of 10, A.F. Rector was fatherless. When he was 18, he came to Chariton County to work for the Chicago and Alton railroad. He became the railroad agent in Slater. It was there that he "read law," as was the practice until he knew enough to pass the Bar exam.

Judge John Pryor Strother of Marshall admitted him to the bar. This same Judge Strother has a stained glass window on the west wall of First United Methodist Church sanctuary donated in his memory by his daughter, Grace Strother Yancey. Mr. Rector became Prosecuting Attorney of Saline County and later Probate Judge.

Alfred Hupp went to Eastwood School, graduated from Marshall High School and attended Missouri Valley College. He volunteered to join the Air Force in 1942, and became an engine change specialist on the B-29. As an air cadet, he was stationed at Santa Ana, California.

In an interesting turn of events, a picture of the young air cadet appeared in the *Marshall Democrat News* just before

Christmas that year. Retta Long, who lived with her son, George Long, at Fairville, Missouri, in the summertime, spent winters in Whittier, California, with her daughter, Margaret Long Parks. Retta suggested to the Parks family that they invite young Alfred for Christmas dinner as he was so far from his Saline County home.

The Parks' daughter, Virginia, a high school student, thought this was a fine idea as everyone was highly patriotic at that time and wanted to do nice things for the soldier boys. Little did they know that the two of them would be married five years later after the war ended.

Virginia grew up in the Congregational Church and remembers being in Sunday School every Sunday morning. During the Sunday service, she and her friends sat in the balcony as quiet as could be because disruptions were not approved. She listened with respect to the sermons by Dr. Lovell, the minister; it was a worshipful atmosphere with silent prayer and organ music. She says it is hard for her to adjust to new ways of worship because of the reverence and formality of the services she knew as a child.

The Parks family lived in the Los Angeles area where her father owned a collection agency and was a successful businessman. Later they moved to a ranch near Whittier, a small acreage with an orange grove.

Virginia remembers her school had lots of discipline. "If you got in trouble at school, you were in trouble at home, too." After graduating from high school, she attended the University of Arizona.

Virginia and Alfred attended First Baptist Church in Marshall in the Hupp tradition. However, their son, Al, was part of a Boy Scout troop at the Methodist church, and their daughter, Nancy, began going to Sunday School there. So they transferred their membership when Dr. Clinton Galatas was minister.

Virginia has been active in a church circle and helped with serving meals in the church kitchen. She remembers that Josephine Lawless Reid was one of the organizers of the kitchen workers. Alfred served on the Finance Committee for years.

Alfred and Virginia both spoke of memories of the depression. Virginia remembers the poor people, referred to as "Okies" who left the Dust Bowl looking for a better life in California. "There was no work or money for them there either; they lived in rundown trailer parks. They worked as migrant field workers seasonally. These families did not create problems; the children respected their parents who made them mind."

According to Alfred, "It was just a day-to-day struggle trying to keep the Farmers Savings Bank open." There were four banks—one on each corner of the square before the depression. Only two remained after the hard years.

When his father was president of the Fitzgibbon Hospital board during the Depression, he sometimes had to milk the two cows that provided milk for patients. Usually this was the responsibility of the janitor, but sometimes he did not show up for the job.

The Hupps reside in a spacious white brick home on Cypress Drive overlooking Stone Hedge Golf Course. Alfred and Virginia feel that they have been greatly blessed in their lives.

Family Traditions

Donna and John Huston   May 2006

Spring sunshine was shining through cobalt glass on the table in the breakfast room when I visited with John and Donna Huston in their home at 407 East North. John Percy Huston III was two years old in 1931 when his family moved into the white house with black shutters built by his parents, John Percy Huston Jr. and Dorothy Curran Huston.

John went to Eastwood School and Marshall High School "just doing the usual things kids do." John would have stuck strictly to the facts about his life, but Donna reminded him of interesting stories. It is obvious to the listener that their personalities compliment each other.

John remembers a variety of jobs as a young person from peddling vegetables for sale from his wagon to working summers on a local farm. When he was old enough to drive a truck for the ice plant, he delivered big chunks of ice on a route door to door. He pumped gas, checked oil and washed windshields at a gas station that was part of the Chevrolet agency at 254 South Odell where the Dolly Madison Bread Store operates at present.

John was active in Boy Scouts; and his Scoutmaster, Dr. E.W. Thomas, influenced his life by taking him quail hunting. Dr. Thomas, a Marshall dentist, started what has become a family tradition of hunting extending to the four Huston sons today.

The Great Depression and World War II influenced the world in his era. John remembers hobos who walked up from the railroad tracks two blocks north of his home asking for food. When he went to the University of Missouri in Columbia, returning veterans on the GI bill swelled the school population to 10,000. Barracks were being built as fast as possible to house the new students. Still a formality existed on the campus; in his fraternity, the college men wore suits and ties to dinner every evening.

After working at Wood and Huston bank for two years, John was drafted into the Army and sent to Sendai, Japan. On the ship on the way to Japan in 1951, he bought a watch for $11 which still keeps time efficiently; he continues to wear it even though today a new band costs as much as the original watch.

John was with the corp headquarters company in an office working with classified documents. He enjoyed being around the Japanese people and seeing the countryside. Two years later, he returned to the bank in Marshall where he has worked for 57 years. John Percy Huston II, John's father, passed the banking tradition down through him to the present generation.

The Huston family history in Saline County begins with Judge Joseph Huston who ran the historic Old Tavern in Arrow Rock. His son, Joseph Huston Jr., started the bank along with Will Wood, an Arrow Rock merchant. The stained glass window of Jesus and the children over the Arrow Street entrance to First United Methodist Church was given in memory of John Percy Huston I, John's grandfather.

One day in downtown Kansas City, John recognized Donna Klepper as a hometown girl when he saw her walking down the street. After a whirlwind courtship, they began a marriage which has lasted 48 years. "He was 29 and I was 25 so we were old enough to make good decisions," said Donna.

Donna, who became a stewardess after graduating from Missouri Valley College with a degree in elementary education, was an instructor in the Trans World Airlines school for stewardess education. In her stewardess days, she had to memorize the names of everyone in the 36 seats of the Martin 404 and the Super Constellation planes. Passengers were asked by name what they wanted from the menu, and meals were served in silver dishes.

Second class passengers entered by stairs on the tarmac through the tail of the plane; first class passengers entered at the front. The flight from San Francisco to New York was eight hours straight. If a passenger wanted to sleep, it was necessary to buy four seats in order to lie down

Stewardesses could get five extra days off in a year if they worked the most unpopular schedule which was three flights a day from Kansas City to Wichita. Requirements for airline hostesses were rigid: young women could not be married, have a bridge in their teeth or dye their hair. Weight guidelines were strict, 100 to 110 pounds with an additional five pounds added for each inch over five feet. Tall women were preferred so they could reach the overhead storage racks.

"During the pre-employment interview, you were asked if you were serious about anyone. It was expensive to train stewardesses, and the airlines did not want to waste their money on someone who was going to get married immediately," Donna said. Bomb scares were not unknown in the fifties, and caused flight delays.

Born in 1933 in Kansas City, Donna moved to Marshall at age two with her parents, Amos Ernest Henry (Jack) Klepper and Midge Evelyn Rogers Klepper; her dad was a Prudential Life Insurance agent. Little Donna loved climbing trees, playing with trucks and swinging on bars at the Latter Day Saints Church near her home on Gordon street. She walked the two blocks to Southeast School where she remembers sitting in the hall quite a bit for talking too much.

In the fourth grade, Donna was sent to the office for standing on the teacher's desk and giving instructions to the class in her teacher's absence. She remembers with pride that she got to be Mary in the school Christmas program; nativity plays in public schools have long since been discontinued because of the diversity of students today.

The Klepper family were members of Our Redeemer Lutheran Church in Marshall. "At age thirteen you had to know the catechism by memory: Scripture, hymns and what Lutherans believe.   We stood before the congregation and questions were asked before we were confirmed.   Her favorite hymns are from the Lutheran tradition: "Just as I am Without One Plea" and "What a Friend We Have in Jesus." She joined First United Methodist Church because John was a member.

Donna remembers being the tallest student in junior high at Marshall High School on Odell Street when the seventh and eighth grades had tea dances as socials.   She took piano lessons from Ruth Storts who gave lessons during the school day near the high school.   Many kids could not afford a piano in the home, and parents paid rent so they could practice on a piano in the Joe and Allie Miller home, 672 South Odell. Donna was in band, orchestra and chorus.

She received band and academic scholarships to Missouri Valley College which reduced the $250 semester tuition fee. Summers she worked from 8:00 a.m. to 10:00 p.m. at the Indian Foothills Park Municipal pool giving swimming lessons, instructing in the Red Cross swimming lesson program and life guarding in order to pay her college tuition.

Donna did not have a car until she was 25 years old. She took buses and cabs in Kansas City, putting away every penny she could for a trip to Europe.   She taught swimming to handicapped students at the Delano school in addition to her stewardess job.   Before she got married, she was able to travel to Europe with her savings.

Donna Huston is an individual with singular style and boundless energy. Many community projects have benefited from her leadership: the YMCA, Jim the Wonder Dog Park, Saline County Historical Society and Friends of Arrow Rock. She and John have been enthusiastic supporters of Indian Foothills Park, Fitzgibbon Hospital and Missouri Valley College.   John has been involved in the Marshall Saline Development Corporation since its beginning.

John and Donna think that summer jobs for teen-agers provide some of the best life lessons possible. Getting used to working with different kinds of people, saving and managing money impart values that prepare kids for what lies ahead.

"Everyone has troubles. You just have to get past them. Whole bunches of good stuff happen in life along with the bad." Donna said, "I have been blessed with a positive attitude. I always expect that the best will happen, and I can stay pretty upbeat. My philosophy is that the world would be a better place if everyone took the Golden Rule seriously."

Work Was Plentiful
Don Keener   June 2006

"Store-bought" toys were not part of Don Keener's youth growing up in Arkansas; in fact, play was a short commodity because there was always work to be done. "Usually we had Saturday afternoons free. We liked to swim or fish in the creek. Things were pretty tight for a family on a farm with four boys. We would find steel rims from wagon wheels and make a semi-circle pusher out of an old tobacco can nailed to a board, and we would push them around.

In the back pocket of overalls, every boy had what we called a 'bean flip' made from a forked branch and bands of rubber from a discarded tire inner tube. A pocket from an old shoe tongue held rocks which could be used to kill birds, snakes and lizards.

"We didn't shoot these weapons at each other—it was too dangerous, but we had corncob fights. Also I would look through the kitchen stove wood pile to find a stick with a knot which could be pried out to hold a rubber ball. It could be balanced over another stick so when you stepped on the end, the ball catapulted into the air for a long way. We made baseballs by wrapping old socks around a hard ball in the center."

Work was plentiful in the thirties for the Keener brothers: cows to milk, eggs to gather, hogs to raise for meat and usually one beef calf which they would ride around the lot for entertainment. They raised corn for feed, sold eggs and milk and used a cream separator to prepare cream for sale locally. The cream was checked for butterfat content at the store; Jersey cream was premium. Higher butterfat paid more, and some cream was shipped to Nebraska from Arkansas by train.

Cotton required the most attention, planting, thinning, hoeing weeds and harvesting. "I have picked a lot of cotton. My dad used to say that we had been over the field ten times before the season was over," Don recalls. The family lived in the hills, but farmed land in the Arkansas River bottoms using a team of mules. He remembers when he saw his first tractor, a brand new Allis Chalmers belonging to a well-to-do farmer in the bottoms. Little did he know that his future work one day would revolve around huge motorized equipment that he would come to know intricately.

Making sorghum molasses for everyone in the community was another Keener family project. The mill with three rollers was set up under a big shade tree near a neighbor's home. A mule harnessed to the crank of the mill walked around and around in a big circle to power the operation. Cut-up stalks of sorghum cane were fed into the mill, and the juice was strained through a feed sack as it emerged. Nearby a fire burned under a long shallow metal pan about six by fourteen feet and six or eight inches deep which held all the sorghum liquid.

Workers moved the stages of thickening syrup through dividers in the pan with a pusher, skimming off impurities in the process. Finally the sorghum molasses was drained into gallon containers. The Keeners received one gallon of molasses for every four they made for a neighbor. Sorghum molasses was ever-present on the table, used at every meal; and Don's mother made cakes and cookies with molasses.

Donald Berman Keener, known as Berman until he was an adult, was born in 1925 in Atkins, Arkansas, to Eathel Herman and Ava Irene Reed Keener. He went to a small country school, Bell's Chapel; the Bell's Chapel Methodist Church was nearby. The minister who also preached in Pottsville, Arkansas, five or six miles away, often came home to Sunday dinner with the Keener family.

When Don was in the ninth grade, they moved to another farm, and he went to Pottsville High School. Baseball was the only sport as transportation was limited for playing games with other schools. He remembers that discipline at the

118

school was generally very lax, although parents were strict at home. In one class students threw erasers when the teacher turned his back to write on the blackboard, and kids routinely talked out loud in class. One teacher had a hamstring strap cut from harness, and Don saw a girl whipped across the back of the legs for misbehaving.

As both of his older brothers were in the Air Force in World War II, Don helped on the farm after graduating from high school. He remembers a trip to North Dakota to help with the wheat harvest. The trip entailed going from Russellville, Arkansas, by train as part of a government program to harvest because the men were all in the service.

Later he went to Houston to work in the shipyards for a couple of months, but he could see that he was going to be drafted, so he volunteered for the Air Force in 1944.

Don was in a cadet program to train pilots, engineers and bombardiers, but the war effort was dwindling. "We were surplus," Don said. After a year he was discharged and the GI bill allowed him to go to Arkansas Polytechnic College in Russellville to study business administration.

The Air Force experience led Don to be interested in planes and pilot lessons in college. After soloing, the young pilots could check out small private planes to fly. He remembers chasing crows on the Arkansas River and ducks on the swamps.

"I had one friend who was either a dare-devil or just plain dumb; I don't know which," he said. "One day he said, 'Do you know these planes can loop-de-loop?' He would fly up to 3000 feet and red-line the engine, that is, push it to the maximum speed of 110 MPH, then fly upside down in a loop!"

Don met his wife, Patsy Porter, when he was refereeing a basketball game in Pottsville. They were married and moved to Fort Smith where he worked in a government agricultural agency. He went on to become a sales representative for

Case, Caterpillar and Fiat-Allis, later New Holland Equipment. Many moves in Missouri finally brought Don and Pat with five children to Marshall in 1966. Don continues to work part-time selling heavy equipment in the central Missouri area.

"When I started selling bulldozers, the popular size cost $28,000 to $30,000. Today the most popular model costs $250,000 and has an enclosed cab, air-conditioning, more horsepower and an expensive transmission," Don comments. He enjoys his part-time sales work as his long-time customers are now old friends, and he promotes sales of equipment over lunch and coffee while they visit.

Don has held many leadership positions at First United Methodist Church, most recently being a member of the new building committee. I asked him what changes he has noticed in church over the years. "When I was young, people thought the minister was almost God, and he was put on a pedestal. Calling the preacher by his first name would have been disrespectful. We would have referred to our minister as Brother Huck, certainly not Dave.

"I don't remember bitter arguments like the current controversy over homosexuality. The things that encourage people to give money have not changed. Every church we belonged to when we were moving around had some kind of a building project. Pat had a lot of insight, and she said once that people need to have something to work toward. She thought that churches that have a debt to pay off are active, thriving churches."

How has he coped with hard times in his life? "I had a good wife," he said simply. Many friends remember Pat Keener as a fun-loving person who always had time to talk, a source of support to many people. Pat died on the Keener's 48th wedding anniversary in 1996.

Don acknowledges that his church friends have helped him through difficult times as well. He has a regular schedule of going out to eat with friends, belongs to coffee groups that get together daily and plays golf. Don is to be admired for creating a new way of life for himself after grief and loss.

Hard Work Was There To Do, So I Did It

Mary Kersten   February 2006

Mary Chevalier Kersten, born in 1915, was raised on County Road YY near Marshall.   Mary was confirmed at the Evangelical and Reformed Church in Arrow Rock because she had an uncle who was an Evangelical minister. She had attended the Lutheran church as a child; she remembers singing in the choir on Christmas Eve at the Lutheran church. It was during the War years that she joined Grand Pass United Methodist Church.

Mary's paternal great-grandfather, Francois Chevalier, came to the United States from France. Her parents were Walter E. Chevalier and Emma S. Eilers Chevalier.

Mary was the only girl in her family, and she often cooked and took care of things at home because her mother went to help other family members at their houses. She remembers it was fun to do cross stitch embroidery as a child. She had chores to do like gathering the eggs.   She rode her horse to Stonewall school, leaving it in a pasture nearby. One day, she recalls someone left the gate open, and her horse ran off! Her father had to come get her and hunt for the lost horse.

When she graduated from high school, her Grandmother Eilers gave her five dollars.   She bought a Kodak camera and a Bible. Mary then read the Bible straight through from cover to cover!   "Actually, I found some of the Bible rather shocking," she said with a smile. Human nature continues to be rather shocking to this day.

Following high school, Mary went to nursing school at Deaconess Hospital in Marshalltown, Iowa, where another family member had attended.   She married Arley Kersten right after graduating.   They had met at the Evangelical church in Grand Pass, Missouri. After they were married they joined First United Methodist Church in Marshall as it was closer to their home.

122

Mary was active in the Keystone Class and remembers the big ice cream socials they had each year on the church lawn. United Methodist Women was also part of her church life; the late Kathryn Bagnell invited her to join the women's group. I asked her if she ever sang in the choir or played an instrument as one of her daughters, Henrietta Fenner, is a musician.

"No, all I could do was whistle. My mother was always whistling hymns. I wonder if children today go around whistling. Electronic music is so available all the time that I don't imagine they ever whistle to make their own music."

The five Kersten children were all born at home. Mary's life centered around farm and family. "Hard work was there to do, so I did it."

One of the Kersten sons, Everett, died in a car accident—an extremely difficult time for the family. "I had to be strong for Arley. It was so hard for him." Arley was blind in his later years; Mary took care of him, and managed things at their farm home. She lived alone for 12 years after his death.

I asked why she thinks she has lived so long. "Because my family insisted that I come live at the Blosser Home, and they take such good care of me here," she said cheerfully.

Mary has taken life as it has come to her. She does not seem to be one to feel sorry for herself; she has done whatever she has needed to do.

Free to Do Whatever You Wanted to Do
Velma Latimer   January 2006

Velma Latimer appears fragile as she sits in her hospital bed at the Grace Rich Care Facility in Marshall. However, she has a strong smile and a bright look in her eyes as she visits. Her mobility has been quite limited since she had to have her left leg amputated three years ago because of complications from diabetes.

Born in 1909, she grew up in Mount Leonard, Missouri, and attended the Baptist church there. "We always went to church, never knew anything else." Mount Leonard had two groceries, a lumberyard, a school, a church and a blacksmith shop.

Her father was teacher of all eight grades at the Mount Leonard School. Velma Grimes Latimer had her father, Carl Grimes, for her teacher the first six grades of school as did her brother; having their father for their teacher did not seem to be a problem for them.

After sixth grade, the Grimes family moved to Marshall where her dad sold insurance. Velma attended Eastwood School and then Marshall High School. Her mother, Hattie, developed asthma, and the family went to Colorado Springs, Colorado, for part of her sophomore year. They moved to Colorado Springs her senior year, and she graduated from high school there. Her mother's health improved. But when Grandpa Grimes died in the 1920s, the family returned to Arrow Rock, Missouri, to take over his farm and to run the Arrow Rock General Store.

Velma met her husband, Dick Latimer, at the Fall Festival in Marshall one year. One of the events of the festival was a dance held in Brown's garage on Eastwood Street, a car dealership. She and Dick were married and lived together for more than 60 years on their farm near Fairville, Missouri.

Velma loved living on the farm. "You were just free to do whatever you wanted to do," she said. It was hard work, but she loved it. The water pump was outside; there was an outdoor toilet, and she had a big garden every year. She cooked on a wood stove and canned and preserved food.

"The Depression was hard. We didn't know it then, but looking back on it, it was very hard." She belonged to a county extension club for more than 50 years. "That is how I learned everything new that came along." Electricity changed the way she lived entirely. "It was the biggest thing that happened in my life."

After Dick died in 1989, she moved to a brand new trailer near the home of her son, Ron, and his wife, Connie. "It was a really nice place to live." She smiles as she thinks about her daughter-in-law, Connie, who is presently the Mayor of Marshall.

Velma joined First United Methodist in Marshall after she moved. She had belonged to the Baptist church at Fairville until it closed, and then she joined Mount Carmel United Methodist Church. For several years, Velma was the church pianist.

Velma's favorite Scripture is the fourteenth chapter of John. "I used to be able to say it from memory, but I can't anymore," she said. However, when I looked it up and started to read it to her, she took over reciting it in a strong voice:

Let not your heart be troubled: ye believe in God, believe also in me. In my Father's house are many mansions, if it were not so, I would have told you. I go to prepare a place for you. And if I go and prepare a place for you, I will come again, and receive you unto myself that where I am, there ye may be also. John 14:1 -3 KJV

Aunt Melba's Favorite Child

Katherine Carroll Lewis   May 2006

Katherine Carroll Lewis knows more funny stories from the past than anyone you could ever meet. Who else could tell you that once there was a farmer in rural Saline County who never washed his overalls until they wore out; and if he had a sick baby calf, he kept it in bed with him to watch it? She is a lively, independent lady who is a spirited companion for her friends.

Katherine Carroll Garrard was born in Shackelford, Missouri, in 1923, to Ruby Akers Garrard and James Walton Garrard. She had a younger brother; and since the neighborhood had 14 boys and only three girls, they mostly played war games, baseball, and football. Shackelford had two groceries, a post office, filling station and a train depot. The Garrards lived next door to the Catholic Church which sponsored dances at a dance hall in town; adults and children came from miles around to these dances.

One grocery store was a neighborhood gathering place. For awhile, her parents ran the grocery, but her dad became a mail carrier. They built their home in Shackelford for $5000; it was the first house in the community to have an indoor bathroom. Katherine Carroll recalls that someone would have to go to the basement every day and pump to get the water pressure up. Many years later the house was cut into half, and the two sections were moved to Marshall to 314 East Rea. The Garrard family eventually lived in this house again after it was moved to Marshall.

Jim Garrard, her father, died when Katherine Carroll was three years old. Her mother, Ruby, continued to carry the mail for a year. Ruby's sister, Melba Akers, moved in with the family and became an important part of the children's lives. Aunt Melba or Nanta began teaching at age 16, and had taught for 49 years when she retired.

Katherine Carroll always thought her brother was her mother's favorite child, but it did not matter, because she was sure that she was her aunt's favorite. The combined family moved to Marshall before Katharine Carroll started school at Benton elementary.

Both sisters worked hard to support the family during the Depression years. Katherine Carroll's mother sometimes did sewing for people. Smocking, a decorative shirring of fabric on the front of little girls' dresses, was popular; and Mrs. Garrard smocked dresses for other children. Katherine Carroll remembers that her mother made all the draperies for the new double residence that Missouri Valley College built across from Murrell Library for the college president and vice-president.

Katherine Carroll does not think she ever went without anything that she needed. Cousins in St. Louis sent boxes of their used clothing, and her mother made them over for her. She remembers having a skirt and three blouses to wear to school; she changed to play clothes immediately after she got home to keep her school clothes nice. Her mother even made their underwear which was washed by hand. Her favorite Sunday dress was a made-over middy white sailor dress trimmed with braid from a real navy uniform.

Later Ruby Garrard got a teaching degree, and she taught grades seven, eight and nine in Independence, coming home on week-ends. Nanta was in charge of the Garrard children in her absence. "When we got into trouble, my brother and I would say, 'Whose children are we anyway?', but Nanta never let that bother her," said Katherine Carroll.

"My mother was a good cook, but when she dieted, the rest of us got hungry so when we went to get our mail at the post office, Nanta would take us to Woody's Hamburger Stand, the hang-out for teenagers which was located across the street from the present Con-Agra parking lot.

"We had to go to the post office for our mail, because at that time mail wasn't delivered to your house unless you had a sidewalk in front." Other favorite places for treats were the Green Mill, 18 South Jefferson, now Sturhahn Jewelers, and Hansbro's, 23 West North, which served homemade ice cream, cokes, and sandwiches. American Family Insurance replaced the original Hansbro's building after a fire destroyed it in the nineties.

When Katherine Carroll went to Southeast school, her aunt was teaching third grade there. She went to junior and senior high at Marshall High School, the present Bueker Middle School on Odell. She remembers learning to knit in a high school class during the brief stay of a rather disorganized young teacher who was not doing much teaching, and the girls took up knitting.

One teacher she enjoyed was Mary Fisher, teacher of English and dramatics. Miss Fisher put on one-act plays each year, and Katherine Carroll was in a number of these. Mary Fisher, born in England, was a favorite of many students; the Mary Fisher Community Theatre in Marshall was named for her. Katherine Carroll says she did not particularly like school; she felt the teachers all knew her Aunt Melba and put pressure on her to do well "for her aunt".

The family attended Odell Avenue Presbyterian Church, 178 South Odell. The Sunday School consisted of a boys' class and a girls' class in the basement. The children sat around a large oval table with the teacher on one side. J. L. Gordon conducted opening and closing exercises each Sunday.

The children were mischievous and liked to sit in a pew that one lady thought belonged to her. The lady would ask them to move, but the next Sunday the children were back sitting in her pew again. She remembers plays for Children's Day and big suppers for the whole congregation. Odell Avenue Presbyterian moved to 710 East Yerby in the sixties and changed its name to Covenant Presbyterian Church; the original church building was later destroyed by fire.

Katherine Carroll met Leonard Lewis at a Young Farmers Camp held at the Lake of the Ozarks. There was a dormitory for girls, and classes and socials were held. After they were married at Odell Avenue Church, they moved to the country and lived on his grandfather's farm where she continues to live today.

"The women in the community seemed to think the marriage wouldn't last long," she says with a laugh. Farm homemakers tended to be skeptical about the ability of "city girls" to handle all the hard work of living in the country. Raising chickens, cooking and farm chores were familiar to her because she had spent time on her grandparents' farm at Norton, Missouri; she adapted quickly. Katherine Carroll and Leonard raised six children in Shiloh Methodist Church and provided leadership in the community in 4-H and other organizations.

"I have always loved living in the country," she says, "and I wouldn't trade it for any other way of living."

During the winter months, Katherine Carroll would work Fridays and Saturdays at Missouri Valley Store, a department store on North Street just off the square. Missouri Valley Store carried nice ready-to-wear women's clothing, men's work clothes, sewing goods, hardware supplies, shoes and jewelry on the main floor.

Pots and pans and kitchen supplies were sold in the basement. China and crystal were on the mezzanine along with an alterations department, and upstairs was a large furniture sales area. Quality merchandise was carried, and it was an important feature of Marshall's downtown.

Katherine Carroll remembers that during the forties, the Marshall Square was a popular destination for all ages on Saturday night. "You went early in order to get a good parking place, preferably on the east side of the Square. Adults liked to sit in the cars to watch the people go by, and there was usually quite a crowd. Nanta would walk around the square holding the hand of my oldest child, Katie, who was a toddler."

Farmers came to town to do their weekly shopping, and Marshall residents turned out as well for the social occasion. In later years the stores were open on Friday nights, but by the late fifties evening hours had been discontinued.

Six children made for a busy household. When they were older, Katherine Carroll drove a school bus and then became a school cook. She enjoyed being around grade school children.

After Leonard retired from farming, he had a severe stroke and was unable to speak clearly. Katherine Carroll found a discarded fifth grade reader and used it to teach him to communicate again. Leonard was confined to a wheelchair, and she cared for him as an invalid for ten years. She feels prayer significantly helped her through these difficult times. Katherine Carroll has stoutheartedly met every challenge before her, and she consistently looks at the lighter side of things. "Sometimes," she said, "you need to laugh to keep from crying."

The Large Power Girl
Mabel Long   April 2006

Her reading materials, the daily newspaper, *U.S. News and World Report* and *Forbes* magazine surround Mabel Long. "Do you keep up with the stock market?" I asked.

"Oh, yes," she smiled.

"You would think that she had money," said her daughter, Helen Griener. Mabel spends her days reading.

Mabel gave up her home in Edwardsville, Illinois, because of health problems and she moved to Marshall in 2001 along with her daughter, Helen, and her son-in-law, Merle. "They have been very good to me," she says.

Immediately I can see her territory in the living room: a recliner backed by two lamps with an additional lighted magnifying light that swings over her chair. The furniture in the living room all belongs to her, and she has her own bedroom and bathroom in this shared living arrangement.

Mabel, at age 98, has macular degeneration and a complicated medical condition of her esophagus. She chuckles as she said, "They sent me home in January to die, and here I am!" There is warm-hearted laughter throughout our interview; she and Helen relate to each other more as old friends than as mother and daughter.

Mabel was born in 1907 in New Lebanon, Missouri, in Cooper County. Her father, Richard Rothgeb, was a former grade school teacher, a farmer and stockman. He raised registered Duroc Jersey hogs and mules and had seven cows which were milked daily. Mabel and her brothers walked a couple of miles to the New Lebanon grade school. In the winter when there were big snows, her father would hitch up a big sled with a horse team and pick up the kids in the neighborhood. Her mother, Jessie Sites Rothgeb, died when Mabel was a young adult, and as she was the oldest of eight, three died in infancy, she assumed many responsibilities in the home.

Mabel was a timid child at times. One of her teachers was her uncle who had been superintendent of Cooper County schools. He was thought to be very strict. In the third grade, when he called on Mabel to read aloud, she fainted! Uncle Dan poured a bucket of water on her head, and she recovered. She fainted on a number of occasions, once in high school at noon time. She was taken to a neighboring house; and when she came to, the whole high school was standing in the room looking at her.

The roads were mostly dirt and mud in those days, and Otterville High School was six miles from her home. Mabel had a beautiful horse named "Shakespeare" who held his head high and pranced; Shakespeare was greatly admired by her friends. One day they stopped to let the horses drink at the Lamine River by Otterville. Shakespeare just would not stop drinking; and shortly afterward, the horse died. A sad time for Mabel.

Her family got another horse for Mabel to ride to school. This horse had been used for racing. Seventeen kids rode horses to school together. One day she was running late, and she let the horse go fast to catch up with the others. As she approached the group, they separated to let her join them.

But her horse didn't pause and shot right through the other riders, running away with Mabel who was covered with mud. The racing horse did not stop until it reached the house next to the high school where it turned into the yard and ran into a tree. After that, it was decided that Mabel would board in Otterville instead of commuting by horseback.

She roomed with two other girls in town. She remembers they all had dates to go to a picnic at the river. When they got home, they hid behind trees in the yard so they would not have to go in. But their landladies heard them, and called, "You girls come in or we are going to call your parents!"

When Mabel was 14 years old, a new boy in the community bought her box at a box supper auction at the school. Her mother had fixed wonderful food for her, sandwiches and desserts. William David Long devoured all the food. He expressed an interest in dating her, but she did not like him. People told her that he swore at times, and she strongly disapproved of this bad habit. Eventually he gave up swearing; and in 1931, she married him. Mabel said, "I worked on him for several years to improve him."

Mabel went to the New Lebanon Presbyterian Church as a child; the church was right next door to the school. "I almost lived there," she said. "I loved my church." She took piano lessons and practiced at the church. She played for Sunday School and occasionally for the church service. At the end of opening exercises for Sunday School, she played "The Battle Hymn of the Republic" while the children marched to their classes. As a young person, she sang "In the Garden" as a solo, making it one of her favorites. She sang at other churches in the area as well as her own.

Mabel and William lived in Pilot Grove for several years, and then moved to Rolla. He was a welder and machinist for the Army Corps of Engineers. Both of them took some night college courses at the University of Missouri at Rolla. Fort Leonard Wood was being built while they lived in Rolla.

Many people were seeking work, and a steady stream of people from Pilot Grove came to Rolla to work on the new army base which was completed in 1941. "They stayed at our house. We had mattresses and cots everywhere. I cooked meals, kept the sheets changed. Sometimes we had day shift people and night shift people who slept in the same beds. They paid me $5 a week!"

During World War II, Mr. Long worked at the army depot at Granite City, Illinois. There was a shortage of workers, and Mabel worked in a war plant on an assembly line building

133

tanks. She wore slacks and had a scarf knotted around her hair.

"You were Rosie the Riveter," I said.

"Yes, she was indeed," said Helen.

After the war she was hired by the Illinois Power company as a credit manager. In spite of the fact that she had made the highest score ever on their pre-employment test, the bosses told her that she would have the job just a few weeks, "until the boys came home." However, she worked for Illinois Power for 25 years. Mabel became known as the "Large Power Girl," keeping huge charts showing the usage demands for their largest customers.

In 1960, Mabel and William built their dream home in Edwardsville, Illinois, 20 miles from their jobs in Granite City. The two of them landscaped the three-acre site. It was a labor of love for Mabel to work all day, come home, and prepare vegetables from their garden to can and preserve.

She loved yard work and won blue ribbons for her beautiful flowers. One day while trimming her own trees, she miscalculated and cut off a limb and fell to the ground along with it; fortunately, she was unhurt. It was hard for her to leave this special place to move to Missouri.

Mabel has serious health problems, but her daughter reports that she eats a healthy diet which probably has kept her going. Her very positive attitude and her humorous outlook on life undoubtedly have added years to her life.

Civil War Connections

Marge and Elwyn Long   July 2006

Eighteen baby dolls sit on the bed of the front bedroom of Marge and Elwyn Long's bungalow at 519 East Summit. Marge has rescued them from the Lighthouse Resale Store; she has restored them to health and made each doll a new dress. Next Christmas they will be given to little girls through the community Christmas project.

For years Marge has knit warm caps which are distributed to children in the winter. Slim and youthful looking, she says, "I can't sit still, I always have to be doing something." Sewing has always been easy for her, "a God-given talent, I guess, I just have always understood patterns and how to construct clothing. I made clothes for my children and grandchildren.

"One of the hardest projects I have done is making Civil War uniforms for the Civil War re-enactors in my family. Once I made a 'great coat' like the ones worn by both the South and the North, a long heavy wool coat with a cape that went around the shoulders."

Marge takes time out from our visit to work on a special pasta salad she is fixing for lunch, "one of Elwyn's favorites." Cooking is also one of her specialties. She remembers the first time she put together a big meal when she was sixteen; her grandmother had died, and her parents went to town to make funeral arrangements. When they got home, Marge surprised them with a complete meal including pies she had baked.

Elwyn, Marge and I gather around the table in the kitchen to visit, and we are joined by Tucker, a fat cocker spaniel. Soon Cleopatra joins us, a sweet-faced Himalayan cat that has just been sheared for the summer and looks like a small animal from an alien planet. Elwyn and Marge engage in light-hearted disagreements about places and dates as we visit.

Marjorie Elizabeth Dennis was born in 1928 on a farm at Blue Lick, near Marshall Junction, the third of five children. When I asked her what she did for fun as a child she said, "Well, did you know that cats can swim? They don't like to, but they will if you throw them in the pond. We weren't really mean to them, we just made them swim!

"I played with my younger brothers, and what one of us didn't think of, the other did. We rode horseback. We had a clay bank in one of the pastures, and we would make clay dishes. We set them in the sun to dry, and it was disappointing when the cows would walk through them and break them up."

Austin Dennis and Hazel Foree Dennis moved the family from Blue Lick to the farm on Highway 41 seven miles east of Marshall when Marge was little. The Dennis family were members of Shiloh Methodist Church.

"I remember basket dinners on long wooden tables on the East side of the church. They lasted until 4:30 p.m. in the afternoon; people just visited and the kids played running up and down the circle driveway. Reverend Tom Harris was a minister I loved. When he left, his replacement would yell and hit the pulpit with his fist. It scared me, and I remember telling Mother I didn't want to go to church!

"I dearly loved Reverend Harris' daughter, Mary Harris Pemberton, who played the piano; I loved to sing 'In the Garden.' Sunday School classes were held in each corner of the church with partitions to separate age groups. No one seemed to be bothered by the noise."

Marge started school at St. Peter's in Marshall because the older children were in high school, and her parents did not want her to walk alone on Highway 41 to Neff School one and one half miles away. But when her brothers were old enough, they all walked or rode horseback to the one room school.

Marge remembers the school was very cold in the winter with a coal stove in the middle of the room and windows on both the north and south sides. "We would take milk to school with sugar and vanilla in it, put it in the window, and by noon, it was frozen into ice cream!"

One exciting time was when the girls' outhouse burned down. "A tramp had set a fire in it. We were very excited when we saw that the outhouse burned because we were sure school would be cancelled. But they went right on and had school anyway." Hobos were common in the thirties, roaming around, offering to work for food. Families would give them a plate of food to eat outside on the porch, and then they would move on.

Marge remembers the frightening experience of hearing the dogs bark at night and chickens squawking because a thief was in the chicken house. "Dad wanted to get his gun out, but Mother would say, 'Just leave them alone, it is not worth getting hurt over.'" Calling someone a "low-down, dirty chicken thief" was one of the worst insults that could be given. The worst name Marge's Grandmother Foree called these criminals was "a scallywag."

Lavinia Elizabeth Wilson Foree, her grandmother, was a true Southerner, from Kentucky and South Carolina. She was born in 1862, the youngest of nine children. Lavinia's mother, Marge's great-grandmother, passed down the story to Lavinia that during the Civil War when the family was living at Pilot Grove, Missouri, Union soldiers came to their home. When they found her husband, Jonathan Wilson, they strung him up with a rope to hang him because he had Confederate sympathies.

Jonathan was 49 years old, older than most of those who were fighting, and he remained at home to take care of his family. Sarah begged them to let him go because she had young children including Baby Lavinia. They let him down, but told him they had better never see him again. Jonathan went to Montana for the remainder of the war.

Marge's Grandmother Lavinia had a difficult childhood as her parents died by the time she was eleven. She then lived three to four months of the year with each of her older siblings. While she was staying with them, it was her job to sew for her nieces and nephews. Perhaps it is from this grandmother that Marge received her gift for clothing construction.

The Civil War figures prominently in Marge's family history. Her grandfather, John Austin Dennis, served on the Union side; and his brother, David P. Dennis, was Confederate. After the war they moved from Kentucky to Missouri and farmed together.

A monument marking their grave is a landmark in Ridge Park Cemetery, a life-size horse ridden by a soldier whose uniform is a combination of both the North and the South. Marge never knew her grandfather who died before she was born. Her father told her that John and David Dennis never talked about the war or their political differences.

After finishing at Neff School, Marge took the school bus to Marshall High School. "High school was not a lot of fun like it is today because World War II was going on. They would let us out of school for scrap metal drives. Gas and tires were rationed so you couldn't travel very far. It was common to have flat tires, and when you changed one, the inner tube would have so many patches on it, it looked like it had the measles!" Kids collected milkweed pods which were used as kapok in life jackets.

The first job for which she was paid was carrying water on her horse to the threshing crew on a farm east of Marshall. While she was in high school, Marge worked at F.W. Woolworth dime store on the corner of North Street and Jefferson Street on the Marshall square.

Marge moved to Kansas City after graduating, living with her sister and working as a secretary at Luzier's Cosmetics. She had no car and rode the city bus to get to work. Later she got a job at the Cooper County Extension Office in Boonville; still she did not need a car because she could walk to work from the room she rented. Here Elwyn Long, her future husband, enters into the picture.

Elwyn was an extension agent in the Boonville office. In 1947 and 1948, the government initiated a Balanced Farming program, and Elwyn had about a dozen farmers with whom he worked. He tested soil, taught the use of commercial fertilizer and lime, laid off contour terraces and encouraged proper livestock feeding.

"At that time the most some farmers knew was just to open the gate and turn the cows out," Elwyn said. Some farmers reported that their income doubled with the new information they learned.

Elwyn Dewitt Long was born in Wellsville, Missouri, in 1920, to Earl Dewitt Long and Nellie Pearl Burkhalter Long. He was the third of three boys. "Mostly we worked all the time. We would go fishing in the creek, or ice skating in the winter, but we had chores to do—12 to 14 cows to milk and we gathered eggs to sell. We drove teams of two or four horses to do the farming. No tractor, no car.

"Nobody had anything, so we couldn't do anything for fun. The picture show was a rare treat, but it cost ten or fifteen cents apiece," he said. "Really, it wasn't as bad as it sounds because everybody lived like that."

The Long boys went to Hazel Dell School. Families contributed wood to heat the school building; coal cost money, and wood was cheaper. When Elwyn was in the eighth grade, he had a key to the building so he could go early to start the fire.

Near the school was a country church the Longs attended. "It was Christian, down the creek a ways was a Presbyterian church and we sometimes went there. Sunday services were all they offered; no activities were held," Elwyn said.

"My mother had been a school teacher, and education was important in our family. We wanted to go to school, so when we had to walk five miles each way down the crooked road to Middletown High School, we didn't complain," Elwyn said.

"Middletown Grade School was in the basement of the high school. Hazel Dell was just a one room school and Middletown was the nearest town. There were no sports in high school. When we had free time, we shot baskets outside."

After high school, Elwyn went to the University of Missouri at Columbia to study agriculture. To support himself, he worked at Gaebler's restaurant across from Jesse Hall. "There was an old streetcar in front of the restaurant where people could sit on stools and order hamburgers. I waited on the counter, fried hamburgers on the grill and washed dishes.

"In the evenings men wore suits and ties to go into the restaurant. I didn't have a car, and I didn't have a quarter in my pocket." Occasionally he drove for two retired ladies in Columbia; Elwyn was paid three or four dollars to drive them to St. Louis for the day.

In the summers, he hitch-hiked to Dekalb, Illinois, to work at detasselling seed corn. Tassels were removed from six rows, leaving two rows of tasselled corn alone to pollinate the corn for seed. Elwyn also worked back home on the family farm in the summer time as detasselling was seasonal.

"My first job after graduating in 1942 was World War II. I joined the Air Corps, but my vision kept me from flying, so I spent two and one half years at Del Rio, Texas, working with airplane parts." Toward the end of the war, Elwyn was sent to the Ascension Islands, a British possession about halfway between South America and Africa to work as a chemist for hydroponically grown vegetables grown fresh for the troops. Planes refueled at an airstrip on the islands.

"When the war was over, I called the School of Agriculture at the University and asked if they knew of any jobs. They told me that the Saline County Extension Office needed a 4-H extension agent. I wanted anything that paid! I bought an old 1936 Chevy for $50 or $60 to get me around. New cars weren't being manufactured, but I put my name on a list. Eventually I got a Ford two-door with a heater for $1300."

The Longs moved several times in Missouri before settling in Marshall. Elwyn worked for Missouri Farmers Association Seed Division and then transferred to Millers Mutual Insurance for the rest of his career, selling insurance for grain elevators and fertilizer dealers. Their three children grew up in First United Methodist Church.

Marge remarks that the biggest change she has seen in the congregation is in the way people dress for Sunday. "Probably dressing casually is all for the best," she said. "I am sure that God doesn't care what you wear."

I asked the couple what has helped them through the bad times in their lives. Marge said, "Prayer—I say my prayers every night before I go to sleep, and if I fall asleep first, I wake up and say them."

Elwyn, who has engaged in gentle teasing of his wife throughout our visit, said simply, "I married her."

"I think he is being quite serious now," I said.

"Yes, he is," said Marge. "Last year he was in the hospital four times and had a pacemaker put in. It was a bad year."

"I am still here," said Elwyn. It is a testimony in few words to a long, supportive relationship together.

Roller-skating Through Childhood
Clara McAfee   August 2006

Clara McAfee roller-skated her way through childhood. "There was always a roller-skating rink in Marshall. If one closed, another opened. We liked the rink behind the Post Office facing Lafayette Street. My folks would take my friend, Kay Bowler Halsey, and me to Sedalia; and we would skate both sessions. I was able to show my grandchildren how I could two-step to music with my skates, and they were impressed!" Clara loved swimming at the city pool which was on North Lafayette Street and playing tennis at Indian Foothills Park.

In high school, she played basketball and enjoyed sports. "Some people remembered me because I wouldn't let them have the ball on the basketball court," she said with a smile. She recalled folk dancing lessons on the second floor of old Northwest School and learning to waltz in gym at Marshall High School on Odell Street.

Clara was breathless and very quiet at the beginning of our visit. She started using a portable oxygen machine two years ago because of her chronic obstructive pulmonary disease. Once she had her oxygen comfortably balanced, she relaxed and quite obviously enjoyed remembering her former athletic self. However, she is a lady who loves life and fills every day with as much activity as she can manage.

On the day of our interview, August 8, 2006, she was 82 years old. "I am not going to sit around, hold my hands and say, 'Oh I can't do this or I can't do that.' I don't have time to complain."

Her parents, Edwin and Agnes Huyett Krumsiek, built the house where she was born at 803 North Hamner, and her grandparents lived on Hamner as well. She remembers riding with her grandfather, Robert McMurran Huyett, in "one of those old square Fords" when the car would not turn because he had broken a tie rod. She jumped out of the running car and ran home because her grandfather intended to keep driving.

"It about scared the liver out of me," she said. "Grandad would not stop at stop signs. He said that people knew him, and they knew he didn't stop at stop signs!"

Her grandfather, who was retired from the brick factory at Shackelford, had a big garden and sold vegetables to Latimer's Grocery Store on the north side of the square. Her grandmother, Molly Kyle Huyett, sold flower bulbs and cut flowers before there were florists in town. Clara said, "I picked peas and strawberries at three cents a box. My grandfather also sold apples and pears."

The Krumsiek family were always members of First United Methodist Church, and Clara grew up in the congregation. She remembers many good times as a child at church such as scavenger hunts for the young people. "No cards or dancing permitted, and no britches for the girls."

Clara married Conley Ahrens after high school; she met him, of course, at the skating rink. She went to work as a telephone operator. "I said, 'Number Please?' and plugged into the switchboard to connect people. There were several of us sitting at a long switchboard. If it was storming and you plugged into long distance, it would shock you! Sometimes callers would get cross with you and expect you to remember who they were and call them back if they hung up before you connected them with their number."

The Ahrens lived in the Miami bottoms until the house there flooded. "I liked the country, but we didn't go back after the flood—I did not like snakes, spiders and the smell that was left in the house." Clara and Conley moved several times in Saline County. Over the years, they had six children, and Clara always had a job outside of home.

She worked at International Shoe Factory for several years sewing leather pieces together. "You had to be fast and precise. I learned to love to sew. I loved to put my foot on that pedal and make it go, make the machine do what I wanted it to do.

"I have a table for my sewing machine in my bedroom to this day. I buy fabric scraps and thread at rummage sales and make patchwork baby quilts and lap robes for invalids. I have 15 ready to go with my son, Darrell Ahrens, and his wife, Marilyn, when they go on the next mission trip to New Orleans to help in the clean-up after Hurricane Katrina."

The reason it was necessary to be fast and precise at the shoe factory is because workers were paid by the piece. Women with the most seniority got the best jobs, working on high tops or work boots paid more; new people were sent home if the workload slowed down.

"I worked in between babies. I had two older kids and ten years later, four younger ones who were 16 months apart. I paid a babysitter one dollar a day for each kid, plus I brought a gallon of milk and a load of cloth diapers each day."

After 29 years, Clara's marriage ended. It took everything she had to manage financially. "I don't believe in welfare; they were my kids and I was responsible for them. All my kids know how to work hard; they had to help me. They brought the wash in from the clothesline, washed dishes, whatever I needed them to do, they did."

Once Clara went to the doctor with health complaints, and she was told her problems were due to fatigue. "The doctor said, 'You get up too early and stay up too late.' I paid three dollars for advice to take a nap every day. I started resting from 3:30 to 4:00 p.m. every day, and it made a big difference. The kids respected that I just had to do it."

Clara worked at Banquet Foods for 26 years. "I learned to do everything. Mostly I had day shifts; I worked the dinner line and the pie line. Sometimes I spent the day grinding onions. Standing in one place holding frozen meat in your hands is hard work. You were not supposed to talk to the other workers. I inspected T.V. dinners for 10 years—a double row coming down the line at 230 a minute, and I had to spot all the ones that weren't quite right."

Clara's favorite job at Banquet, later Con Agra, was in the laundry. She operated two enormous machines that each held 28 coveralls. Heavy starch was used for the food inspectors' coveralls. In addition, she got to mend using her favorite tool, the sewing machine.

Clara was skeptical about getting married again; but after a number of years, she met Lee McAfee, a mechanic at Con Agra. "Lee was a wonderful person. He could do anything with metal or wood; he fixed cars and had a shop on Boyd Street. We traveled to other states, bowled, danced, fished on the Missouri River. He didn't roller-skate though!" she laughed. They had been married 25 years when Lee died last year.

"He had Alzheimer's disease for two years, but he wasn't any trouble. I took care of him, he was just forgetful."

Her son, Darrell Ahrens, a member of First United Methodist Church, is a contractor who built the triplex at 612 West Clara in which she presently lives. Her children moved her hostas and peonies into a new garden from her old place. They are hard workers, as Clara says. Vickie Ahrens Leslie keeps the church nursery and is the part-time church custodian.

Clara has these words of advice for her family: "If you have anything cross to say, keep it outside my house. I don't want anyone raising 'Old Billy Ned.' My house is peaceful."

She feels she has much to live for; she loves to see her great grandchildren playing. "I don't believe in crying over spilled milk. You have to learn to look ahead, you can't look back."

In the Shadow of the Depression
Jessie and Bob McDonough   December 2006

The Great Depression of the nineteen-thirties cast a shadow on the teenage years of Jessie and Bob McDonough. Thomas Edward McDonough and Nellie Jane Crank McDonough farmed on the edge of Marshall, the present site of the Saline County Criminal Justice Center, 1915 West Arrow. Bob remembers helping with the annual hay baling by sitting on the seat to one side of the baler and punching the wire through to wrap the square bales.

Bob, born in 1925 and the youngest of five*, was 13 years old, he began helping at the Crockett Dairy Farm a half mile from their property. He got up at 3:30 a.m. to help milk the 30 cows and deliver milk before he went to school and returned for the evening milking. "I got $15 a month, but I had to quit after my freshman year because I kept falling asleep at school."

"Didn't you want to quit?" I asked, "Didn't you complain about having to get up so early?"

"My parents didn't have any money," Bob said simply. "You were just glad to have a way to earn something."   "After working at the dairy, I got a job at Temple Stevens grocery store on North Street. I was in Diversified Occupations class, and I got out of school to work every afternoon. The teacher would go to your employer to see how you were doing in order to give you a grade.

"I worked 12 hours on Saturdays because the old Mary Lou Theatre was next door, and the grocery stayed open till midnight to catch shoppers after they left the double feature; the second show started at 9:00 p.m. With the $7.50 I got each week, I had enough to buy my clothes and pay my expenses.

"My older brother had a job working in Kansas City for Wilson's packinghouse, and he got me a summer job when I was fifteen. It was hard work. . .I pushed a cart with the internal organs of the butchered cow and emptied it after the heart and lungs were examined for disease. If you need money, you will do about anything! I got 60 cents an hour that summer and I was on a roll. I opened up a bank account at Wood and Huston when I got back to Marshall.

"My brothers and I had fun pitching horseshoes, rolling hoops or old tires, riding hogs and having corncob fights. We always had enough to eat even though it was hard times."

Jessie recalls, "Sometimes I was sort of halfway hungry because we were short of things during the Depression. We lost our 80 acre farm by Blackwater; but my father, Ludwill Cramer, drove a dump truck, and he was a good mechanic so we got along okay."

Jessie was born in 1923 in the country between Pilot Grove and Blackwater, Missouri; her mother was Nellie Annie Tally, and Jessie was the youngest of four children. "The Cramers were originally from Holland; they were called 'wooden shoe Dutch.' My grandfather, Harmon Cramer, lived with us.

"I walked two miles each way to Peninsula School in the rain, snow and sleet. When I was older, I rode the school bus to Blackwater High School. There were 16 in my class." Jessie was a star basketball player; she and her team were the champions of Cooper County.

The Cramer family walked to Peninsula Baptist Church. "When I was baptized, we rode in the back of a truck to Blackwater River; the minister tipped me over backwards and dunked me in the muddy water."

After high school, Jessie rented a room with her sister in Boonville, Missouri, and worked at Viertel's Café for $3.50 a week plus her tips, usually a quarter. International Shoe

Company in Marshall offered a better job, so she moved to a boarding house on North Street to go to work there.

She substituted occasionally for a friend who was a waitress at The Spot, a restaurant on North Street that served hamburgers from the grill and had a wooden dance floor in the back with a nickelodeon. Jesse was waiting tables one day when Bob McDonough came in to eat. They were married in 1943 in the home of the Marshall Baptist Church minister, Reverend William M. Taylor.

Bob thinks back on his grade school years at Elm Grove School with eight grades in one room. "You learned from the others when they recited their lessons. An insulated shield stood around the stove that burned wood or coal. Gladys Ruff was the teacher. I went to Benton School for a short time, and it was an experience for a country boy—the bell ringing, and kids going to different classes.

"We lived in town for a while because my dad was able to get a job with the Works Progress Administration (W.P.A.) in the building of the Marshall swimming pool. He was the night watchman from 12:00 to 8:00 p.m. When the project was finished in 1937, we moved back to the farm."

Bob was drafted into the Navy after graduation from high school. After his gunnery training, he traveled through the Panama Canal to Sydney, Australia, and on to New Guinea and the Philippines on a transport ship. He was part of a Navy armed guard accompanying Merchant Marine ships.

Jessie worked in Kansas City at the Pratt and Whitney plant in the underground caverns that later became the Bendix corporation.

"The women did important work during World War II," Bob said, "People tend to forget that."

"We were making clutches for Corsair airplanes," Jessie said. "You never saw so many gears. The work site was heavily guarded, and you had to have the right identification to get in. My brother's wife and I stayed at the Alcazar Hotel and we took a streetcar to work."

Jessie remembers that she was in downtown Kansas City when she heard that the war was over. "The news was announced on loudspeakers. People just went wild; everybody was kissing everybody else. They tore the sockets right off the electric tracks, and the street cars couldn't run! Traffic came to a stop because the streets were full of people."

The McDonoughs came to Marshall to live after the war; Bob's first job was changing tires for Harold Sherwood on Eastwood Street. Then he began billing, shipping and keeping inventory for Missouri Farmers Association Seed Division when Harold Swinger was manager. For a while, he worked for Red Comb Pioneer Mills, later returning to M.F.A. Seed Division as manager.

Bob started his own business, Mid-State Warehouse, with Eidson-Ussery trucklines. Jessie did the books and inventory. Several years later, he sold this business and started his own seed brokerage. Jessie has always been a active partner in the family businesses.

Jessie needs oxygen almost continuously now because of her emphysema. In spite of health problems, Bob and Jesse attend First United Methodist Church regularly; Bob has been a member for his entire life, and their son and daughter grew up in the congregation.

Jessie finds inspiration in Billy Graham's column in the Kansas City paper that she reads every day. Bob says, "You can't give up when things go wrong; you have to keep believing things will get better. You just have to be thankful for what you have."

*Bob's older sister, Mary Frances McDonough Coad, is interviewed elsewhere in the book.

Generations of Methodist Circuit Riders

Lucille and Harry Major   July 2006

In the Normandale Highlands United Methodist Church in Bloomington, Minnesota, the "Harry Major Sunday School Class" continues to exist; it is named for Harry Merritt Major of Marshall, Missouri, who started the class and taught it for 12 years. Harry Major comes from a long line of Methodist Circuit Riders that has skipped a couple of generations, but he has left his mark none-the-less.

Harry is highly regarded as a Bible scholar and a lay speaker, and he has served as Lay Leader of First United Methodist Church three times since he and his wife, Lucille, moved to Marshall to retire in 1985.

Harry, born in 1923 in Armstrong, Missouri, was named for his grandfather, Reverend John Merritt Major, who was still actively riding his horse between services in Armstrong and two other churches at the time of Harry's birth. Reverend Major had circuits in Tennessee and Colorado before he was married at age 42 to Mary Jane "Molly" Benson, settling in Missouri.

Two horses were required to keep up with the circuit as services were held twice a day in a week of traveling, and a change of horses allowed one to rest a few days. Reverend Major was paid in food or money and given room and board on his way; Harry thinks he probably made $100 a year at the peak of his career.

Harry's great-grandfather, Reverend James Merritt Major, was a circuit rider in Tennessee and Kentucky, and his great-great-grandfather, Reverend John Major, rode on a circuit in South Carolina. John McFall Major, Harry's father, and John's wife, Narcissa Shores Major, lived in Armstrong, Missouri, at the time of Harry's birth. Later John Major rented land to farm near Clifton Hill, Missouri, in Randolph County.

"We were quite poor folks. Eventually my father bought land, but we were sharecroppers really. I started driving a team of workhorses when I was about eight years old," Harry said very matter-of-factly.

Harry was the middle child with an older and younger sister. He fished in farm ponds and walked and wandered through the woods with a neighbor boy when he was finished with his daily chores.

Harry started school in Armstrong, but after the move to Clifton Hill, he attended Smith School; and he walked the mile and a half from his home. "If you got a whipping at school, you got one at home. My dad was strict, but I never begrudged him that, he was not unfair."

"Surely you did not get whippings at school?" I asked.

"Oh yes, most all the boys got whippings, and once in awhile a girl, too.

"My sisters always told on me, so I got it again at home. I would pinch the girls, throw marbles over my shoulder and let them roll on the floor, sass the teacher. We had to cut our own switches. A boy in my class who went to jail as an adult would get me into trouble with the other boys. I learned from that experience to choose your friends well and to get to know people before you trust them."

Church in Clifton Hill was Presbyterian one Sunday and Methodist the next. Sweet Springs Union Church had preaching services only, no Sunday School. As there were not many kids, there were no activities like churches have today.

Mt. Airy, Missouri, was the closest town to the Majors' home. The little town, which no longer exists, had two grocery stores which were highly competitive, and the owners did not speak to each other. Each business built a dance hall which served liquor, and riotous times were enjoyed by patrons. John Major strongly disapproved of these activities.

Harry went to Roanoke High School for three weeks but had no interest in classes, and he began to get into trouble. His parents arranged for him to take the school bus to Huntsville, Missouri where he enrolled in vocational agriculture under a teacher named John Hoff who influenced Harry to become successful in school.

Competitive judging teams in vocational agriculture gave state and national awards at that time. Farm boys developed expertise in judging poultry, dairy products, dairy husbandry and livestock as well as entomology, identifying insect pests and crop damage. Harry's specialty in his freshman year was entomology, and he took first in state at the University in Columbia.

His sophomore year he competed in the dairy products division, tasting milk, identifying sourness and judging the quality of butter. Again, he took first in the state competition and went on to compete at the national level at the American Royal in Kansas City.

His junior year he participated in the poultry department, judging confirmation of roosters, and choosing the best of breeds. Candling eggs was another skill required. The judging contestants examined an egg with a tube containing an light bulb that revealed if the yolk was centered and if the white was thick or thin. In eggs that were not fresh, the yolks dropped to the bottom of the shell. Harry thrived on this scientific knowledge; once again he got first place in state and went to the American Royal.

Now the rule was that a student could not participate in the nationals at the American Royal if they had ever participated previously, and Harry had. But his teacher told him to enter the contest under another student's name, Felix Colo. "Wouldn't you know that Felix Colo won the national award, a plaque and $50?" Harry said. He is still upset over that incident!

After graduation in 1941, Harry started the University of Missouri in Columbia, majoring in agriculture. Financially, times were difficult, and he took a summer job with Union Pacific Railroad in Wyoming. He was a member of a steel gang that spiked rails and ties laying a second track from Laramie to Grand River, extremely hard work.

Immediately after he returned to the University, he was drafted. Applying for officers' training, he says he became a "90 day wonder" at Fort Benning, Georgia. Second Lieutenant Major went to the South Pacific as a platoon leader in combat, landing on Luzon Island in the Philippines. Later he was part of the Army of Occupation at Nagoya, Japan, where his unit functioned as military police.

"The Japanese people were afraid of us," Harry said, "The soldiers who had been in combat were jumpy and suspicious and would over-react to situations with local citizens. It was my job to control problems. There is nothing good you can say about war."

Harry returned to finish his degree at the University of Missouri on the GI bill; and after graduating, he took a job in Excelsior Springs to give "on the farm" agricultural instruction to veterans. Coincidentally, Lucille Eaheart was a new science teacher at Excelsior Springs High School, and the two met at a party for new teachers sponsored by the Lions' Club.

Lucille was raised on a farm in Saline County, one of twin girls born to Edwin "Ned" Eaheart and Louise Brown Eaheart in 1927. She and her sister Louise walked a mile each way to Union Elementary School which did not have many children their age. The school day began with lessons for the youngest and progressed to the older classes. "If you knew the lesson, you didn't listen, but often you listened to the older kids' classes and learned from them."

Union Baptist Church near Malta Bend, Missouri, was their family church. Lucille and Louise were members of the Girls' Auxiliary and the youth program. Union Baptist Church burned, but has been rebuilt and re-opened in July 2006. It was a thriving church with many young people when the Eahearts attended.

In Marshall High School during the war years, there were no extracurricular activities, no yearbook, no frills—gas was rationed, and the girls took the bus straight home from school. Lucille enjoyed being on her own when she went to the University of Missouri, living in Hendrix Hall her first year; the last three years she lived in a private home on Conley Street.

"It was a 'boom time' at the University as the GIs were returning to school. I had good friends in college, and there were lots of fellows in proportion to the number of girls," she said.

After graduation, she was hired to teach high school biology, chemistry and physics. Lucille was teaching when she and Harry were married at Christmas, 1949.

Harry and Lucille both remember the Depression vividly. Harry remembers the newspaper headlines when a group of poor people marched on Washington, D.C. to demand some kind of help from the government. President Hoover called out the military to break up the protest marchers. Poor people clustered together in shantytowns to try to survive and the settlements were called "Hoovervilles."

"We made do with what we had," Harry said.

"It was a sin to waste something," Lucille commented.

Harry took a job with the United States Department of Agriculture Soil Conservation Service, moving several times in Missouri before becoming the State Resource Conservationist. The Majors family moved to Wisconsin when he became Assistant State Conservationist, then on to Minnesota where

Harry was the State Conservationist for 15 years, retiring after 30 years.

Lucille is renown for her pies—blackberry, cherry and gooseberry. Cooking has always been her specialty; at one church to which they belonged, she was in charge of catering wedding receptions. After retirement, Harry and Lucille gardened extensively on a large plot west of Marshall, and Lucille loved to can and preserve food.

When the Majors retired to Marshall, they remember Carolyn McCombs, wife of Reverend Bob McCombs, coming to their house with a pecan pie to welcome them. "One of the first people I saw at church was Virgil Zahn, an usher, and I remembered him as a 4-H leader when I was young," said Lucille.

"It was a very friendly congregation," Harry said, "and in the time we have been here, there has been a complete change in membership, young families and new people joining the church all the time."

The Majors have been active in the Lamplighter class, and Lucille has been a member of Circle 6 of United Methodist Women. Harry has held many leadership positions in the church and community. They delivered Meals on Wheels for years. Health problems have caused them to slow down in their schedule recently.

"I lift up my eyes unto the hills," Psalm 121, is a Scripture Harry appreciates, as well as the fifth and sixth chapters of Matthew, the Sermon on the Mount. "When you have troubles in life, you go to church to receive the strength to go on," he said.

Lucille tends to be the quiet one of the two. I reminded Harry that he seems to get all the credit in the family. For example, one Lent in First United Methodist Church when a symbolic Seder Passover meal was served, this conversation was overheard:

"Who fixed the lamb for the dinner?"

"Oh, it was Harry Major."

Now the reality is that Lucille fixed the lamb; Harry just gets the credit. "But Harry is the one that makes it all happen," said Lucille.

Harry just chuckled and patted her hand affectionately, "Still waters run deep, you know," he said. In 57 years of marriage, Harry and Lucille have perfected the way to work together as a team.

A Lesson to be Learned

Evelyn Marshall   August, 2006

"The best lesson you can ever learn is not to ask for much; do with what you have and appreciate it." Evelyn Marshall speaks of moving to her husband's family farm near Marshall Junction after World War II. "My mother-in-law, Sally Mary Keys Marshall, raised four kids when her husband, William Benjamin Marshall, died young.

"She was a remarkable woman. She taught me how to do the laundry in a tub, can vegetables and raise chickens. I was always afraid I would find a black snake in the nest when I gathered eggs! Women who were born in the 1880s, like Mrs. Marshall, didn't waste a thing. They had big gardens and canned and preserved. The pantry was full of food.

"We had outdoor toilets and water from a well; I learned to cook on a kerosene stove and ironed with flat irons heated on the stove. We dressed chickens for frying. We cooked huge quantities of food for threshers, and something always broke down so you would have the crew an extra day or two. Mrs. Marshall knew how to manage; sugar was rationed, and still we had pies and sweetened ice tea!"

"Wasn't that something of a shock for you when you had been raised with electricity and plumbing growing up in North Missouri?" I asked.

"It was a lesson to be learned. You just did it. People did not complain. People did not ask for a lot. They just did not expect as much from life as people do today."

Evelyn Roach Marshall was born in Faucett, Missouri, in Buchanan County near St. Joseph in 1916 to Lutie Jane Dye Roach and James William Roach. She was sickly as a child and learned to love to read books. Reading continues to be an important part of her life today.

157

"I remember being the bride in a Tom Thumb wedding when I was seven years old. My sister, Betty Lou, was the flower girl, and we dressed for the part. Everyone came to see the performance."

The original Tom Thumb was a dwarf with Ringling Brothers Barnum and Bailey circus; his marriage in 1863 to a short bride was highly publicized. Americans were captivated by the spectacle. Mock weddings were scripted for children and often were fundraisers for community organizations.

The Roach family moved to St. Joseph, and her father went into the insurance business when Evelyn was in the third grade. St. Joseph was quite a city compared to Faucett. She remembers hucksters selling fresh vegetables from their horse-drawn wagons in her neighborhood. Evelyn's grandfather was a banker in St. Joseph, and she enjoyed spending time with her grandparents.

"When my mother and grandmother went downtown, my sister and I would go along, and we would go to vaudeville performances while they shopped. I remember seeing on stage two women who were Siamese twins. I also remember seeing the first 'talkie', Al Jolsen in *The Jazz Singer*.

"We had such a carefree life in those days. When I was 11 years old, I would take a bus downtown alone, go to my piano lesson, transfer to another bus to go to the library and then get on the bus again to go home."

Mr. Roach later became a Ford car dealer in Maitland, Missouri. Evelyn remembers the Methodist church in Maitland. She taught a Sunday School class of nine year old boys when she was a junior in high school. "They were very attentive and well-behaved; once I had a party for them. I remember reading poems or selections in the Sunday service. On Sunday night, we had Epworth League and got together for activities.

"My mother was a good manager; she had a way of doing things so that we got along very well. I remember my junior year I had a dress for a banquet that cost $16.95. I was so proud, but I knew my parents had sacrificed so that I could have it." Evelyn's mother always had cookies or a cake when the girls got home from school. "She was a real homebody," she recalls.

One adventure Evelyn remembers happened when she went with a date to visit his grandmother near the Iowa border. An exhibition at Grant City, Missouri, offered a ride in an open cockpit airplane, and Evelyn and her date went up. "I was scared to tell my father," she said. "He was very protective of my sister and me, and he never encouraged us to learn to drive. He would not have approved of a ride in an open cockpit plane!

"My senior year in high school, we moved to Jefferson City. I walked to school, as we didn't have a car then. We lived in a building with four apartments; no air-conditioning, and heat records were set in 1934 to 1936. I remember my mother ironing in the basement to keep cool!

"I was studious, and after graduation, I took a business course in Jefferson City. In 1935, when Guy Parks was governor, I got a job in the state highway department as secretary to the bridge engineer. I walked to work right by the Capitol for three and one half years. There were social events with other girls who worked in the office. I went to the Methodist Church, and I was part of a women's group."

Evelyn met her future husband, Bill Marshall, when she traveled to Warrensburg with a Jefferson City friend where the two had dates with Marshall Junction boys. Evelyn's blind date was Joe Marshall, Bill's brother. She met Bill that night, and they began to go out. "I would take the train to Sedalia to meet Bill; we would go to Marshall to the show, then back to Sedalia where I would take the train to Jefferson City and be home late that night.

"Once we met in Sedalia and decided to go to Kansas City. We planned to be back in Sedalia in time for the train to Jefferson City as usual. As we were driving back, we saw that the train had already left Warrensburg headed for Sedalia. Bill had to drive fast to get to Sedalia in time to catch that train! It was close, but I made it and got back to Jefferson City that night. I never told my dad that story!"

Evelyn and Bill were married in 1938 and moved to Marshall to an apartment on North Brunswick. Bill Marshall was a conservation agent for four counties. Bertha Mae and Leonard Van Dyke were neighbors. "If we had a dollar, we would light out for Kansas City. Bertha Mae would drive and sometimes we would pick up her mother, Mrs. Carmean. We had so much fun."

In December 1943, Bill was drafted and went to Fort Benjamin Harrison in Indiana and later to Camp Atterbury in Kentucky serving in a Military Police Unit. He was next in line to go overseas, but never had to leave the country. As there was little housing for families around military bases, Evelyn stayed in Marshall with her three year old daughter, Judy, now Judy Marshall Streu of Liberty. Her son, William James or B.J., was 18 months old when Bill was discharged.

Evelyn says she has always had excellent friends and neighbors who helped her manage since she never learned to drive. "I never would have gotten through World War II without Dub and Doris Campbell who lived across the street from me."

After the war, Bill and his brother, Joe, ran the Marshall farm near Marshall Junction until Bill's sudden death from a heart attack in 1971. Evelyn's son, B.J., took over management of the farming operation when his Uncle Joe died less than a year later. Over the years, farming had progressively changed from raising chickens and threshing crews to huge equipment and large-scale acreages.

Evelyn and B.J. lived at Marshall Junction on the farm until recent years when they moved to a light and airy, spacious townhouse at 1625 Sunset. In the room where Evelyn and I visited, George Caleb Bingham prints hang on the walls of the living area along with historical art. Memories of the farming years are evident in a collection of black and white photographs.

"All my life, I have been in involved in politics," Evelyn said. Evelyn's uncle, Fred Roach, was circuit clerk in Buchanan County. As a child, she attended picnics and round-ups for the Democratic Party, passing out circulars encouraging people to vote for her uncle. In 1990, the Missouri Federation of Democratic Women gave her their "Woman of the Year" award.

"The Democratic Party was good to me and my family, and I have never forgotten it," she says. Serving on the Saline County Central Democratic Committee for years, Evelyn has been described as "short in stature, but tall in endeavor." Other community service has included helping to organize the Fitzgibbon Hospital Auxiliary and working with the American Cancer Society for 35 years.

Seven deaths affected Evelyn and her family in a three-year period beginning with her father's death in 1970. "How did you survive in the face of such overwhelming grief?" I asked.

"The Good Lord will not give you more than you can handle," said Evelyn.

"I have heard that said, but sometimes it is hard to really believe it," I said

"If you take one day at a time, God will give you strength," Evelyn said. "Yesterday is gone, so take this day and enjoy it." Evelyn Marshall is blessed with a steady sense of optimism that has enabled her to adapt to the changes in her life.

Amy and George Carey, parents of Mary Lou Porter, dressed to go to the movies in 1933 — stopping on the way in a booth that took photos three for quarter.

Muriel Weinreich, 10 years old, 1945.

Evelyn Roach Marshall, 1935.

Evelyn Woirhaye and Ervin Campbell, about 1939.

Corporal Elmer Hare,
1944.

Sarah Tittle Hains as Madame
Ernestine Von Liebedich in *Little
Mary Sunshine* performed in
Arrow Rock, Missouri, in 1966.

Donna Huston
TWA Hostess, 1956

John Huston — Quail hunting 1940s.

Ronald Hackler and Margaret Collett in 1920.

Bertha Sutton
Heffron in her
mother's shoes.

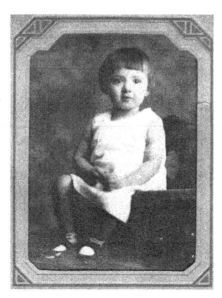

Virginia Bell Clough Schilb, age three.

Hubert Schilb — Fir
grade at Sunnysid
School. Bertha Ma
Carmean Van Dyk
was his teacher.

164

Ed Weinreich on his 1949 Harley Davidson

Betty Jackson Stone, Charles Neal Jackson, Jane Jackson Stonner, about 1931.

Bertha Mae Carmean Van Dyke
with Jane and Bob, 1951.

Second Lieutenant Harry Heinemann,
Hakaido, Japan, 1945.

Pat and Ed Richards, 1961.

Winnie Warnock,
about 1945.

167   Margaret Sutton Waters' graduation
from Marshall High School, 1944.

Nelson Weber— Marshall High
School Band, 1955.

Jane Shaw Weber — Marshall
High School Band, 1951.

Barbara Svoboda Prichard on Chesty, 1952.

Ray Pritchard,
University of
Minnesota Marching

Clay and Lela Mead, 1958.

Carol Mallman Raynor
University of Missouri,
Columbia, 1961.

Jane Stonner, about 1997.

Richard Raynor, 2006.

Deep in the Heart of Missouri
Cristine and Bill Martin   December 2006

Cristine Martin gave me a tour of their farmhouse that sits deep in the country 12 miles from Marshall and 12 miles from Sweet Springs.   Built in 1913 by Will and Florence Thompson, Bill's maternal grandparents, the comfortable home has been updated and remodeled to standards of today.   I saw the upstairs bedrooms which were once an apartment where Cristine and Bill lived as a young married couple.

Downstairs in the living room stands a revolving Christmas tree worthy of a department store window display with mirrored ornaments and crystal garlands. We drank coffee from Christmas mugs in the kitchen.   The Martin's grandson, Billy, is the fifth generation to live on these farms.

In 1919, Bill Martin was born in the bedroom just off the kitchen to Catherine Thompson Martin and J. Francis Martin. He had a younger sister, but mostly he played with cousins in the country.   Bill used to get tired of eating fried chicken as a child.   They raised, dressed and ate chickens; a real treat was to visit in a home that served baloney.

When Bill was growing up, Sweet Springs was a busy community.   "All the farmers came to town to shop on Saturday night, and it was hard to find a parking place. There were five grocery stores."   "The Gusher" was, a fountain in the Sweet Springs park that attracted many visitors.   In 1901, a group of entrepreneurs drilled unsuccessfully for oil but hit a spring of sulfur-tasting water that was considered to have medicinal properties, and they called it "The Gusher."*   "I never liked the taste of it myself," Bill said.

The Martin family attended Antioch Baptist Church.   Bill walked two and one-half miles to Green Mound Grade School. His aunt, Florence Martin, was his teacher.   Years later, his son, Jimmy, also had Aunt Florence as a teacher.

Bill started young working on their farm, and he drove a team of workhorses; he remembers shucking corn with a shucking peg on his hand. He was driving a Case tractor before he went to high school.

Bill drove a Model T Ford to Sweet Springs High School when he was 14 years old and a freshman. Four neighbor kids rode with him. "It was mud road for five miles to Old Highway 40. If you turned the other direction, it was five miles of mud road to Highway 20."

"Did you ever get stuck?" I asked.

"You bet! We would get a neighbor with a team of horses to pull us out. You soon learned where the worst mud-holes were, and you tried to avoid them."

At Sweet Springs High School, Bill was president of his senior class and a member of Future Farmers Association (F.F.A.). Physics and science were his favorite classes.

After graduation, Bill enlisted and was a bombardier navigator in the Air Force, but he never left the United States. He was stationed at an air base at Sioux City, Iowa, when friends introduced him to Cristine Whitcanack.

Cristine said, "I was born in Lucas, Iowa, in 1920, but most of my growing up years were in Schaller, Iowa, the popcorn center of the world. Popcorn Days is a big festival in Shaller. Next year I will be going to my 70th high school class reunion during Popcorn Days. My family moved to Canada for a year where my dad, Claude Whitcanack, raised wheat on a farm in Saskatchewan, but we returned to Schaller.

"While Bill lived way out in the country, we lived right in town. My mother, Velma Woods Whitcanack, shopped for groceries and went to the post office for the mail every day. My three sisters and I roller-skated on the sidewalks, played house, climbed trees and walked down the railroad tracks. We liked to get together and make up stories with the neighborhood kids.

"School was two blocks from home. Fire drills were exciting because there was a tube leading from the second floor to the outdoors, and we slid down to get out of the building! When I was in high school, there were square dances in barns and in rental halls.

"Bill used to play for square dances. His dad played fiddle and guitar, and he made Bill learn to play the banjo. Bill and I used to be in a square dance club in Marshall years ago."

Cristine belonged to the Epworth League in her Methodist Church in Schaller. She remembers going with high school friends to Sunday School at the Presbyterian Church because the kids liked the teacher, A.K. Reniger.

After graduating from high school, Cristine went to live with an aunt and uncle, Sylvester and Leah Smith, near Chicago. Her uncle was a Nazarene minister. She could make good money working in a defense plant on an assembly line. For a while, she attended college at Olivet Nazarene in Kankakee, Illinois, getting her basic courses.

"War stuff was everywhere around you. I moved back to Iowa, to Sioux City to be a secretary at a defense plant there. I was with a group of friends when I met Bill. We were married in 1945."

After the war, Bill and Cristine returned to Saline County. They moved in with Bill's parents and lived in an upstairs apartment in the farmhouse for about a year. But they were young and restless and moved to Porterville, California, with Baby Jimmy. Bill was a parts manager for an International Harvester dealer.

Both Cristine and Bill went to night school to learn new skills. Bill wanted to learn to type because they did not teach typing at Sweet Springs High School when he was a student. Cristine studied shorthand to improve her secretarial skills.

"A turning point of our life came when Bill's dad had a terrible car wreck on the way to Nebraska to go pheasant hunting. His two friends were killed, and he was crippled for life in the head-on collision. Bill immediately came back to Missouri to take over the farm," Cristine said.

Cristine grew to like the rural life. "My philosophy is 'Bloom where you are planted!'" she said. "At first, the washing was done in the washhouse using a plunger to move the clothes up and down in hot water with lye soap and hanging them out on the line. I raised chickens, gathered eggs and dressed chickens to eat. We had baby pigs, cows, and calves and 'big time gardening.'"

The Cretcher Home Extension Club of which Cristine has been a member for 60 years continues to have regular meetings even though it is no longer affiliated with the extension service. In October, the group met in the Martin home, and Cristine dressed up like a witch to entertain her friends.

When the boys were teen-agers, Cristine went back for a teaching degree at Missouri Valley College. She taught remedial reading and learning disabilities in Marshall for 13 years, eventually getting a master's degree from Central Missouri State University. "I loved going to school. I would still take classes if it were possible to do it," she said.

Cristine and Bill have been faithful members of First United Methodist Church. "Going to church adds so much structure to your life. You can listen to services on television, but it is not the same as being there in the sanctuary."

Bill, who is confined to a wheelchair, said, "When you live 12 miles out in the country, and you can't drive anymore because of Parkinson's disease, it is hard."

Cristine said, "Bill complains so little about his health problems. He has a wonderful attitude. He is just not one to get depressed." Last winter they went to live for three months at the Good Shepherd Home in Concordia when Bill got pneumonia. They are pleased to be back on the farm again now. Regularly, they have helpers in their home, and their son, Mike, his wife, Jane, and grandson, Billy, live down the road.

The Martins are interested in many things. Cristine reads various books, and Bill keeps up with the Marshall, Sweet Springs and Kansas City newspapers. They entertain friends at their home. Sometimes Bill just sits on the enclosed back porch and watches the farm cats, but he said, "With no wheels, you have to get out of the house." Their home assistants take them somewhere almost every day. Maintaining structure and routine in their lives helps them cope with health challenges.

"Years ago, I stumbled across a book in Davis Pharmacy, a little drug store on Lafayette street between the old hotel and Van Dyke's insurance company, now part of the Jim the Wonder Dog Park," Cristine said. "That book, *A Guide to Confident Living* by Norman Vincent Peal, influenced my spiritual life. It was based on a Bible verse that often comes to my mind."

I can do all things through Christ who strengthens me. Phillipians 4:13.

*Saline County History, A.H. Orr, Editor 1967

A Long Methodist Heritage
Lela and Clay Mead   June 2006

Methodism has deep roots in Clay Mead's family. A 1795 document in his possession was signed by Francis Asbury appointing Clay's great-great-grandfather, Reverend Stith Mead, as the first ordained elder of the Methodist Church in the United States.

John Wesley did not approve of the idea of having bishops, but Clay suspects that Reverend Mead did serve as a bishop when the church later began such appointments. Mead Memorial United Methodist Church in Lynchburg, Virginia, is named in memory of his great-great-grandfather. Clay also has a journal penned in beautiful, scratchy script, written by Reverend Mead in 1779.

Sophronia Rowena Hibbard Mead and Samuel Taylor Mead lived in Slater when Clay was born in 1925. His father was a general family doctor who graduated from University Medical College, which later merged, with the University of Kansas; he had an eye, ear, nose, and throat specialty from Northwestern University.

Accepting payment with country ham, eggs and sausage, Dr. Mead had his office on Main Street in Slater, and Clay remembers spending hours sitting on the curb outside watching people in the busy downtown district. Fishing and hunting were father-son activities that have remained central to Clay's life to this day.

The Meads lived on a dead-end street with 22 boys in the neighborhood. Clay rode bikes, roller-skated and played at damming up the creek that ran alongside their property. The boys made rubber band guns with a small board and nail and a clothespin to hold the rubber cut from strips of tire inner tube.

Clay says he was a mild-mannered kid; however, once a fifth grade teacher got so exasperated with his talking in class that she threw an eraser at him. Clay's childhood was stable, secure and happy with an uncle and aunt, J.W. and Martha Belle Pool, like another set of parents to him.

A framed watercolor of the church of his youth, Slater United Methodist Church, hangs in a prominent place in his home. Years later, his own two children were baptized in the old brick church which was torn down in the sixties as the structure weakened, and bats took residence in the belfry.

At Slater High School he had lead roles in *Where's Elmer?* and *One Wild Night*, the junior-senior plays. Clay learned the Twenty-third Psalm as a requirement for memorizing poetry in high school.

Clay remembers dance cards carried by girls at high school dances. The boys signed for partners. "You had to dance with other people except for the first and last dances when you danced with your date for the evening."

After one year at the University of Missouri, Clay was drafted and served with the 104th Infantry in combat in Holland and Belgium.

"In the Battle of the Dykes, we crossed the Mark River. As Holland was below sea level, we waded canals in 40-degree weather without waterproof boots. At night, we slept in slit trenches 18 inches deep with the dirt pulled up around us.

"For three weeks, we wore the same clothes, and we were always wet. An artillery shell went off directly behind me, and it threw me, but I didn't think I was hurt. I got trench foot because my feet had frozen; and when I was examined, the medic discovered I had a minor shrapnel wound from the artillery shell."

When Clay was immobilized in a hospital for two months in Charlberry, England, to allow his feet to recover, the toes had turned black; and the treatment was amputation. One night when it was quiet, Clay got out of bed and crawled into the office where he read the latest bulletin on trench foot care saying that amputation was not always necessary.

A friendly nurse caught him and offered him coffee and cookies before sending him back to bed. Because of his new found information, Clay stubbornly refused to allow his toes to be amputated, and he made a full recovery.

After recovering, Clay was sent back to Europe in a quartermaster depot company which handled supplies in Belgium, and he later issued clothing and equipment at Mannheim, Germany.

"I was not in combat again, but you could hear the guns in the distance from our post." In March 1946, General George F. Patton was killed in a jeep accident 50 feet from Clay's office. The war was coming to an end, and several months later Clay was discharged.

Returning to the University of Missouri, he worked as a bus boy at Stephens College while he finished school. After he graduated, he took a sales job with the William Volker furniture company.

Volker was a prominent Kansas Citian for whom Volker Boulevard and Volker Fountain are named; his furniture company had a branch in Oklahoma City to which Clay was attached. The providential move led him to meet a pretty blonde Oklahoma girl to whom he has been married for 51 years.

Lela Edge Mead was born in 1930 in Weleetka, Oklahoma, to Lee Elmer and Ella Ledbetter Edge. Her father died when Lela was six months old. "I know it must have been hard for my mother alone with my brother and me, but I was never aware that we were short of money. My grandfather, Jacob Marshall Ledbetter, was a very important person in our lives," she said.

When Lela was young, her family went to the Church of Christ, which permitted no musical instruments; but as she got older, they changed to the Disciples of Christ church. Lela grew up in central Oklahoma, walking to school in Okemah and going home for lunch.

"I remember I always had skinned knees from riding bikes and roller-skating. We could go to the movies for 12 cents; the grown-ups paid 35 cents. When I was older, I worked four hours a day after school in the box office of the movie, selling popcorn and candy. I got paid 25 cents an hour."

Okemah did not offer many activities for young people, but they gathered at "The Pig Stand" for hamburgers and at an old fashioned soda fountain for ice cream sodas, phosphates and flavored cokes.

After high school, Lela was a telephone operator in Okemah asking "Number please?" when customers picked up the receiver before the days of dial telephones. She moved on to Oklahoma City plugging lines into the switchboards, sometimes on the night shift.

Later she became an airline hostess for Central Airlines, a regional passenger service which eventually merged with Frontier Airlines. "We flew to Kansas City, Amarillo, San Antonio, Tulsa and Wichita, mostly three hour flights. The DC-3 planes carried 22 to 25 passengers. Most routes were pretty routine, although once the landing gear didn't lock going into Tulsa which was frightening, but we made it safely."

Lela and Clay met on a blind date arranged by mutual friends and were married in December 1955. They lived in Oklahoma City for two years before coming back to Saline County to be closer to his family.

Clay operated a furniture store just off the square beside the Farmers Savings Bank Building; later he built a new store on

North Highway 65.   Lela's flair for color and fashion is reflected in their new home at 2313 Cypress Drive.

Both have been active in the First United Methodist Church in Marshall for several decades.   The Meads appreciate Reverend Dave Huck, the present minister for his down-to-earth sermons. It is not surprising that Clay is a life-long Methodist, as it seems to have been part of his genetic heritage.

Clay Mead at the church in Lynchburg, Virginia, named in memory of his great-great-grandfather, Reverend Stith Mead

Blessed by Two Baptisms
Charles Nicely   August 2006

Charles Niceley is probably the only member of First United Methodist Church who has been baptized twice by immersion. When he was about 12 years old, the congregation of the Nelson Christian Church in Nelson, Missouri, gathered at a farm pond to baptize him in water four or five feet deep.

When the Christian Church burned and did not rebuild, Charles joined the Nelson Assembly of God church which believed baptism should be done in running water, so the second ceremony took place in nearby Blackwater River in Saline County.

Charles was born in Los Angeles, California, in 1926 to Pearl Howard Niceley and Willis Elmer Niceley. Mr. Niceley was first a motorman and then a street car conductor in Los Angeles until his wife decided she had enough of earthquakes.

Charles remembers glasses falling out of the cupboard one day; and looking out of the window, he saw telephone poles waving back and forth. He held up a tall clock in the living room to keep it from toppling. "It seemed like the end of the world," he said. Shortly after this earthquake, the Niceley family moved back to Missouri where Charles' parents had grown up.

Mr. Niceley began to operate a grocery store two miles east of Pipertown. Now an outer road for I- 70, Pipertown was a little town six miles east of Marshall Junction, on Highway 40.

His father drove him to a one room school, Ridge Prairie, where his favorite teacher was Miss Virginia Whittaker. After they moved to a house on Bar Hollow Hill, three miles north of Nelson, Charles went to Cotton Patch School.

After a time, the Niceleys operated one of four grocery stores in Nelson, Missouri. For a time, the Niceleys lived upstairs in a building that had once been a hotel before they bought a house on the edge of Nelson. When Charles was 12 years old, his father died. Mrs. Niceley continued operating the store with the help of a cousin, and Charles finished his school years in Nelson.

In summers, Charles worked on a railroad gang that replaced rails and ties by hand; the crew worked up and down the tracks from Boonville to Waverly. "The heat never bothered me in those days; I could work hard and never sit in the shade for a break."

Charles received 56 cents an hour for his railroad work, exactly the same hourly salary as his first full-time job at the shoe factory in Marshall. He and two other employees were "dye carriers" to 30 shoe cutters at machines that cut leather quarters or the sides, vamps, fronts and heel pieces.

When the shoe cutters received a new order, it was necessary to move the dye or pattern shape for cutting to their machine for the change. The shoe factory was busy with Army contracts for boots and work shoes.

Charles worked as an attendant at the Missouri State School until he was drafted at age 23 for the army in the Korean War. After basic training at Fort Knox, Kentucky, Charles became a gunner using the 105 Howitzer. His artillery unit was an attachment of the First Calvary Division in Korea.

"It wasn't a picnic," Charles said of his combat experience, "It was the Fourth of July every day." He was transferred to the rear echelon as a gun mechanic before his discharge in 1952. Charles wears an Army ring from the First Calvary Division as a reminder of his military services.

When Charles began work at the Missouri State School, his salary was $105 a month including room and board. He saw the name of the institution change three times during his work career; it became the Marshall State School and Hospital and later the Marshall Habilitation Center. He started as a developmental assistant, became a supervisor, and later a Certified Med Technician giving medications to the clients.

In recent years, teaching clients how to do things on their own became a big focus—programs outlining how to wash dishes and other activities of daily living. Charles saw many changes in the numbers and types of disabilities of the people who lived at the Habilitation Center. He became attached to some of the residents; and at times, several would accompany him when he worked at another part-time job, projectionist at the Auditorium Movie Theatre.

Charles ran the reel projection machines for Steve Sutter and then for Leo Hayob, managers of the theatre. Sometimes Leo Hayob would arrange a special showing at the theatre for Habilitation Center clients, and Charles would work as projectionist without pay. Skill was needed to thread film into the cogs which wound into the bottom reel, and if the film broke, the film had to be kept moving by hand so the movie would run without interruption.

If problems occurred, the film would run out onto the floor and would have to be rewound by hand. Two machines were used; cues on the screen told the projectionist when to switch reels. *Mary Poppins*, *The Music Man*, and *Green Beret* were shows he remembers showing as projectionist. Charles appreciates good movies; his personal favorites are from 1944, *Back to Bataan*, and *30 Seconds over Tokyo*.

Charles continues to work part-time in his retirement as a school crossing guard. He has also been an active member of the Saturday morning breakfast Optimist Club for 13 years.

In the First United Methodist Church sanctuary, Charles presides over the electronic soundboard which has become more and more important in the services. He says it is an easy job to keep the microphones balanced for speakers and music, but the task seems mysterious to most of the listeners. Charles joined Marshall First United Methodist Church in 1956.

He was relieved when Dr. Clinton Galatas told him that it would not be necessary for him to be baptized again.

People-to-People

Leona Odell   November 2006

During the last eight years of Leona Odell's twenty-seven year teaching career, she was a leader in the People-to-People Student Ambassador program. Through this travel program, she was chaperone to eight to ten students in a group of 40 traveling to foreign countries.

Leona loved to travel, and this program gave her an opportunity to see many Asian and European countries including Russia, Czechoslovakia, Hungary, Korea, China, Poland, Yugoslavia, Italy, France, England, Spain and Germany.

In each country, students and leader paired up to spend several days and nights with home stay families. Leona felt visits in the homes of local people were the highlight of the People-to-People program.

Leona said, "I never visited a country I wouldn't like to visit again." She was able to travel extensively with her husband, Woody, in their retirement, often with friends from his World War II 711th Tank Battalion.

Leona Frances Sharp Odell was born October 18, 1917, in Pittsburg, Kansas, to Myrtle and Jesse Sharp. She graduated from Higginsville High School and has attended almost all of their 70 class reunions. She received her bachelor of science in business education and her master's degree in vocational education from Central Missouri State University.

In 1943, she married Woodrow Wilson Odell while she was working as a secretary for Trans World Airlines. She was a secretary for Huff Business College and the War Bond Headquarters in Kansas City.

Her teaching career began in Lexington where she taught for two years. For many years, she taught business classes at Marshall High School. Leona was pleased to participate in the move to the new vocational school in Marshall in 1968 and in starting a Future Business Leaders of America club. Leona truly loved young people, and she felt that all students need business skills.

After moving to Marshall, Leona and Woody were active members in First United Methodist Church. She taught Sunday School, led youth activities and made sure that church was an integral part of the lives of her daughters, Sharon Lee and Carol Ann. United Methodist Women's activities were important to her; sometimes she was the speaker on Laity Sunday.

Her community activities included the Missouri Business Education Association, Missouri Vocational Association, now MACTE, and Marshall Chamber of Commerce; she is a lifetime member of the Missouri State Teachers' Association. Leona was a Worthy Matron of the Order of Eastern Star and held a state office in that organization.

Leona's motto and attitude toward life is, "If it is worth doing, it is worth doing well." Her daughters remember her as one who never did anything half-heartedly. Her dedication showed in every area of her life.

In 1999, Woody and Leona moved to John Knox Village in Higginsville. As Leona is no longer able to communicate well, her daughter, Carol Ann Odell Strodtman, has provided the details of her life.

The family remembers how important music was to Leona. She loved church music, especially "Amazing Grace," "How Great Thou Art," and "You'll Never Walk Alone." Medleys of Christmas carols filled the house on Christmas and Christmas Eve. A special family tradition was the piano solo, "Bless This House", on Thanksgiving Day.

Bronze Star

Woody Odell   November 2006

Woodrow Wilson Odell, born in 1917, remembers mostly work when he was growing up. Woody was born in the country near Lexington to Bessie Bell Eatherton Odell and George H. Odell; the family of five children moved to Lexington where he went to Arnold Grade School, and he graduated from the old Lexington High School at 16th and Main.

Woody recalls working before and after school. "I learned lots at Scott's Dime Store; the boss taught me all kinds of things. I swept the front walk, waited on customers, stocked shelves and managed the store when the boss took vacation." Woody also worked at a gas station and as an agent selling and distributing a weekly independent newspaper.

When the first bridge over the Missouri River at Lexington was officially opened in 1925, Woody went with his parents. "It was quite a big event; they released a flock of homing pigeons at the ceremony. The new bridge put an end to ferries across the river."

After eighty years of service, the 1925 bridge was demolished, and Woody was present when the new bridge opened in 2005.

After attending Wentworth Military Academy for two years, Woody began working at J.C. Penney's Department Store. He met Leona Sharp of Higginsville, his future bride, through her brother, Mel Sharp. Leona attended Central Missouri State University in Warrensburg and spent weekends with her sister in Lexington.

"As soon as I heard about the attack on Pearl Harbor in December, 1941, I was ready to enlist, but my boss talked me out of it until the end of January. After enlisting in Kansas

186

City, I was sent to Jefferson Barracks in St. Louis where I found my buddy, Ike Entine, whose family owned Entine's Department Store in Lexington; and we signed up to be quartermasters because we knew about clothing and supplies.

"However, the military put me in mechanics because I had worked at a filling station; they put Ike in cooking and baking! We got $21 a month as privates. Ike's sisters sent him packages of Jewish food and black cigars, and I looked forward to those boxes because he shared them with me.

"Eventually I was sent to San Antonio and trained as a mechanic at Normal Depot Motor Base." Woody was a maintenance officer, working on tanks and other vehicles. "While in Texas, I attended chapel and sang in the base choir. I grew up Methodist, and that's what I always have been."

From San Antonio where he had applied for officer training, Woody went to Camp Carson, Colorado, assigned to the 89th Mountain Division. There he received word to report to Fort Knox, Kentucky, for officer training. "I was to leave that afternoon on a train with a layover in St. Louis on the way to Louisville.

"Leona worked as a secretary for TWA in Kansas City and she met me at Union Station. In order to see my family in Lexington, I took the streetcar as far east as I could go, then hitchhiked to Lexington and had dinner with my family. Then someone drove me back to Union Station to catch the train to St. Louis."

Second Lieutenant Odell was sent to Fort Riley, Kansas, and on to Needles, California, where his unit lived in tents and practiced maneuvers on the desert with tanks. "We about wore those tanks out," Woody said.

"While I was stationed at Needles, Leona came to see me. We took the train to Los Angeles, and we decided to get married. We went to a Methodist Church, and the preacher and his wife stood up with us. I joined Leona at the Boulder

Dam Hotel in Boulder City, Nevada, 90 miles from Needles, whenever I was not out on maneuvers. Once when I arrived at the hotel, she said, 'We don't live here anymore.' She had located a bedroom in a home for us to rent."

The 711th Tank Battalion next spent several months in Hawaii and was scheduled to go to the Philippine Islands. "After preparing for the move to the Philippines, we left Schofield Barracks for Honolulu Harbor." Woody was at the rear of the column of tanks and other wheeled vehicles.

"The column was moving a little fast; and before we could get them slowed down, three tanks rear-ended each other. The delay to repair the tanks gave me an opportunity to see my brother-in-law, Merle Sharp, again before our departure."

Woody was put in charge of army troops on the landing craft in the convoy leaving Hawaii. "Our convoy was to pull out late that afternoon, but our skipper needed more cooks." Due to the need for more cooks and the tank repairs, the convoy left without Woody's ship.

Because the tide had already receded when the tanks were repaired and cooks located, it was necessary to wait until morning to depart. Woody's ship left alone the next morning for the journey through the Pacific to the Philippine Islands, eventually catching up with the other ships while they were docked at a Pacific island.

The 711th Tank Battalion made it to the Philippines without further incident and was stationed there two or three months, long enough for Woody to run into his cousin, Earl Baird, with the 96th Infantry Division.

Eventually Woody was sent to Okinawa, "as close to Japan as you could get. It seemed like a long time before Easter Sunday arrived, and we hit the beach. We experienced little resistance, dug in and spent the first night on a little airstrip. We heard that a suicide plane had hit some of our ships, including the ship we had just left. We did not know who was lost, but we did know who never reported to the unit again.

"After the seventh day ashore, three tanks were going around a hill; and the first tank hit a land mine; the third tank was hit by a satchel charge, and the middle one was caught in between. Our men were evacuated, and one had his feet mangled."

It was in Okinawa that an act of heroism led to Woody's receiving the Bronze Star. I had to ask many questions to get the details as Woody was modest, "The guy that writes it up makes you sound good."

Later I saw the letter, which stated, "Under enemy fire, Lt. O'Dell led a party which succeeded in recovering two tanks which were saved from destruction by the enemy."

Woody continued, "One day the company commander called me and told me one of the platoons had a track thrown on three tanks. He told me that when I found them, I should take over the platoon. I found the platoon and talked to the platoon sergeant." With that, Woody became a platoon leader with five tanks.

Once on the front lines the unit was trying to clear a minefield. "We pulled up near the other tanks, and I got out of the top hatch and talked to the men. I reached inside for my radio, and was squatting down behind the turret. I rolled off the tank and pulled up my pants leg; there was blood on my knee and a bullet sticking out of the skin on top of my kneecap.

"The men were unable to get the bullet out with tweezers so I had to go to the aid station. The medics took it out and gave me the bullet, saying that called for a purple heart. They then took me back to work." Woody still has the bullet.

"Our company commander told me I would need to stay in the next day to get a tetanus shot; his tank crew had wanted to go up there and see some of the action. I learned later that a corporal was killed in action while on my tank that day.

"Several months later, after the atomic bombs were dropped on Japan, the end of the conflict was announced by President Truman at 1:30 p.m., Hawaiian War Time, August 14, 1945, 1,347 days after the sneak attack on Pearl Harbor. The rest of that night, the sky around Okinawa was lit up like daylight by the happy soldiers who were glad to see the end of that conflict."

By the end of the war, Odell's unit was in Korea to help in the occupation. After landing at Inchon Harbor, D company left the beach with Odell in the rear again. The natives ran out of the hills to see the tanks. The troops were showered with flowers and food of all kinds.

The Battalion moved into an enclosed Japanese post with a three-story barracks. "The Japs had left in a hurry; we had to clean it up. We had no clean-up supplies so we cut up blankets to make mops to scrub the floors. We would take Jap rifles down to the navy to trade for things like brooms and canned condensed milk to put on our dry cereal," Woody recalls.

In Korea, Woody received his Bronze Star medal for meritorious achievement against the enemy during the bloody struggle for Okinawa in the Ryukys Islands.

Woody finally boarded a ship for America on Thanksgiving Day in 1945. "When we arrived in Fort Leavenworth, Kansas, I was promoted to Captain. After putting on my captain bars, I was ready to go see Leona at her home on Broadway in Kansas City. My new bars were a surprise to her."

Following a brief time in Kansas City, Woody and Leona moved to Marshall where he operated a Skelly Oil Station at 250 West Arrow for 37 years. "I remember when gas was five gallons for $1.00," he said with a smile. Woody leased from

Skelly for about ten years and then purchased the station when it relocated in a new building across the street.

After living in Marshall for two years, Woody, Herbert Butterfield, Harry Heinemann, Marshall Sloan and many other World War II veterans joined the Missouri National Guard and helped to form the 35th Quartermaster Company. Herbert Butterfield was Division Quartermaster, and Woody was Company Commander. While Woody went to Quartermaster School, Leona very capably managed the service station. Before his retirement, Woody received his promotion to Major and Lieutenant Colonel.

The two Odell daughters were raised in the First United Methodist Church, and Woody and Leona provided leadership in many ways. Woody served as Commander of the local American Legion and was a member for over 60 years. Woody was also Worshipful Master of his Masonic Lodge and a member of other lodge units. He recently received a 50-year pin for membership and service in the Ararat Shrine.

Woody and I visited in the conference room at First United Methodist Church following a dinner celebrating the opening of the New Life Center. Woody and Leona moved to John Knox Village in Higginsville several years ago. I was pleased to have an opportunity to interview him as the Odells have many friends at First United Methodist Church.

Woody proudly wears a U.S. Army star lapel pin on his jacket, along with his 50-year Shriners' pin. Woody and Leona have led full lives with many contributions to their church and community.

Life Revolved Around Church and School

Mary Kay Peterson December 2006

When Mary Kay Moore and her brother, Joe, were nine and eleven years old they were joined by a baby brother, far better than a new pet for the two of them. Mary Kay regarded herself as Harrison's second mother.

"Harrison was our plaything—we spent hours and hours with him. When we were in high school, we took him to all the ball games and special events. When we went to college, Harrison felt abandoned."

The Moore family lived in Ash Grove, Missouri, until Mary Kay was nine. Her father, Joseph Clayton Moore, was a high school agricultural teacher who went on to be supervisor of agriculture teachers and FFA chapters in Southwest Missouri.

Mary Kay's family lived across the street from the school in Ash Grove. Born in 1935, Mary Kay went to school well before she was old enough for kindergarten. She knew the neighborhood children and the teachers in the small community. She would run away to school and knock on the door of a classroom, saying, "I have come to see Wanda," or whoever she knew in the class.

The teachers would kindly let the preschooler come in and sit with her friend. Presently Mary Kathryn Moore, her mother, would come to the school asking, "Is Mary Kay here?"

Mary Kay remembers grade school in Mt. Vernon, Missouri, during the war years. "We saved our pennies until we got 10 or 25 cents, then we turned them in at school for defense stamps which applied toward the purchase of savings bonds. By the time we went to college, the bonds were worth $25 or $50 dollars.

"Mr. Claypool, the janitor, rang the bell which stood on a stand in the school yard to announce the beginning of classes.

On Mondays, we brought our scrap iron to him at the bell stand. He weighed the scrap iron, and posted a chart with a thermometer indicating which class had the largest amount. At recess, we played "war"; the boys were pilots flying around and shooting at each other; the girls were nurses and would drag away the "wounded" to a safe place.

"On Sundays, we never missed Sunday School or church at the Mount Vernon Christian church. Sunday afternoons we went to visit both sets of grandparents regularly.

My grandfather, Harry Moore, was the first county superintendent of schools in Lawrence County. He and his wife, Laura, lived in Mt. Vernon. My other grandparents, John Henry and Harriett Sehnert, owned a dairy farm. They bottled milk in their basement and delivered it to homes.

"When I discovered that there was a soda fountain at the drug store, Joe and I told our parents we would like to walk home after church. We would keep back five cents from our Sunday School money to stop by the fountain and buy ice cream which we ate before we got home."

Eighth grade graduation was an important occasion in Mt. Vernon. Mary Kay's class planned a pageant on the United Nations, and she was to represent America, a starring role with 14 pages of memorized speech about each of the other countries.

Just before the big program, her father took her to Springfield to buy a watch for her graduation gift. As they were returning to Mt. Vernon, they had a car accident; Mary Kay had stitches in her leg, and her father had broken ribs. On the night of the pageant, "America" entered on crutches and had to sit down instead of standing like the rest of the class.

"Everything in our lives revolved around school and church. In high school, I was a twirler with the band. I wore a white military-looking top with green braid and brass buttons, a short white skirt and white boots with tassels. We were in parades in Springfield. I played flute in the band when it was not the marching season. As a senior, I got out of school to play background piano music during the weekly Rotary Club meeting; I rode to the meetings with the superintendent and principal who were Rotary members."

Mary Kay had enjoyed high school home economics, and she went on to major in home economics at Drury College in Springfield. "You have to approach home economics with caution," she said. "Home economists can get to thinking everything has to be perfect or get caught up in meticulous details, and they begin to think they should make their own underwear. Consequently they never get anything done."

Mary Kay met Bill Peterson at Drury and went out with him once or twice, but she was still partially tied up with a high school boy friend who was playing football in Springfield. Bill was a sophomore at Drury on a track scholarship. He was raised on a farm in the Herndon community near Marshall; he was born in 1934 to Marjorie Elizabeth Mallot Peterson and Rufus Otis Peterson.

In 1954, Bill was accepted by the Naval Air Cadets for flight training. Eye problems kept him from becoming a pilot, but he served on an aircraft carrier in charge of supplies during his two and one half years of military.

When Bill returned to Drury after his discharge, Mary Kay was a senior. The romance began in earnest, but she had signed a contract to teach in Aurora, Illinois, 40 miles from Chicago. She was excited to be near the big city with commuter trains leaving her community once an hour. She rented a room, and taught junior high school home economics for a $4200 yearly salary. At the end of that year, she and Bill were married.

The young couple settled in St. Louis; Bill got a job making maps in a government office, using his degree in geology. Mary Kay taught home economics at a brand new high school, Parkway.

Cartography was not the career that Bill wanted, and he was accepted into Washington University Law School. In order to manage law school expenses, the Petersons took on the management of a Howard Johnson's Motel at 6929 Lindberg Avenue.

They were paid for their office work in addition to getting an apartment with free rent. Mary Kay operated the switchboard and ran the office from 7:00 a.m. to 3:00 p.m. Some reservations were made by teletype between motels.

Bill took over the evening shift until 11:00 p.m. and managed the swimming pool. These arrangements allowed them to be debt-free when he graduated from law school three years later.

Bill practiced law in Malden, Missouri, for eighteen months before he was appointed to work as an assistant attorney general to Attorney General Norman Anderson in Jefferson City. For three years, he was counsel for Secretary of State Jim Kirkpatrick. In 1968, the Petersons returned to Bill's hometown where Bill shared an office with Bob Rasse.

In moving to Marshall, the family was looking for a home near a neighborhood school for their three children, and the big house at 503 East Eastwood seemed like an ideal spot so they purchased it. The only problem was that it had been converted into a duplex, and you could not get from the downstairs to the upstairs.

Bill went back to Jefferson City to finish his work, and Mary Kay moved in...putting the children down for their naps and going outdoors to get to the kitchen downstairs. Quickly her father-in-law restored the stairwell to allow access between the two floors.

Reclaiming the house for a single family dwelling was a colossal project, but today the 100-year-old structure shows no remnants of its apartment years.

The first Sunday after moving, Mary Kay pushed a stroller holding Mary Margaret and Clayton, with Laura walking alongside, to First United Methodist Church. She walked into the Lamplighter Class and was greeted by friendly people who made her feel quite welcome.

Mary Kay became active in United Methodist Women, and she has served as a member of the Board of Trustees among other responsibilities. Bill was active in church leadership and was a Lay Speaker for several years.

Over the years in Marshall, Bill served as prosecuting attorney of Saline County and municipal court judge as well as state representative of the 46th District. Mary Kay was a full time mother involved in community activities. When their fourth child, Sarah, was born, Harrison Moore, the little brother, came to help her with the newborn as he had just been discharged from the military.

When the children were older, Mary Kay had part-time jobs as a Home Economist at a child abuse program at Blosser Home for Children and as a nutritionist at the Saline County Health Office. For the past twenty years, she has been parent educator for the Slater Public Schools Parents as Teachers program.

"My parents set an example of perseverance, strong morals and valuing education that have been a lasting influence on my life. Then, too, I think always being able to count on your mate helps you through any hardship. Bill always felt that I was right behind him, no matter what happened," Mary Kay said.

Bill experienced deteriorating health and died in 2004. The Petersons had been married for 46 years.

Mary Kay said her favorite hymn, "Because He Lives," states her spiritual philosophy. "It is an avowing of Christian life...from birth to death."

From Minnesota to Missouri
Barbara and Ray Prichard   December 2006

The holiday season was approaching as I visited with Barbara and Ray Prichard in their home on Mar Drive. Fergus, a three-month-old Scottie puppy, romped over our feet. Scottie dogs have always been part of Barbara's life, and when the last one departed from the household, her daughters, Joanie Arth and Wendy Davis, located Fergus in Iowa. Barbara grew up playing with kittens and dogs and riding horses; she has always loved animals.

When she went to first grade in Olivia, Minnesota, Barbara remembers the thrill of going to the library to pick out books. An avid reader from the beginning, one of her first reading books was *Scalawag the Scottie*, and the book is part of her extensive collection of Scottie artifacts that range from embroidered tea towels to stuffed dogs.

Her father, Frank Svoboda, was the county agent in Renville County, Minnesota. Barbara, born in 1934, was the youngest of three children born to Frank and Ethel McCrum Svoboda. The Svobodas lived in a neighborhood full of large families of children who played together year round.

In the winter, water was flooded into the baseball diamond to form a skating rink; nearby was a warming house with a pot-bellied stove. In the summer, they swam in farm ponds. Five of her friends formed a club called "The Lucky Five" and without any adult leadership, the girls conducted their meetings.

Barbara remembers showing 4-H sheep in the county fair and in the state fair in St. Paul. "We stayed in the 4-H building for the entire week, sleeping in triple bunk beds."

At Olivia Methodist Church, Barbara memorized the books of the Bible to earn colored tickets for their own Bible. "Mother-daughter banquets were special times. The men at our church had very good voices, and the singing was great. Every morning my dad would sing "Bringing in the Sheaves" at the top of his lungs as he got ready for the day."

But some of the best memories of her youth took place on the farm where her friend, Margaret "Mugs" Erickson, lived. Mugs' mother was head of the ration board during the war, and the two girls made ration books and used them as they played dolls.   The Ericksons had workhorses and let the girls ride on their backs when they came in from the field.

Another of Barbara's friends had a Welsh pony, Chesty, and Barb's family became the caretaker of Pete, a five-gaited horse whose owner had taken him to school with her at Stephens College in Columbia, Missouri.   The two girls rode their horses everywhere all over town and country and in parades.

When Mugs and Barbara were teen-agers, University of Minnesota agriculture students came to work summers on the Erickson farm. City students were placed on farms to work in the summer because it was necessary to have a year of experience before the agriculture degree was awarded.   One summer Mugs dated their farm helper. Barbara teased her, "The next one is mine." The next summer, Ray Prichard was the University student on the Erickson farm.

"On our first date, he was two hours late. He got involved in a band playing polkas on his clarinet in a parade. I said I wouldn't go, but my mother said he had a good excuse, so I went anyway," Barbara said, not knowing at the time that this was a forewarning of Ray's passionate involvement with his special interests.

Ray, born in 1931, grew up in a disciplined family with a mother, Jean Hastings Prichard, who made her two sons practice their musical instruments 20 minutes, three times a day. The boys played in the Schmitt Music Company band in Minneapolis.

Ray's father, William Prichard, worked for Ford Auto Company and for Minneapolis Moline Implement Company. Tractors were made in Minneapolis; plows were made in Moline, Illinois, and threshing machines in Hopkins, Minnesota.

The Prichard family attended Minnehaha Congregational Church, an active congregation of 250 members who did all the maintenance on the church themselves. "The Men's Club sent 25 to 30 young men to a conference every year, and boys couldn't wait to be 18 years old so they could join the Men's Club."

"I grew up one and one half blocks from my grade school, and eight blocks from the Mississippi River. I went to Sanford Junior High and Roosevelt High School. I loved band and orchestra but also took college courses and basic courses in the manual arts, woodworking, mechanical drawing, printing and typesetting.

"My parents also liked learning new skills, and they would take classes at the vocational school. One year they took a course and chopped up an old sofa and converted it into a sectional for the living room," said Ray.

"When I was 15, they sent me to work on a dairy farm in Wisconsin for the summer. Polio was everywhere, and the idea was to get kids out of the city. The Sister Kenney Institute, pioneers in polio treatment, was six blocks from my home. Everybody was scared of polio. Anyway, that summer job got me interested in farming. I drove a Minneapolis Moline tractor on that dairy farm. The outdoor life appealed to me."

Ray went to the University of Minnesota at St. Paul studying for a degree in Animal Husbandry and Economics with a minor in Engineering and Farm Mechanics. During his college years, he played with the University of Minnesota Marching Band, the university orchestra, and in the concert band which preformed with the Minneapolis Symphony. Reserve Officer

Training Corp (ROTC) training at the University prepared him to be an officer; and three months after graduation, he left a job with Dekalb Seeds and was activated as a second lieutenant during the Korean War.

Meanwhile, Barbara Svoboda was in her third year at Mankato State Teachers College, now the University of Minnesota at Mankato. The romance had been on going for five years. That fall, Ray called her when he got his orders and said, "Let's get married; I am headed for Europe." She hesitated, telling him she would tell him at Thanksgiving. Her father counseled her against getting married, "It will never last. You will never go back to school to finish your teaching degree."

In spite of this advice, Barbara said, "Yes." They were married on December 18, 1954. Ray left for France, and Barbara went back to the dormitory to finish the year at Mankato State.

In June, Barbara went to France. Ray had accumulated six days leave from his work, selling tires and government surplus items to the French. "There was still World War II destruction," said Barbara, "We moved into a small house in which two officers had the other bedroom.

"There was a hand pump at the sink, a wood stove and a toilet with a chain-pull to an overhead water reservoir. We had electric lights, but one window was broken. The only living thing I saw while Ray was at work was a cat, but she didn't understand English. I cried and cried. I wanted to go home so badly."

Later they got a nice apartment; she learned enough French to get by, and they were able to do some traveling. The American hospital was 150 miles away in Landsthul, Germany; when she was pregnant, it was necessary for Barbara to go to the hospital two weeks before her baby was due. After Baby Ron was born, his care was turned over to the new mother in her hospital room. "It was a nightmare!" she recalls.

200

Returning to the U.S.A., Ray went back to work for Dekalb in Redwood Falls, Minnesota. He worked the night shift with the corn drying operation, and he found another job in the daytime to supplement their income.

"You can't say Ray is lazy, can you?" I said.

"No...he is obsessed with work. I spend more time with my dog than I do with Ray," said Barbara.

Several moves and promotions later, Ray became assistant manager at the Marshall Dekalb plant. Barbara went back to school at Missouri Valley College and finished her teaching degree. She taught elementary school for over 28 years. Her father would have been proud—she also received a master's degree in education from Central Missouri State University.

The Prichards moved to a country home near Malta Bend. Ray and son Tom invested in some farm acreages. Barbara had a horse again, and Ray began collecting Minneapolis Moline tractors and equipment.

One of Ray's proud accomplishments is his 43 years with the Boy Scout troop at First United Methodist Church in Marshall. He began as Scout Coordinator when Ray McClure recruited him, later becoming Scoutmaster with five assistants and 52 boys. The troop has produced 19 Eagle Scouts including the two Prichard sons.

Ray took Scouts on trips to the boundary waters in Minnesota, to Philmont Scout Ranch in New Mexico, to the National Jamboree in Morain Park, Pennsylvania, and to Strawberry Park, Colorado where they hiked 20 miles on the Continental Divide.

Ray has served in every position on the church board except treasurer. They joined the Lamplighter Sunday School Class, a new group for young couples. Barb and Ray say their closest friends in life have always been from church.

In the eighties, corporate take-overs and downturns in the economy brought major changes in American business, especially in the agricultural base. Downsizing companies gave the axe to middle management people. Along with many other business people in the area, Ray faced employment changes. To stay in Marshall, he eventually took a job on the assembly line at Con Agra Foods.

"Instead of telling people what to do, I was doing it," Ray said. "Lifting boxes of potatoes onto the line for the assembly process. After awhile, I became in charge of maintenance on the 3:00 a.m. to 12:00 p.m. shift. It became necessary for me to work past retirement age in order to have insurance coverage for Barbara. Sometimes I would have to work seven days in a row."

"Then he would take a ten minute nap and go to work at one of the farms," said Barbara. "He is a workaholic." Ray explains that he usually only needs six hours of sleep.

Ray is planting walnut trees and developing 65 acres for quail habitat on his properties. "In pieces at the moment, I have a 1931 Model A Ford, a disk, two lawn mowers, two manure spreaders, three antique camelback trunks, six Minneapolis Moline tractors and. . ." he paused, thinking about his current agenda.

"And a partridge in a pear tree?" I asked.

"If he was in school today, he would be on Ritalin for attention deficit disorder!" said Barbara. Ray points out that he does complete projects, but he always has several others started.

Barbara stays busy gardening, reading and keeping up with three bridge clubs, as well as Beta Sigma Phi, P.E.O., Red Hatters and Coterie Club. Barbara had one of the first water gardens in area, and they have been active in the Saline County Water Garden Club. Ray is one of the Water Garden

Club volunteers who help to maintain the Jim the Wonder Dog Park.

The Prichards have been able to travel extensively over the years; they are ever on the lookout for additions to their Red Wing pottery that originates in Red Wing, Minnesota.

Ray has maintained a consistent interest in music, playing clarinet in the Marshall Municipal Band for 42 years. Another of Ray's special interests is the American Legion, Malta Bend Post 558, of which he is a Past Commander and a member of the firing squad.

Church and friends have kept them going during times of trouble. Both say their adult children are a tremendous source of support in life. Ray believes that the secret to success is "Gotta Wanna." "Don't give up; you can have anything you want, if you are willing to work for it."

Lieutenant Ray Prichard, Barbara and
Ron Prichard   France, 1956.

None of Us Were Rich or Famous

Mattie Ray   December 2005

I walked unannounced into Mattie Ray's room at Mar-Saline Manor one cold, snowy December day. She was dressed neatly in her denim skirt and coordinating top with her hair fixed and wearing earrings. Her cozy room was decorated for Christmas with a couple of small trees on top of the television. The room definitely had the feel of someone's home with a colorful Christmas scarf she had embroidered herself draped over the television.

As we visited, I asked her what year she was born. "1905," she said.

"Why, Mattie, you are one hundred years old!" I said.

"I know it. Can you believe it? I can't," she responded with a smile.

Mattie Odell grew up on a farm north of Hardeman, Missouri. Church was not part of their lives as Dora Watts Odell and William Letcher Odell had no transportation to take the family, and it was too far to walk.

"My brothers and sisters and I grew up poor; we worked hard and made our own fun," she said. The boys liked to build things in the workshop, and Mattie remembers making toy wheelbarrows from scrap wood.

Mattie went to Clay Center School near Hardeman. "I didn't get to go to school as long as I would have liked to. I have tried hard to educate myself by keeping up with what goes on around me," she said.

Mattie met Charles Ray during World War II when she was making clothing at the Rice-Stix factory in Slater. The factory made men's clothing for Penney's; but during the war, they had a contract to make underwear for the military. Charles, a little older than those who were recruited to fight, was also working for Rice-Stix.

After they were married, Mattie and Charles attended the "Come Join Us" Sunday School Class at Slater United Methodist Church, meeting new friends and working together on projects. Later Rice-Stix transferred Charles to Denver, Colorado, and then to California for 10 years. "We went to a great big church in California, and it was hard to get acquainted."

Mattie says she has felt most inspired in life by nature. She loved to garden, especially planting flowers. She loved growing up on a farm with the change of seasons. "Living on a farm gives you a foundation that helps you a long way."

She recalled that her great-grandfather, Jeremiah Odell, gave the land for the town of Marshall in 1839. I said, "You must be proud to be part of that history."

"Oh, no, none of us were rich or famous people. We just worked hard and did the things we were supposed to do."

Mattie and Charles moved to Marshall in the early seventies when he retired, and they joined First United Methodist Church. She has been continuously active in Circle 4 of the United Methodist Women.

Until a few months ago, Mattie lived by herself. It was hard to sell her home and give up everything, being alone as she is. Did she ever feel bitter or sorry for herself without close family around?

"Well now, that would have been a waste of time, wouldn't it?", she said smiling. She seems to have an admirable knack for making a pleasant life for herself whatever the circumstances may be.

I asked her if it had been hard to adjust to the nursing home.

"I had lived alone since 1985, and I know how to do that."

Years ago, she used to sew for other people, and she has always loved sewing. At present, she reads a lot, mostly mysteries, "And the Kansas City and Marshall newspapers, I always keep up with the news. I think the wrong people are making the news. Sometimes I wonder how much of what we read is true!"

She commented that she does not enjoy much television. "Missouri basketball. Some football, but I like basketball better."

"Why do you think you have lived so long?"

"I don't know; I never intended to," she laughed. "No one else in my family has lived this long. Sometimes, I do wonder what the world is coming to, though; everything is so different than in my lifetime."

"I expect your ancestor, Jeremiah Odell, felt the same way when he got old."

"Well, I guess he did at that! He and his bride left Virginia on horseback and came all the way to Missouri to homestead. We would all be too lazy to do that." It seems if you live long enough, you are going to be out of step with the next generation in some ways. Mattie has kept her perspective on life exceptionally well.

Shiloh United Methodist Church

The Church in the Wildwood

Carol Raynor   March 2006

The childhood goals of Carol Raynor were to become a nurse and to marry a cowboy. Born in 1939, she has lived the greater part of her life in rural Saline County. Her parents, Dorothy Elizabeth Weber Mallman and William Leeper Mallman, shared a home east of Marshall with her grandparents, Jake and Alma Seibert Weber.

All of her great-grandparents and her grandparents were from Saline County; Jake came from Germany when he was six years old, Alma Seibert was from Sweet Springs as was her paternal grandmother, Lou King Mallman. Her paternal grandfather, William Peter Mallman, was from Hardeman, Missouri.

"Growing up on a farm with the changes of four seasons, the planting, the harvesting and being around many different animals was a wonderful childhood," Carol said. Carol spent hours riding her horse and playing in the hayloft of the barn near the farmhouse on Highway 240-41. Every summer was busy with 4-H projects, sewing and raising sheep.

An only child, Carol attended Jester School located near her home. Her piano teacher, Ruth Mead Storts, stands out in Carol's memory as someone who influenced her; Mrs. Storts was a member of First United Methodist Church, a gracious lady who traveled, read lots of books and led a very interesting life.

After graduating from Marshall High School, Carol went to the University of Missouri at Columbia and received a bachelor of science in nursing. There she met Richard Clark Raynor, a medical student from Kansas City; they have been married for 45 years.

For 20 years, Carol was a full-time mother; she then earned a master's degree in nursing and worked for 20 years as a Child and Adolescent Psychiatric and Mental Health Clinical Nurse Specialist. Before her retirement, she was a clinical therapist at Butterfield Youth Services in Marshall.

About her childhood church, Shiloh Methodist, Carol said, "Most of all, I remember people—Ben and Mary Pemberton, Ray and Minnie Bernice Leimkuehler, Willanna and Milton Fuqua, Chester and Mable Barnes, Miss Edith Eddy, Leonard and Katherine Carroll Lewis, Elmer and MaryAnna Zimmerman, Ott and Marjorie Windmeyer and Phil and Charlene Humphreys among others. All of these people have left legacies continuing in the Marshall community today.

"I remember many ministers, Missouri Valley College students, whom we shared on a circuit with Smith Chapel Methodist Church. We had "preaching" every other Sunday. My mother studied Bible history seriously before she taught her Sunday morning adult class.

"The time came when I was the only person in the congregation to play the piano. For some time we could only sing #124 in the Cokesbury hymnal, "What a Friend We Have in Jesus," as it was the only piece I could play. The oil heaters made the sanctuary intensely hot in the winter. Sometimes the wasps would hatch out from the attic and dive-bomb around my hat while I played—very distracting for a young pianist.

"I always experienced God in the out-of-doors as a child, and my memories of Shiloh are rooted in nature. From the choir loft window, I could see quail in the cornfield. In the spring, Jack-in-the-Pulpit, Spring Beauties and Sweet William grew around the church foundation.

"We had wiener roasts over bonfires in the fall. Always after church services, everyone stood outside in the driveway visiting with each other before leaving. I remember once after a night revival meeting in the summertime, I looked up at the night sky; and while I was looking up, I saw shooting stars, and I felt sense of awe.

"Basket dinners on wood planks placed on sawhorses outdoors were big events in nice weather. The table sagged with plates of crispy freshly dressed chicken fried in lard, garden vegetables, angel food cakes whipped with a dozen eggs from the chicken house, deviled eggs. Experienced cooks advised that boiled eggs do not peel nicely if they are less than a day old.

"Before the church closed, the fare had changed to chicken purchased at the meat counter and prepared with 'Shake and Bake,' cake mix cakes and the famous green bean-cream of mushroom soup casserole with canned, deep-fried onion crumbles on top.

"In the next two or three decades, contributive dinners at churches progressed to buckets of Kentucky Fried Chicken, store-bought cookies, Kool-Whip salads mixed with powdered Jello and canned fruit, and creative desserts made with instant pudding.

"Presently the trend is toward meals cooked by a kitchen crew and paid for by money thrown into the basket. The zeal for food preparation has dwindled.

"Shiloh opened in 1884 and closed 100 years later when the congregation dwindled. Eventually the building was torn down with only a marker left on Highway 41 about six miles from Marshall. I can get teary hearing the words from the hymn about the church in the wildwood, 'The Little Brown Church in the Vale.'

"I remember the first time I went to First United Methodist Church with my parents; I was probably about eight years old. Possibly, it was because the driveway up the hill to Shiloh was impassable if it snowed. I had never heard an organ played before, and the congregation sang 'Holy, Holy, Holy.' The majestic sound seemed to fill the entire sanctuary.

"When I reached high school age, my mother insisted that I join the Methodist Youth Fellowship group at the Marshall Church as there wasn't anyone my age at Shiloh. We had many good times with Dr. Clinton Galatas, the minister. To make money, we had newspaper drives; a truck took the paper to Kansas City to sell. I went to church camp in the summers at Eldorado Springs.

"Every Sunday night at 5:00 p.m. we brought a covered dish: and after eating, we had a program, a discussion or some kind of activity. Some of us often walked to the movie after Methodist Youth Fellowship. There was a slight feeling of wickedness about this because some adults did not think you should go to the movies on Sunday.

"When Richard and I moved to Marshall from Columbia in 1966, we joined First United Methodist Church; and we raised our four daughters in the congregation. We served in many leadership positions. There were family camp-outs with the Lamplighter Class at the Lake of the Ozarks and wild game dinners with duck, turkey, quail, deer and rabbit donated by the many hunters in the group.

"The music has always been outstanding. At one point, Harold Lickey conducted a church orchestra for special services. The Chancel Choir, organ and piano duets by Jane Huff and Donna Zahn, children's choirs and cantatas led by Pam Riggs and accompanied by Pam Reeder, organ music by Virginia Schilb, the bell choir, vocal soloists, and Mary Lou Porter's flute performances all have enhanced our worship services. With every change in ministers, the congregation has developed and grown in a different direction.

"Hats, gloves and business suits were the rule on Sunday morning. Children required Sunday coats and Sunday shoes; little girls wore black patent, buckle-strap shoes with ruffled anklets. Women never wore slacks. Adults today often wear jeans, and children wear school clothes or shorts and tee shirts in the summer. There is an increasing informality about services which is more welcoming. People are much more aware of strangers, and hospitality to visitors is greatly improved.

"When I think about what has been most important to me spiritually as an adult, opportunities to learn rank high. The person who teaches Sunday School or leads a Bible study always learns more than the listeners. For several years, I have been a member of an early morning book study at Covenant Presbyterian Church. I believe that Christians of every age can always step up to a higher level by learning new things."

Keeping a journal has always been a means of maintaining steadiness in life and a source of inspiration for Carol. "When I get anxious, I write prayers. Re-reading what I have written at the end of a year, I can see the ebb and flow of life, and it becomes clear that prayers are answered. The human mind cannot visualize change and response unless life events are recorded on paper."

Carol appreciates the positive outlook of her husband, Richard, and believes that looking for what is right and

211

focusing on the good are guiding principles that have been important in her life. One of her favorite Bible verses is Phillipians 4:8.

Finally, brethren, whatsoever things are true, whatsoever things are honorable, whatsoever things are just, whatsoever things are pure, whatsoever things are lovely, whatsoever things are of good report; if there be any virtue, and if there be any praise, think on these things. (ASV)

One Wonderful Horse

Richard Clark Raynor   March 2006

Born in 1936 in Tuscon, Arizona, to Sarah Kathryn "Kitty" Barnes Raynor and Harold Godard Raynor, Richard Clark Raynor moved frequently during his childhood. His father managed Montgomery Ward stores and was transferred every time he was promoted to a larger store, about every nine to 18 months.

Richard had three brothers close to his age, and they always played together; they grew accustomed to playing with each other as they did not have time to make friends after each move.

Richard really did not like school very much. He became adept at running away from kindergarten and going home. After kindergarten, he went to school willingly, but he always just tolerated school.

In Bakersfield, California, Richard recalls that the fourth grade had 40 kids in both morning and afternoon sessions because of overcrowding in the school district. In their free time, he and his brothers played Cowboys and Indians and rode bikes all over town.

For a time the Raynors had a boxing ring in the backyard, and boxing matches were held with the neighborhood kids. From the third grade through high school, the family owned horses which began an enduring hobby for Richard.

Housing was scarce during World War II, especially for families with children. Richard remembers his mother negotiating with a landlady in a house they had found to rent. Outside, the four little boys found a hose and began squirting each other with it. Water sprayed through the open window, hitting the landlady. The rental contract was off, and the family had to search elsewhere for a place to live.

The Southern California coast was alert to the possibility of enemy craft sailing into the region. Heavy curtains were hung over windows for blackouts at night; an air raid warden checked and told people if any light was visible from the outside. Soldiers walked the beach with guard dogs, scanning the horizon for Japanese boats or planes.

Children collected scrap iron and saved tin foil from cigarette packages. Schools held contests to see who could collect the largest ball of aluminum foil. Richard's mother saved grease from frying meat; at the meat market, she received a small amount of money for the grease which was used in the process of making munitions.

The Raynors always attended a Protestant church within walking distance of their home, as Kathryn Raynor did not drive. Usually it was Congregational or Presbyterian, but one brother was baptized by immersion in a Baptist church.

Richard and his brothers always wore suits to Sunday School and church; often their mother cut the suits down from old ones that had belonged to their father. "We were not very reverent little boys; as I recall, we were quite mischievous," Richard said.

The Raynor brothers attended 12 or 13 schools through junior high. Richard went to North Phoenix High School in Phoenix, Arizona, for all three years playing junior varsity football. "I sometimes got to play the last two or three minutes of the game. I was never any good, but it was fun."

Richard always had a job when he was old enough to work. The boys together raised chickens when one place they lived had a chicken house. They bought 500 chickens in the spring and then sold them for $1.25 each in the summer. Customers would point out which chicken they wanted, and the boys would catch it. Sometimes they had to catch several before a customer was satisfied that it was the best one. In the fall, leftover pullets were sold to a chicken farmer for 50 to 75 cents each. Richard bought a Montgomery Ward Hawthorne bicycle with his share of the profit.

Later he delivered newspapers and carried out groceries at Camelback Pay-and-Take It in Phoenix. "You could not get $20 worth of groceries in one cart—it would have overflowed." Richard said. He also mowed yards with a reel-type push lawn mower without a motor for a dollar a yard.

After high school, Richard continued to move with his family and attended city schools where they lived. He went to the University of Denver for most of his undergraduate work but also attended the University of Houston, finally graduating from the University of Kansas City, now the University of Missouri at Kansas City. Consequently, he studied Colorado, Texas and Missouri history as an undergraduate. All through college, he worked 40 hours a week in the Montgomery Ward catalog office and at Burt's Shoes in Kansas City.

Richard decided to go into medicine his senior year in high school because someone told him that pre-med was easier than pre-law. Science was his favorite subject. In Kansas City, he applied and was accepted into the University of Missouri School of Medicine in Columbia.

During his first year of medical school, he met Carol Mallman, a student nurse, "The love of my life," he said. "I have always been lucky and just stumbled into things. It reminds me of the old saying, 'If the good Lord gives you a choice between brains and luck, take luck every time.'"

"I really enjoyed practicing medicine. I took a general practice residency, and I liked doing many different kinds of things. My cousin, David Rice, a psychiatrist, told me that medicine is intellectually stimulating, and that you learn something new all the time, and it has been true.

"I enjoyed my patients and the people I worked with; there is nothing else I would rather have done. Now that I am retired,

I really enjoy my cows and horses, but I am just thankful that I did not try to make a living at farming."

Medicine has changed drastically since Richard started practice in 1966. When he started in Marshall, he gave anesthesia, did gall bladder surgery, hernia repair, appendectomies, tonsillectomies, cesarean sections and amputations. House calls were the rule for doctors.

Richard delivered about 1500 babies. He set broken limbs and reduced dislocated shoulders, elbows, wrists and hips. During most of his practice years, Richard worked 10 to 12 hours a day, getting up at night for emergencies and deliveries; and he made rounds twice a day at the hospital seven days a week.

When doctors with medical specialties began to move into Marshall, it was a welcome change. Having a doctor in the hospital emergency room improved the quality of life for family doctors.

Medications improved, as well; high blood pressure problems and heart disease became better controlled. Antibiotics became more effective. The advent of anti-depressant medication made life easier for scores of people who would not have admitted to depression years before because of the stigma.

Richard was married to Carol Mallman in First United Methodist Church in 1961 and has been a Methodist since their marriage. "I have never been 'born again,'" he said. "I was born once and that was enough." Richard served several terms on the Board of Trustees and has always faithfully supported his church.

He enjoys organ music, especially "Joyful, Joyful, We Adore Thee" which is a Beethoven composition. "I like hearing the organ played by Jane Huff. At my funeral, I want the organ played so loud that they can hear it on the Marshall square," he said.

When asked if he had any advice for young people, Richard was thoughtful and then said, "Do a job that you enjoy, don't just work at something for money or prestige. I wish that everyone could be blessed as I have been with a wonderful spouse, wonderful children, work that I loved," and he added, "one wonderful horse."

The Best of Two Worlds
Jean Redford   February 2006

Frances Georgene Curtius was born in 1921 and has always been known as Jean. In August 2006, she will have been a member of First United Methodist Church in Marshall for 50 years. She well remembers the first time she attended Circle 5 of United Methodist Women, the night circle, at the home of Mrs. Wittrup who owned a floral shop and green house on Summit Street. Jean remembers outstanding teachers in the Keystone Sunday School Class, Earl Burdock, Harold Lickey and Elizabeth Guthrey among others.

Jean was born and raised on a farm belonging to her grandparents about a mile west of Blackburn. In 1895, her grandfather, Luman Birch Curtius, came from Carrollton, Illinois, with his wife, Colville Mungel, who had been born in Scotland. Jean's father, Ben Curtius, was six years old when the family made the move to Missouri. The people for whom Blackburn was named met them at the train.

Her grandfather bought sheep to clear the brush from the property. Luman Curtius was quite well-educated for the times, as he had graduated from Blackburn University in Carlville, Illinois, and he could read Greek and Latin. Jean recalls that he read the *World Book Encyclopedia* for pleasure.

Frances Curtius, her mother, saw that the children attended the Blackburn Methodist church regularly. Jean remembers that the Sunday School hour began with a general assembly of all ages. Then the men and women separated into different corners of the sanctuary for their classes, and the children went downstairs to the basement where curtains separated areas for different age groups. Miss Edith Sunderbrink was one of her Sunday School teachers.

Jean would recite from memory at Children's Day and Christmas programs that were big events in the rural church.

At the front of the sanctuary was the single furnace register; in the winter it got intolerably hot if you sat too close to the heat. She remembers that Leland Suggett, the father of Lucille Humphreys, was one of the singers in the choir.

The Blackburn church shared a minister with Malta Bend. The pastor always went home for dinner with Jean's aunt and uncle, Lily and Sam Wegener, who lived in town. Her mother, Frances, always took some of the single ladies home with her for Sunday dinner.

Jean had two sisters and four brothers; she was right in the middle and somewhat of a risk-taker as a child. She recalls that one day when she was about four, her mother went to visit a nearby farm neighbor, Mrs. Hoeflicker, in the car. Jean wanted to go because she had a new dress with pockets shaped like ducks, and she was very proud of it. Her mother said, "No." So Jean got on the running board of the car, and crouched down so she could not be seen. She secretly rode all the way to the neighbor's farm down Highway 20 which they called "the big road", more dirt than it was gravel. When her mother found out, Jean got a whipping and was sent back home.

The Curtius children liked to ride horseback, and the boys enjoyed hunting. They walked to Halley School, about a mile from their home. Snow would drift up to the fence posts at times, and her dad would take the team of workhorses and break the drifts so that the children could walk to school.

Jean was four when she first went to school with the older kids. When the County School Superintendent, Mrs. Marjorie Hoy, paid the school a visit, she told them that Jean was too young to start as she had an October birthday which was too late for the cut-off date. It was disappointing, so Jean's older sisters taught her to read at home. The next year she skipped first grade and went on to second. When she started Blackburn High School, she was 12 years old.

Jean always enjoyed school; she remembers especially Mrs. Margaret Buie, the English teacher. Most of the students were of German descent, and the Lutheran school in Blackburn taught grades one to eight in German. Consequently, Mrs. Buie was teaching Shakespeare to kids who could hardly speak English.

After graduating from high school, Jean stayed at home to help for a couple of years; however, she was able to have some interesting adventures. A cousin managed an exclusive resort in Sarasota, Florida, and one winter Jean took the bus there and managed the dining room.

Her first cousin, Loula Grace Erdmann, was getting her master's degree at Columbia University. She took Jean with her by train to New York City; she stayed with Loula, and she remembers going to see *Life with Father* on stage with the original cast. Loula Grace Erdmann later became a well-known author, writing 21 books, many about life in central Missouri.

Following her visit in New York City, she took the bus to Lake Champlain, Vermont, where her cousin had moved from Florida to another resort; Jean managed the dining room there for several months.

In 1941, she enrolled at Missouri Valley College in Marshall, and she met Grover Redford who was two years ahead of her. They were married in 1943 just before Grover left to serve in the Marine Corps in World War II. Jean stayed with her sister in Kansas City. She wrote a letter to Grover every day that he was gone. Grover served in the Pacific Theater; after the atomic bomb was dropped, he saw the terrible destruction of Nagasaki.

Jean's four brothers served in the war. One brother, Bill, was killed in the Pacific Ocean when his ship was torpedoed.

After the war, Grover went to work in Hardin, Missouri, coaching five sports and teaching classes in addition. Jean thinks he made $2200 a year. Later he coached football at William Chrisman High School in Independence for seven years. Volney Ashford, football coach at Missouri Valley College, recruited Grover to be basketball coach.

Jean gave up a nice little house in Independence so she and Grover could be house parents at the Alpha Sigma Phi fraternity house with their three sons. She chaperoned the boys, planned receptions for parents and went back to take some classes. Little by little, she finished her teaching degree over the years.

In 1962, Jean began teaching in the Marshall Public School district. She taught elementary school primarily at Eastwood School, but the last three years she taught fourth grade at Northwest School when the school district reorganized the neighborhood schools into a grade level in each of four buildings. "I had the best of two worlds," she said. "I was at home with my children until the youngest was in fourth grade, and then I taught for 22 years."

Grover and Jean looked for a farm to buy near Marshall, and they found 40 acres on Watermill Road with a house, barn and outbuildings for $25,000; the Redfords lived there for 45 years. Her present well-kept brick house across from the municipal golf course is on the original farm property.

Jean's background in managing dining rooms was utilized well in volunteer work with First United Methodist Church. For many years, she was in charge of church dinners with Helen Chamberlain as her co-leader. She remembers on a Sunday near Thanksgiving the Keystone class served a holiday meal for the entire church; sometimes they baked four turkeys, making dressing and gravy. The congregation brought dishes to complete the menu.

Those who have worked in the kitchen testify to Jean's energy and ability to get tasks finished in double-time. She contributed food and helped in the church kitchen with the late Kathryn Bagnell who organized the serving of banquets to the community over the years.

Jean assisted Dorothy Stonner, a faithful United Methodist Women member, who organized a system for volunteers to cook and work at funeral dinners, a wonderful help to families who get together in the church dining hall after the funeral to share memories and support each other in their grief.

When asked how she has coped with hard times in her life, Jean's first response was, "Grover." She said he always made her feel cherished and that he felt he was lucky to have married her. In return, she would never have done anything that would upset him. A strong statement about a loving marriage—Jean and Grover celebrated their fiftieth wedding anniversary in the dining room of First United Methodist Church in March, 1993, two years before he died.

Jean credits her mother as the other big influence in her life. "She had so much work, so many people to care for, and so little to do it with. She loved people and always wanted to have them come to her home."

During the depression years, it was very hard for the Curtius family. Her dad was glad to sell wool from the sheep to have some ready cash in the spring. Families helped each other; her mother's sisters helped with the mending. Jean wore clothes that had belonged to Loula Grace Erdmann and her sister Blanche; her mother remade them for her.

In the winter, butchered pork and beef hung outside in the cold, and slabs of meat were cut off for cooking. Relatives shared meat when supplies got low. In the summer field corn in its early stages was a big treat for roasting ears, but times were hard.

"Everyone was poor then, honey, I remember when it was hard to get a three cent stamp. Our family charged groceries at the store and paid the bill when the crops came in." Jean feels this family heritage of working hard to manage has kept her going through tough times in her life.

The Creative Spirit
Marie Reeder   July 2006

Marie and I sit on the long narrow deck behind her house under the shade of a huge tulip tree. The round table is covered with a sunflower cloth and matching chair cushions she has made. Hanging baskets, caladium in pots and patches of daylilies in bloom make this a wonderful summer retreat.

Creativity has always been an important part of Marie Reeder's personality. "Even as a child I noticed sunsets, the varying shades of colors in trees. I always wanted to be able to paint what I saw." She has painted both pictures and china, sewed, cooked and gardened in extremely creative ways.

Marie Anderson Reeder was the oldest of six children born to Clarence and Ruth Goeakler Anderson in 1920 on a farm ten miles northwest of Topeka near Elmont, Kansas. Clarence had been adopted by his Kansas family who made no secret that he had been adopted to help get the work done on the farm.

Clarence met Ruth when he was stationed at Fort Dix in New Jersey during World War I. Marie does not have many memories of grandparents because her mother's family was from the East Coast; her father's family were not very affectionate nor were they close to their grandchildren.

Marie and her siblings spent much of their childhood outdoors, building leaf houses out of branches and playing in the water-ditch at the bottom of the hill across from their house. The Anderson children were attracted to playing in the mud. Marie tells of walking to their one-room school one day after a flood, and her sister was stuck in a mud hole. Marie got in trouble because she just left her there and went on to school.

One childhood incident that Marie will never forget is when one of her friends playfully cut out huge clumps of Marie's hair, and she was taken to the barber in Topeka who shaved her head.

"What I don't understand is why we didn't study in school about the Civil War and Quantrill and his gang that burned Lawrence, Kansas? It all happened right in our area and was never mentioned in the textbooks. I think people were ashamed of that history. We mostly learned reading, writing and math. I probably didn't learn enough to pass junior high school today," Marie said.

The Andersons attended Bethel Chapel, a non-denominational Protestant church started in 1916. Then a congregation of about 60 people, the church is celebrating its 90th anniversary this summer and is enlarging the building. Marie's family donated a stained glass window in the sanctuary.

For years and years, there was no preacher and church services were just a glorified Sunday School class. Marie remembers singing "Jesus Loves Me" with a variation at Christmas, "Santa Loves Me", somewhat of a blurring of theological thinking which would not do at all in present times.

Elmont was "a wide place in the road," according to Marie, and North Topeka had one department store. At that time, North Topeka and South Topeka were quite separate from one another. Marie graduated from Silver Lake High School, seven miles from her home, riding with someone else before she could drive herself. She played basketball, was in band and took home economics classes.

"Mother always made our clothes, I learned in 4-H, too, and we sewed our own dresses when we were old enough. Dad raised corn and wheat on our farm. He had a big garden, and he started his plants in a cold frame," Marie said.

When Marie graduated from high school, she had the opportunity to go with a family, Ray and Elizabeth Kinney, to New York City for two years to take care of their children while Ray went to Union Theological Seminary, and Elizabeth went to Columbia University. The Kinneys had been missionaries; Ray was paralyzed from the waist down from polio as a child.

New York City expanded the world for a Kansas farm girl. Marie took the subway alone to go to night classes at Traphagen Fashion and Art School. She learned pattern designing, sketching fashion art and skills such as how to make a big collar that would stand up in back by putting in strategically placed darts. Marie sewed her own clothes at the Kinney's home.

"I can still make patterns for clothes, but why would you spend 10 hours making a pattern when you can buy one for five dollars?" she said.

Marie and Fred Reeder went to high school together. While she was in New York City, Fred attended Kansas State University for a year, but his parents' house burned down, and they had no insurance. Fred quit school to go home and help rebuild the home.

Later he went to Alhambra Air College in Los Angeles, California, studying aircraft mechanics. Fred and Marie were married in 1941 in San Diego. He traveled the country as a technical representative for Consolidated Aircraft Company.

The Reeders moved to Long Island, New York; and Fred worked for the company at Newark and LaGuardia Airports. Back to California again, he was at Hamilton Field in San Francisco.

"The war was going badly, and the company wanted to keep Fred out because they needed his skills," said Marie, "but he was drafted into the Air Force and sent to mechanical school in Biloxi, Mississippi. It was pretty basic instruction; they held up a pliers and said, 'This is a pliers.' Fred quickly became an instructor."

Eventually Fred went to Panama where his job was to keep planes running. There was a desperate need for co-pilots so he learned to "fly by the seat of his pants." Later he took formal lessons to become a licensed pilot. During most of the war, Marie could go with him; but when she could not, she went to Topeka and taught sewing at the Singer Sewing Machine Company.

Fred's brother, Bill Reeder, was killed at the Battle of the Bulge in World War II. "He was able to apply for a discharge because if you had a brother killed in the war you were eligible to be discharged."

After his discharge, he owned an aircraft repair shop at the Topeka airport, but repairing airplanes was not a thriving business at the time. He took a job as Director of Aircraft Maintenance in Moultrie, Georgia, for Hawthorne Aviation out of Charleston, South Carolina. Hawthorne was a civilian operation with a contract for training cadets for the Korean War.

The Reeders lived in the South for a number of years. One adventure for Marie was teaching junior high art for a year. "Without a year of college, I was asked to take the position. The class had a textbook that did not suggest anything anyone would want to do. So I made up my own curriculum. We created a town out of cardboard the kids designed and built houses to scale. We made pottery in a kiln that had no temperature monitor. Another project was making pictures with tin can lids. We had an art show, and someone told me that our show was better than the college art exhibit at Tallahassee College nearby!"

The government contract with Hawthorne was cancelled which led Fred to investigate a career with National Automotive Parts Association, an auto parts franchise store. The family moved to Brighton, Colorado, but returned to

Georgia when Hawthorn Aviation decided to get into the growing field of VIP jets.

The company had begun work on their first project rebuilding a Twin Beach plane for private use and had it completely torn-up with only blueprints for re-assembling it. Those in charge called Fred to return and train a crew for re-building it.

In 1963, the Reeders moved to Marshall as they wanted to return to the Midwest to be closer to family. Fred took on NAPA dealerships in Marshall, Sweet Springs, Concordia and Carrollton. They built the house on South Lincoln as development was beginning in the southeast section of town

"We sort of outgrew this little house," Marie said, "but we were all so sick of moving, that Fred decided to finish every inch of the basement." Downstairs is a laundry room, bathroom, bedroom, family room, sewing room and Marie's china painting studio where she has given lessons.

"Fred called the paint room 'The Berry Patch' because I painted an entire set of china with berries for my son, Tim and his wife, Pam, when they were married." Marie has done custom china painting for customers, and has aquired an assorted collection of kilns, paints and greenware.

"I learned china painting from Aileen Knight, wife of the Methodist District Superintendent. Fred sang in the choir at First United Methodist. Because I worked right along beside him at the store, I didn't have time for many extra activities." Marie did serve as Financial Secretary for 10 years.

Fred was a commercial pilot in addition to his auto parts business. When he was sixty, he was flying a plane to the Grand Lake of the Cherokees in Oklahoma on business. He stayed overnight, and when he woke up, he could not see very well. In spite of his vision problem, he started on the return trip to Marshall.

It became evident that he had lost his peripheral vision, and he guided the plane between radio signals from two towns in South Missouri. In Kansas City, he found the stadium and headed for home. When he reached the Marshall Airport and circled to land, his vision impairment would make the airport disappear. Unable to reach the Marshall Airport by radio, as it was not manned 24 hours a day, he was radioing for assistance.

Someone at the Higginsville Airport heard his radio message, recognized his voice and said, "Fred, are you having trouble?" The individual at Higginsville gave him wind and flight information, and Fred returned to Marshall Junction and radioed all flights in the area that he was going to land at the Marshall Airport on a straight approach which was an irregular procedure. It was the end of Fred's flying career because he had suffered irreversible damage from a stroke.

For eight years his health deteriorated, and Marie took care of him at home with hired help as she continued to run the business with her son, Tim. "He could not be left alone. Fortunately, he only had to be in the rest home for two weeks before he died. We had been married 47 years. We had the NAPA business for 27 years. I kept the books, knew the inventory, and took care of stock orders. We had some excellent employees; among them was Chester Dooley who was faithful for years."

Is she bitter about the difficulties of Fred's degenerative illness?

"You have to 'roll with the punches,'" Marie said. "It is part of life, and you have to take the bad with the good. I can tell you that when someone has trouble in his or her life, it means a lot just to say 'I am thinking about you.'"

Marie is modest about her creative ability. "I am a jack-of-all trades and a master of none," she said with a smile. "I do believe that the most important thing an artist has is imagination."

People who know Marie are always impressed with her incredible energy. "I don't like to sit still. Sometimes I just cook all day even though I am alone. I like to have two meals in the freezer that will feed six people. If I have left-overs, I bake something—I have a couple of sour cream cakes in the freezer right now."

Marie is preparing to catch a plane in Kansas City tomorrow to join her daughter, Peggy, and her husband, Todd Starbuck, in Philadelphia to sightsee for a few days. As the old saying goes, "Grass does not grow under her feet."

West Virginia Hill Country
Pat and Ed Richards   December 2006

Ed and Pat Richards came to Missouri in 1990 because their two sons and families had moved to the Kansas City area. They felt their children had missed getting to know their grandparents, and they wanted to be around their grandchildren.

Pat's parents, Alice Fair Royster and Raleigh Royster, had a grocery store and filling station in Troy, West Virginia. Pat, born in 1935, was the second of five children, and life revolved around playing with neighborhood kids and community activities. Square dance parties held in schools were popular with young people, and live music was provided with guitar and violin.

The Roysters attended a small Methodist Church in Troy. "We shared a minister with five or six small churches," she recalls. "The Frymeyer family provided most of the leadership in the congregation. I played the pump organ and later the piano. My family still refers to certain hymns as 'the Frymeyer songs'—their favorites."

Pat played basketball and softball, worked on the school newspaper, was a cheerleader and belonged to Future Homemakers of America at Troy High School. After graduation she went to college at Glenville State in Glenville, West Virginia.

"College students could ride the county school bus, boarding at 7:20 a.m. and arriving in time for an 8:00 a.m. class." Her mother, a teacher in one room schools before her marriage, had a teaching certificate from Glenville State, and all five of the Royster children graduated from the college which was 13 miles from their home.

Pat met Ed Richards when she was a college student, and Ed came to teach biology and agriculture at Troy High School. He had her brother and sister in his classes. They were married when she was a senior in college and remained in Troy until she graduated in 1957 with her degree in home economics and business. When Ed went to graduate school at Ohio State University, Pat worked as a secretary; and by the end of their four years in Columbus, she was working in the office of the Director of Agricultural Extension.

Ed remembers his school years in Gilmer County, West Virginia. "Until I was nine years old, we lived in a hilly rural area of the state called Slab Camp Run. My older brothers and I walked one and one half to two miles to a one room school, the same one that my dad had attended. The roads run along the low areas by streams, and the hills seem steeper there every time I return home. I remember wearing my four-buckle Arctic overshoes in the mud.

"Dad made many of our toys, whirligig tops from old wood spools, pop guns from hollowed out branches, pea shooters from forked branches and old inner tube strips. When we were older, we fixed metal hoops from buggy wheel parts and had contests rolling them over rough terrain to see who could go the fastest.

"When I began at Spencer High School, I had never seen a football game. I had an image of violence and quite expected that maybe players got killed. I went on to play football for three years, but I was never very good, so that ended my thoughts of becoming a coach.

"In Future Farmers of America, my enterprises included growing potatoes and corn and raising pigs. In 4-H, my last project was personal accounting, and I kept track of every single cent I spent, candy bars and all."

No one had gone to college in Ed's family, but a teacher of a one room school, E.E. Romine, made an impression on him when he commented on the civil engineers who were

232

surveying for road work in the rural area where they lived. "They make good money, but you have to go to college," said Mr. Romine.

The only way Ed could afford college was to work his way through. He chose to go to Potomac State School of West Virginia University, 225 miles from his home, because he was promised a job on the school farm. As he did not have a car, he hitchhiked to get there.

"I lived in a farmhouse with other boys who worked in two shifts. My shift got up at 4:20 a.m., milked 40 Ayrshire dairy cows and took care of a cowherd of 100 before breakfast; we fell into bed at 9:00 p.m. We received 50 cents an hour. I vowed that I would never do that again, even if it meant I never got through college!"

In his second year, life improved; he got to be a lab assistant in the farm shop and received $20 for the whole semester. On Sundays he earned a little extra money by being the collection agent for the local laundry, picking up and returning laundry to individuals in the dormitory.

Ed completed four years at West Virginia University majoring in agricultural education. The first summer he filled grocery orders at Krogers, and next he worked two summers for the United States Department of Agriculture in soil conservation work.

Ed took a class on officiating in order to make 75 cents a game officiating at college intramurals. With pride, he relates that during his officiating career, he was able to call fouls on two individuals who later became pro-football players, Joe Marconi and Sam Huff. Sam Huff was eventually named to the Hall of Fame.

Certainly, a good education proved to lead to excellent jobs for Ed; his Ph.D. in agronomy and soil sciences took him to college teaching and administration and research in the fertilizer industry.

"Unfortunately, I had more than my share of job losses," Ed said with a smile, "Every company I went with went either went broke or sold out. The fertilizer industry was closely tied to big oil companies. The business was cyclical, and fertilizer companies would be sold off in mergers and spin-offs with bad results for the employees."

Pat said, "We figured there's always another job somewhere."

Along the way, Ed became acquainted with marketing and business. He invested in duplex apartments in St. Louis; and subsequently, he and Pat bought the NAPA auto parts business in Marshall, Missouri, to relocate closer to family. Pat was involved in the business as bookkeeper.

Pat learned to sew from her mother and grandmother, and creative sewing has been continuing interest for her. "I made the majority of my clothes until about ten years ago. When the grandchildren needed dance costumes, I could put them together. I used to make quilted wall hangings, and I taught quilting classes at one time." Ed and Pat share an interest in buying collectibles at flea markets and garage sales and re-selling them on E-bay.

Ed has pursued writing in his free time. Inspired by Jesse Stuart, a Kentucky writer, he resolved to record his early life experiences. He is a disciplined writer and has worked on a family history for over 40 years, finding ancestors who fought in the Civil War and in the American Revolution. In 2004, he published a 218-page book on the Richards' family history. Because of his fascination with history, he is currently at work on a history of First United Methodist Church in Marshall.

In retrospect, he feels that his Ph.D. program was well worth the time investment...learning how to do research and developing confidence in solving problems. "I learned one gem of knowledge I was able to share with others in my field—I guarantee everyone will get another job if he loses the one he has, and often the new job will be better than the old one.'"

Listening and Encouraging Others at 101
Mary Sheetz Riley   January 2006

Mary Riley was not expecting my visit the morning I came to see her at Mar-Saline Manor. I complimented her on her nice appearance, a black pants suit with a cream-colored blouse tied at the neck with a bow; she was wearing ear-rings and make-up.

"I don't want to just let myself go," she said. We talked about the weather which was windy; she commented that the wind is coming from the South, a little unusual. I went to the window to check, as I am easily confused about directions; she was right. It brought to mind experiments on the weather when she was my ninth grade science teacher. I was in awe of her then as I continue to be at this moment.

Mary joined First United Methodist Church in Marshall in 1943 when she first starting teaching for Marshall Public Schools. She rented a room in town so she would not have to drive the 14 to 15 miles to her rural home. Soon she and her husband, Walter Sheetz, bought a home at 258 South Redman, and she has lived there until the last few months.

Mary Diggs was the only girl with four brothers in her rural home south of Arrow Rock. Her parents valued education for their children because they only went to school through the eighth grade. Every evening before bed Mr. Diggs read from the Bible, going straight through it; they all got on their knees for prayers. Every morning her mother did the same, and they had group prayers. The family traveled to the Methodist Church in Arrow Rock three miles each way in a horse and buggy on Sundays and on many Wednesday evenings as well.

Mary graduated from Central Methodist College, now Central Methodist University, in 1927. Her first two years in Fayette were to finish high school. Arrow Rock had no high school, and it would have been necessary for her to rent a room in one of the nearby towns; commuting would have been impossible at that time because of poor roads.

Juniors and seniors in the degree program taught the College Academy for high school students. Mary taught physical education and helped with the biology lab when she was an upperclassman. She had two brothers in school at Central, and Mary remembers that Cupples Hall had the dining room for everyone on campus. After supper, Josephine Shepard from Pilot Grove would play the piano, and they would gather in the Cupples Hall parlor and sing both popular music and hymns.

It was very special to her when Dr. Clinton Galatas was minister in Marshall in the fifties and sixties. He was a friend at Central Methodist and like a brother to her.

Mary said when she began going to First United Methodist, she knew it had a reputation as a "high hat church." I was never one to go up to strangers and visit, so it never bothered me!" Over the years, she made many long-lasting friendships.

It was while she was president of the Philathea women's class that the men's Rector Class merged with them at her suggestion about 1989-1990. Both were dwindling in numbers and having trouble finding teachers so it was a good solution for both.

Mary was a widow for 16 years, and then married Wallace Riley, also widowed. Wallace and his wife, Margaret, were also long-time members of First United Methodist church in Marshall.

Wallace was killed in an unfortunate auto accident that seriously injured Mary as well. I remarked that it seemed unfair; life events like this often make people become chronically depressed and bitter. Yet, I knew that Mary led a full life in the years after this, too.

"I had to; there was no choice." It obviously never occurred to Mary that she could have become stuck in poor spirits. "I had lost one husband," she said, "and I knew I had to get through it. Death is part of life. People come and they go."

Mary remembers that her oldest brother was in World War I in 1918. She and her mother knitted frantically in Red Cross meetings in neighborhood homes. They ate lunch together and knitted sweaters, socks, caps, gloves and scarves for the soldiers. Her brother never went "over the pond" as he was so good at marksmanship that he became an instructor. Her brother almost died in the 1918 flu epidemic.

Her favorite hymn is "In the Garden," also the favorite of her mother. About 1967, she went with a busload of teachers to San Francisco for a national meeting and afterward north to Vancouver Island. While there she visited a beautiful sunken garden, Butchart Gardens in Victoria. From that time on, the images of this garden come to her mind when she thinks of the hymn.

"To what do you attribute your long life?" I asked her.

She replied humbly, "Why 101 years? I ask God that every night and ask Him if there is something else I am supposed to do. If so, I ask Him to push me in that direction." She prays every day. "I watch the news, but I don't dwell on it. There isn't anything I can do about it."

Reflecting a moment, she said, "I wish I had a lot of money. There are young people here who push mops and brooms. They were not encouraged to finish school; in fact, they were encouraged to quit. They come in here and pour their hearts out to me. I try to encourage them." God seems to be providing a direction for Mary at 101. She is a listener and encourager to others.

Love of Music
Virginia and Hubert Schilb   November 2006

It is a wonder that Hubert Schilb lived to adulthood considering the dangerous play activities of his youth. Born in 1927, the youngest of four brothers, he kept right up with their adventures. "I was five years old when my father, Sylvester Schilb, bought a 331 acre farm in Saline County. Finnis Creek ran along the back of the property. When we had rainstorms and water was running to the top of the banks, we would jump in and dog-paddle around a curve in the creek, hanging on to the roots of a big tree to stop ourselves in the current. We would do this even when it was thundering and lightening.

"We had an old buggy at the farm which we would pull to the top of a hill with a rope around the axel then coast down. Sometimes it turned over with us into a ditch full of brush. In 1937, my father bought a Farmall F-20 tractor with rubber tires. We tried to coast it down the hill, but my father put a stop to that pretty fast.

"We would make tunnels using the square bales in the barn loft and crawl through them. Once I tried to hide from my dad who was calling me, and I dived into a tunnel which had a board with a nail hanging out and cut myself on the head.

"Even before we moved to Saline County from Montserrat, Missouri, which was near Warrensburg, we were into mischief. We lived with my great-uncle who was a bachelor. We would play in the hog wallow, getting completely muddy and then jump in the stock tank to wash off. Uncle John would bring his team of work-horses for a drink, and they wouldn't touch the dirty water."

Hubert and his brothers went to school at Sunnyside, District 67, where the teacher was Miss Bertha Mae Carmine. Leonard Van Dyke would come to school to pick her up in his Ford coupe. "We though it was pretty nice that Teacher had a boy friend!" Hubert said.

Amazingly, Hubert survived his adventurous childhood. He and his brothers drove a Model A Ford to Marshall High School until it quit when the engine fell out of it. They were unable to go to football practice and other after-school activities because they had to ride the bus.

Hubert enjoyed his FFA projects; and when he took shop classes with Stewart Sherard as his teacher, he began a life-long interest in woodworking. A cradle made by him for grandchildren is a family heirloom, and he continues projects for his family in his retirement.

After high school, Hubert was deferred from the draft because of farming; in 1946, he enlisted for 18 months and was a clerk-typist. The GI bill allowed him to attend the College of Agriculture at the University of Missouri at Columbia. After receiving a bachelor of science in agriculture, he returned to Saline County to farm for the next 40 years.

Virginia and Hubert Schilb are long-time members of First United Methodist Church. Virginia was baptized here as an infant; Hubert became part of the congregation when he was five years old.

Virginia Bell Clough was born Christmas Day, 1929, to Forest Clough and Virginia Bell Nicolds Clough. Little Virginia Bell was called by her double name, a Southern custom. The original Virginia Bell was her great-grandmother who lived on a plantation near Boonville, Missouri, not far from Bellaire, a town on Highway 5 to this day.

Virginia claims she was a tomboy and liked climbing trees and roller-skating in the basement of her country grade school, Thorp. Water was pumped into a cooler for the schoolroom; the bathrooms were outdoor privies. In the winter, the children took sleds to school and would slide down a hill from the pump across into the road ditch.

Miss Eskew, her first grade teacher, took it upon herself to retrain five-year-old Virginia to use her right hand for writing instead of her left which was more natural for her. "It slowed me down some," she said.

She especially remembers her third grade teacher, Miss Thelma Cochran, who included art and music in the curriculum. "There were six or seven kids in the whole school and only two girls. The teacher alternated teaching different grades because they didn't have to cover every grade with so few students. Miss Cochran taught me piano lessons for free after school." A teacher paid by the W.P.A. government agency gave violin lessons twice a week.

Virginia spent her first two years of high school with her grandmother, Ella Stouffer Clough, who lived at 361 West Yerby, in order to attend Marshall High School. The last two years, she rode the school bus from her home to the high school as the Napton school district had merged with Marshall. She studied piano with Mrs. Ruth Storts throughout high school leaving the school building on Odell to go to lessons in a house across the street. Virginia enjoyed vocal music in high school; and by the time she was a junior, she knew that she wanted to major in music in college.

Growing up in First United Methodist Church, Virginia has memories of Janie Crosswhite who taught the High School Sunday School Class. "She told Old Testament Bible stories in such a fascinating way that it was like a soap opera. You wanted to read what happened before you came back the next Sunday." Paul Green was the Methodist Youth Fellowship sponsor, and the group met in homes for programs and socials.

At Central Methodist College in Fayette, she focused on piano and organ, studying with well-known teachers Louise N. Wright and Opal Hayes. She also sang in the college chorus and remembers participating in performances of Handel's Messiah. She was a member of Phi Beta professional fraternity, switching from a performance major to a degree in music education in her senior year.

After graduation Virginia was employed by Jamestown School District in Jamestown, Missouri. Plunging deeply into her new job, she started the band and taught vocal music and English. She also taught baton to some of the grade school girls, studying from a book to learn how to twirl. Virginia didn't drive until she was 23 years old; she rented a room and commuted with another teacher to Boonville to catch a bus to Marshall to visit her family on week-ends.

Virginia had known Hubert Schilb since they were seven or eight years old. Their families were both in the Farm Bureau, and a Fourth of July celebration with fireworks was held at the Clough farm each year. All the children played together at the event. In the summer of 1954, Hubert drove several girls to the State Fair in Sedalia, and Virginia was one of the group. Shortly afterwards, he and Virginia began to go out together.

The first summer after teaching, she went to Northwestern University to work on a graduate degree in music performance. The following summer, she transferred to the University of Missouri at Columbia studying piano and music history.

One night after returning to her parents' farm home from a date with Hubert, she felt like she had the flu. The next morning when she woke up, she could not walk. The family doctor, Dr. S.P. Simmons, asked her if she could touch her chin to her chest, the common diagnostic screening for polio, and she could not.

Virginia said, "It caused a big scare in the campus dormitory where I had been staying because polio was so contagious. Going back to school was out of the question. I could not put any weight on my left leg. They put me in the old University

Hospital and put hot packs on my back, the Sister Kenney method. Even though there was no air-conditioning and the fans ran constantly, the hot towels felt so good; I love heat close to me to this day. It was scary as there was an iron lung respirator outside my door all the time in case I started having trouble breathing. They were not sure I would ever walk again."

"That sounds terribly depressing," I said.

"No use crying over it, you couldn't do anything about it," Virginia said. "I had physical therapy for several months with Viola Lacey at the Blosser Crippled Children's Home on Eastwood."

"She has strong will and determination," said Hubert. "I admired that. I asked her to marry me before we knew whether she would walk again."

"He had to carry me on dates," Virginia laughed. "We could park the car on the track at Missouri Valley College sports field, and he would carry me up into the stadium to watch the football game." In 1955, Hubert and Virginia were married and moved to the Schilb family home southwest of Marshall while a new home was being built for them.

Virginia finished her master's degree at the Univerity in 1971. She taught high school music, then taught keyboard at Missouri Valley College for nine years. After Stewart Chapel burned, the music program was discontinued for a number of years.

Virginia has taught piano, off and on, for 50 years; and for 30 years she has taught Suzuki piano and violin to private students. A music studio with a private entrance was added to their home on Leawood street. Two grand pianos, side by side, along with music stands for violins and stacks of music on shelves make the studio an impressive sight.

Virginia has been church organist for the first service for 30 years. She plays the violin in the Marshall Philharmonic

Orchestra, and she and Hubert have been members of the Marshall Community Chorus for years.

Music has become important to Hubert over the years as well. "My mother, Myrtle Genevieve Steele Curtis Schilb, tried to make musicians of us boys, but she couldn't get us to practice. My younger sister took piano lessons from Mrs. Marguerite Fichthorn in exchange for a dozen eggs from the farm." Hubert has sung in the chancel choir for over 20 years. "The words and the music of "A Mighty Fortress is Our God," just make chills go up my back," he says. Virginia especially likes, "Joy to the World." "Most people don't realize that it is classical music by Handel. I guess I like it, too, because of my Christmas birthday."

Big corporations began to take over farming. Hubert had run a hog operation for many years. Prices went down, and small farmers just could not compete. "My children were not interested in farming so it seemed like the best plan to sell the farm, and proceed in another direction. I took a job with a wholesaler for veterinary supplies for several years.

"Now I am a grain inspector for the State of Missouri. I get samples for the people who establish the grade of grains, certify weights and check the barges and rail cars used for transporting. Ethanol plants have decreased the need for grain inspection, however, because more corn goes straight to the plant."

Hubert says he was baptized by Reverend Clinton Galatas in Warrensburg early in his ministry. Reverend Galatas served the Marshall church two different times. During his second pastorate, he baptized two of the three Schilb children. As a young person in First United Methodist, Hubert especially remembers John Irvine, a Sunday School teacher who could keep the attention of the kids in his class.

As a young married couple, the Schilbs became part of the Lamplighter Class founded about 1956. Janie Crosswhite and Gladys Haynes were teachers of the large group of new young people who had moved to Marshall. Hubert is teacher of the Lamplighter Class at the present time.

"My first job in First United Methodist Church," Hubert said, "was teaching Junior High Sunday School. Helen Weeks had the class, and they felt perhaps that a man could help with the problem situation. Bob James, now a well-known jazz musician, played the piano for the opening exercises before age groups divided, and he would change keys after each verse of the hymn so that by the fourth verse, it was too high for anyone to sing.

"It was a particularly lively group of junior high kids," he laughs as he thinks back. "Bob James and Fred Winkelmeyer would talk to each other instead of listening to the teacher. I made them sit in the hall, but that didn't do any good. They left church and went to the fountain at Red Cross Pharmacy on the square. Who knew what to do with them?"

In almost 52 years of marriage, the Schilbs have survived job changes, health problems and a house fire. Virginia remembers the help the church gave to their family after the fire. "Ed Zahn organized a dinner that raised money to help us. Church members helped us move furniture. We had to sort through the ashes to find belongings that remained. Monty Fenner let us live in a house at no charge until our home was rebuilt."

As Hubert looks back at family troubles, he gives credit to his wife. "She has helped us through the bad times." He smiled and said, "She nagged me to do what I ought to do. She was an excellent mother; our kids never got into trouble, and they have turned out well. She stood by me through it all."

Growing Up in Slater Missouri
Anna Marie Sharp   September 2006

Anna Marie Sharp comes from a family of railroaders in Slater, Missouri. Her paternal grandfather, John Julian, was an engineer on the Chicago and Alton Line; and her maternal grandfather, Clyde Dresser Sargent, was a brakeman who later became a superintendent. Her father, C.P. Julian, was a crew dispatcher.

Anna Marie remembers that during World War II, troop trains stopped in Slater, the point at which crews changed. Girls went down to the depot to meet the trains and fellows would throw scraps of paper from the windows with their names and addresses. Pen-pal correspondence begun in this way continued throughout the war years.

When prisoners of war were transported, Slater residents knew because the train stopped for a crew change, and armed guards stood at the doors. Trains carrying the wounded were identified by a Red Cross symbol.

By appearance, Anna Marie Julian Sharp could be at least 20 years younger than her 80 years. She stands with erect posture; she is agile and vivacious and is interested in many different things.

In her home on East Highlander, we sat at her dining room table, and she showed me an antique painted chalk cat as she told me about playing "Chalk in the Corner" outdoors with neighborhood children.

"One person would hide in a corner, writing chalk messages giving directions for those who were hunting. We would run out of chalk. Painted chalk animals like this cat were prizes at the traveling carnivals which set up in Eiler's pasture on the west edge of town at the present site of the Countryside Motel. Someone would drop one of these chalk animals and break it into pieces for chalk for the game."

246

Anna Marie was the only child, but her mother, Dora Sargent Julian, was the oldest in her family. The children of Dora's sisters, or Anna Marie's aunts and uncles, were close to her age. Mr. and Mrs. Julian both worked full-time and Anna Marie often stayed with her grandmother, Christine Souza Sargent, who lived nearby. The children played together on a vacant neighborhood lot.

Anna Marie went to all eight grades in the Alexander building in Slater. She especially remembers Miss Effie Fowler who taught second grade. "She was a buxom lady with a sweet personality. She treated children with kindness, and you knew she enjoyed her work as a teacher. She was a good storyteller." Miss Fowler fostered a love of reading in Anna Marie.

When she was in junior high, the Slater high school building burned, so classes doubled up to include the senior high students in the Alexander building. When Anna Marie graduated in 1944, her class was one of the first to graduate from the new high school.

Anna Marie remembers that a small group of girls in a high school sorority planned a dance in the high school gymnasium. "During the war, there weren't any local dance bands because all the young men were in the military. We were able to get the Prison Band from Jefferson City to come to play for our dance. The band wore prison band uniforms, and they spent the night in the Marshall Jail after playing. We were all a little scared at the thought of prisoners providing the music!"

"One of the festivities for the seniors was a 'Hobo Day' when everyone dressed like a tramp and had a picnic. It was a free day from school and my class decided that we would take the train to Glasgow, 'the plug' or 'the puddle jumper' as we called it. We planned to catch the return train back to Slater in the afternoon. To our dismay, the conductor would not let us get on the train because he thought we were all skipping school!"

After high school Anna Marie attended Central Methodist College for two years. "Not much was going on in Fayette during the war years. With the V-12 program for Navy officers at the college, many of the girls dated sailors." Central Methodist was one of the many colleges and universities with short-term educational programs for the military during the war.

Anna Marie returned to Slater and worked for Arion, a factory that made radio speakers for planes. After a year, she began commuting to Missouri Valley College, taking business classes in the morning and working for E.E. Hailey in the Farm Bureau Insurance office in the afternoon. She traveled to and from Marshall by bus, leaving from Slater at 7:00 a.m. and getting on a 5:00 p.m. bus to return.

The insurance office was located in the Chamber of Commerce building, now the Marshall City Offices parking lot on the corner of Eastwood and Lafayette. Mr. Hailey's office faced Merle Sharp's service station at 202 North Lafayette, and Mr. Hailey would send Anna Marie over to the station to buy him cokes. "I suspect he was trying to be a matchmaker," she said.

Sometime later, there seemed to have been a bet on whether Merle could get Anna Marie to let him drive her home to Slater at the end of the day in Bill Fluty's gasoline delivery tank truck. He did drive her home that day, and it came to pass that Merle and Anna Marie were married at the Slater Christian Church in 1949.

After graduating from Missouri Valley College, Anna Marie worked for Stanley Hayden, Director of Admissions at the college. Later she taught business classes, first at Slater High School and then at Marshall High School. She loved teaching, and she remembers many funny incidents with students.

Students who had Mrs. Sharp for typing and bookkeeping in high school can attest to her stylishness. She was always trim and fashionable. Backcombed hair in a bouffant style was the rage in the 1960's. "One day I was especially proud of my new hair-do. A boy in one of my classes said, 'Mrs. Sharp, your hair looks like it went through a washing machine wringer.' "My ego went down to my knees!" she said.

In the seventies, wigs were popular. "I had several wigs, some in different colors," she recalls. "One day a student said to me, 'Don't you have any hair of your own?'" Kids can be trusted to keep teachers humble.

Retirement has been busy for Anna Marie. She has worked in First United Methodist Church in many positions, serving as chairman of the education committee, secretary of the Methodist Men's Family Club and working on the capitol campaign for the new building. She delivers Meals on Wheels, and she is active in the Daughters of the American Revolution.

Anna Marie and Merle had been married for 45 years when he became terminally ill with melanoma. She took care of him at home, and the last weeks were extremely difficult. "Reverend Roger Wreath was very supportive to me. It meant so much to me that Merle's sister, Leona Sharp Odell*, was often with me helping with his care. Family, friends and God helped me survive."

Near the end, one of Merle's customers came to see him and told him about a near-death experience during cardiac surgery. "He told Merle that he had found himself in a beautiful place with lovely music like he had never heard before, and that he had not wanted to return to life. He told Merle not to be afraid to die.

"Merle did not say a word during his last week of life, but just before he died, he opened his eyes and said to me, 'I will wait for you in heaven.'... Not another word. I believe he had to have seen or experienced something. I know there is a heaven."

Anna Marie says that First United Methodist church has become like family to her. "I am very comfortable here; it is my church home, and it has been a blessing to me."

*Leona Sharp Odell and her husband, Woodrow, now reside at John Knox Village in Higginsville; their stories are included elsewhere in this book.

Strong Minded and Independent
Alice Ann Shelnutt   February 2006

My interview with Alice Ann Shelnutt, a life-long Presbyterian, took place at Westport Estates. Methodist residents told me that Alice Ann is the niece of Georgia Brown Blosser who was instrumental in the building of Marshall First United Methodist Church.

Georgia Brown married Alice Ann's uncle, Louis Blosser. She recalls that Georgia Brown Blosser was one of the most gracious ladies she ever met. "She was very wealthy, but she made you feel completely at ease...she was never a person who overpowered you." Alice Ann went on to say that her Aunt Georgia was crippled and walked with canes, and she was always helping somebody. She left money for the Blosser Crippled Children's Home and for a home for older women, both on East Eastwood.

Georgia Brown Blosser was chairman of the building committee for First United Methodist Church; and as Alice Ann understands it, she did much of the planning for how the sanctuary would look.

"Aunt Georgia had her chauffeur take her to Columbia where Missouri Methodist Church was being built on Ninth Street. Ideas from that church influenced the design of the Marshall church. The Columbia congregation had ordered a carving of the Lord's Supper from Italy for their altar. When it arrived, the freight bill was so much more than expected that they could not pick it up from the railway station. The story is that Aunt Georgia gave them the money to have it delivered. In addition, she donated all the pews in the Marshall church sanctuary. There are just no words to describe all the good that she did," Alice Ann said.

Alice Ann Blosser Shelnutt was born in 1915 in Malta Bend to Alice (Allie) Lantz Blosser and Dr. Ervin E. Blosser, a veterinarian. She was their only child, and she attended

Baker School, a country school on Clyde's Corner on Highway 65.

The Blossers were members of the Old Saline Presbyterian Church that no longer exists. Alice Ann graduated from Malta Bend High School and went to Christian College in Columbia, Missouri, now Columbia College. "Christian College was known as a 'finishing school' for girls. I studied to be a teacher, but I never got around to it," she said. Alice Ann met her husband, Orson Wendell Shelnutt, in Columbia; they returned to Saline County to farm with her father.

Alice Ann's home east of Malta Bend was built in 1880 and is on the National Register of Historic Places. She has heard many stories about the history of the area. Salt Fork Creek seemed to be the boundary in that part of the county for the division of Northern and Southern sympathizers in the Civil War. Quincy Blosser, a Northerner, and Betty Gauldin, from a Southern family, planned to be married. Problems arose about where the wedding would be held.

Finally, it was decided that the wedding would be held on the south side at Union Baptist church, but the reception would be held in a home on the north side.

The wedding of Henry Blosser and Mary Heskett was held in the historic Blosser home, a double wedding as Henry's brother married Mary's sister at the same ceremony. The reception was held on the third floor of the house and seven hired girls carried the food up from the basement to serve the 50 guests.

Alice Ann said that she was a housemother at a fraternity house at the University of Missouri in Columbia from 1973 to 1980.

"Did you enjoy being a housemother?" I asked.

"There were times when I did," she said, "Those boys used to say that they could ignore me when I said 'No,' but that if I stomped my feet and said, 'No,' 'By damn, you had better do what she says.'"

One day after a football game, several students were watching television in her room. Some scuffling was taking place in the hall outside, so she went out to check. A strange boy was in the house fighting with someone who lived there. "I took him by the collar and told him to get off the premises."

Her actions stopped the fight, but she resigned as housemother at the end of that year. "I figured if I didn't have better sense than to deal with a fight with a college boy who had been drinking, I needed to get out of there."

In the late fifties, Alice Ann found herself solely in charge of the family farm. She managed the farm herself with the help of a hired hand. She had hogs, cattle, corn and hay.

She remembers eventually getting a new Case tractor and baler. One summer she baled 300 bales of hay; then someone took her to the Kansas City Airport that same day and she flew to Billings, Montana to visit her daughter. "I accomplished more that day than I had for years!" she said.

Alice Ann is a strong-minded woman with ideas of her own. Although she is not a member of a church at present, she remains a staunch Presbyterian. "God knows who belongs to Him."

A Cheerful Worker
Sally Sherwood   June 2006

Sally Sherwood lives an active life working at two part-time jobs and keeping up with community activities. We met at her office, 315 Banquet Drive, SBJ Real Estate. Dressed professionally with matching jewelry and shoes, she sat at her desk surrounded with plaques and awards for the achievements of more than 25 years in the real estate business.

In her other business, Marshall Greeting Service, Sally calls on new people moving into Marshall. In 1953, the Welcome Wagon Greeting Service was calling only on professional people. Sally became the Welcome Wagon representative and expanded its service to every new resident; she continued with the company until it switched to direct mail contacts several years ago. Marshall Greeting Service evolved from these roots.

Sally remembers the move from Clinton to Marshall with her family in 1944. "The whole town was like an iceberg! They did not want change; they wanted everything to stay the same. Not many new people moved into the community, and the town seemed to like it that way. It was terrible, and First United Methodist Church was the same. No one spoke to us."

"When the boys came back from service, the Keystone class was formed for couples at the church. We made good friends: Margaret and Ronald Hackler, Pat and Jim Reid and many others." Apparently, the community's attitude toward strangers gradually began to change after World War II. Perhaps these experiences spurred Sally into the greeting service business.

Sally loves meeting new people, and she enjoys working with the Hispanic community, often selling houses. "I saw one family so often that the children started calling me ''Grandma,'" she smiles. I asked if she has a language problem.

"There is usually one child in the home who can speak some English," she said.

Sarah Frances Gray was born at home near Clinton, Missouri, in 1921, to Cecil E. and Mary Jane Stansberry Gray. She remembers a busy household with church meetings and parties at her home. Her parents were very involved in Norris Methodist Church and school activities. "We called all the neighborhood men and women 'Uncle' and 'Aunt.'"

"Daddy was on the district school board, so we always attended one of the four grade schools with the lowest enrollment, usually Norris, one mile away, or Victor which was further. We rode the horse in the rain, sleet, hail or snow—whatever the weather," she said.

Clinton was affected by the sluggish economy just as was the rest of the country. "I remember we didn't have any money," she said, "Daddy was on the bank board, and he knew the banks were going to close; but he wouldn't take his money out when other people were going to lose their savings."

Cecil Gray sold Dekalb seed corn, and he traveled from one local fair to another with an exhibit to promote sales to farmers. Young Sally would go along with him; and on one occasion, she was alone in the sales booth when customers stopped by. As she knew the entire sales routine, she proceeded to share the information. It was an early sign that she was destined to be a businesswoman.

Sally walked to Norris High School. A friend played the piano by ear; and at noon they would sneak into the auditorium which was off-limits to sing and dance to her friend's music. One person kept watch for teachers who might put a stop to their fun. Sally took piano lessons from her aunt. "I hated every minute of it! But I did play occasionally for church."

After high school, she went to Central Missouri State Teachers College in Warrensburg and graduated with a degree in home economics. She took a job as assistant hostess in the servicemen's dining room at Whiteman Air Force Base while living in Warrensburg.

Cecil and Mary Jane Gray moved to Marshall in 1944 when Cecil took a job with Dekalb Seed Company; Sally decided to move with them. Shortly after coming to Marshall, she met Harold Sherwood who was operating a service station on Odell Street with his brother. She taught home economics for one year at Malta Bend High School after they were married.

Eastwood Street was central in their lives—Harold ran a service station and tire re-capping business at the corner of Odell and Eastwood, and they lived at 845 East Eastwood. Sally's parents lived at 710 East Eastwood. Harold and Sally were active in many roles at First United Methodist Church; and their daughter, Mary, was involved in youth activities.

Harold began to have health problems, closed his business and sold insurance for several years before his death. Sally has been a widow now for more than 20 years.

Sally's answer to dealing with trials in life is "Work." Keeping busy and having a schedule full of things to do describes her life. She plays bridge and is active in Eastern Star and Optimist Club. You need to know her cell phone number if you want to find her—she is a person who is involved in the present with no time to ruminate about past sorrows.

Educators First and Foremost

Irene and Morris Shikles   September 2006

Morris and Irene Shikles are educators, first and foremost. The Shikles began teaching school when they were 18 and 19 years old respectively. They knew each other and had classes together when they got their undergraduate degrees in 1953 from Central Missouri State University, but their relationship began several years later when they were both in graduate school in Warrensburg.

At the time of their marriage, Morris was teaching in Lee's Summit, and Irene was teaching in Shawnee Mission, Kansas. In the 1956-57 school year, she joined him in the Lee's Summit School District where they remained until retirement.

A point of pride with the Shikles is their connection to the Reverend Steve Burbee, former pastor of First United Methodist Church. Morris was principal of Steve's school when he was in first grade. Later, the Burbee family moved a half-block from the Shikles' home.

Both the Shikles and the Burbees were members of Lee's Summit United Methodist Church. Irene was his seventh grade teacher. "Steve was above and beyond the rest of the students. When I started talking about Adolph Hitler, Steve was reading *Mein Kampf*. He could have gone into any field he chose and been successful, and he chose to become a Methodist minister."

Irene Mette Shikles was born in Independence, Missouri, in 1932. Her father, John Mette, was with the Missouri State Highway Department. Her mother, Mable Bomhake Mette, was born in Marshall on the farm to which the Shikles retired in 1989. Irene's grandparents, Herman and Fredricka Bomhake, helped to found Our Redeemer Lutheran Church in Marshall. The family property was purchased by Irene's great-grandparents, the Bomhakes, in 1906 and was recognized as a Missouri Century Farm in November, 2006.

Irene's aptitude for learning showed up early. When she was in second grade at Oldham School in Independence, the play, *A Christmas Carol*, was to be performed. All grades went to the school cafeteria during rehearsals even though only older students were the performers.

Little Irene memorized all the lines as she listened. At the last minute, the eighth grader who was to play Tiny Tim's mother got sick. Who could substitute? The second grader who knew the part by heart.

After taking lessons as a little girl, Irene played with the Ludwig Accordion Band in Independence. When she was eight years old, she outgrew her small accordion and was ready for a larger one. Her father asked her if she would rather have a new accordion or a pony. It was not a difficult choice, and Irene got Tony, a black and white pony who lived to be 30 years old. Horses have been always an important part of her life.

The Mette family moved to Warrensburg at the end of World War II. There was a housing shortage, and they bought a big old house at the edge of town with space for horses. Irene got a six-month-old American Saddlebred colt named Pal which she broke and trained. She rode Pal in parades and taught him 21 different tricks.

Irene enjoyed drama in high school and was in several one-act plays. She remembers *The Ladies of the Mop* in which they did a flea-hop dance. The high school band was recruiting members. "If you could carry an instrument, you could join," she said. "I could read music from playing the accordion so I played clarinet. Band was fun, and we made bus trips to other towns."

Irene's father, John Mette, was raised Lutheran as was her mother, Mable; so Irene was baptized Lutheran, but later she was confirmed in the Evangelical and Reformed Church, now the United Church of Christ. When they moved to Warrensburg, she joined friends at the Christian Church.

259

When it was time for college, Irene "stayed home with the horses." Morris, who had classes with her, thought she was a complete bookworm.

She was always in the library in the daytime," he said. However, Irene was busy afternoons and evenings with horses. By this time, she was breaking horses for other people, and they were bringing her horses with problems to be corrected. "I drew the line, however, when someone contacted me to see if I could train two pet buffalo to pull a cart!"

After graduation, Irene took a job teaching in Shawnee Mission, Kansas. During summers, she returned to Central Missouri State University to enroll in graduate school. She and Morris had their first date to a Graduate Students Club watermelon feast.

Morris William Shikles was born on a farm in Cole County about 18 miles from Jefferson City. He and his brother had chores to do on the farm and they walked two miles each way to Mount Carmel School in a building which today is a residence. Rural schools were built every four square miles in Missouri in those days, and the country schools then paid tuition to an area high school.

Morris went to Eugene High School, halfway between Jefferson City and Eldon, and he walked two miles between his house and the bus stop. World War II was going on when he was in high school, and activities were limited. Morris enjoyed school plays and playing basketball.

Morris and his family were members of a rural Baptist church. The men of the congregation sat on one side of the church, and the women and children on the other side. Basket dinners on the grounds in the summer were a big treat. "There was no church nursery; if the kids misbehaved, they were taken out of the sanctuary."

The last year that high school students could take a teacher's examination after graduation was 1948, and Morris took advantage of the opportunity. He went to summer school at Central Missouri State University and then taught in a rural school making $1500 for an eight-month school term.

"I built the fires and swept the floors. We got water from a well and had outdoor toilets. At Christmas, the older boys would go out and cut a tree for the school to decorate. I had 13 students in eight grades, and I visited in every student's home."

Morris was deferred from the draft for two years to finish college, and then he was drafted immediately after college graduation which occurred during the Korean War. As fate would have it, he was stationed at Fort Leonard Wood, 65 miles from home. After basic training, he spent eight weeks in engineering training, building a bridge over the Big Piney River.

The remainder of his military service was spent on the post keeping personnel records. He entered the army at a salary of $78 a month and left as a sergeant making $135 a month. Morris was able to buy a $25 savings bond every month.

Discharged from the military at 25 years of age, he was hired to teach sixth grade and be principal in the Lee's Summit district at the Greenwood School with a salary of $4000 for a ten-month year. There was a shortage of teachers, and Morris was pleased with the position. Two years later, he was hired to be principal of Westview, a new school in Lee's Summit.

With no central library for the Lee's Summit elementary schools, and Morris started a donation drive to establish one— at first it was a single bookshelf. After his retirement, a beautiful new library was built and named the "Morris Shikles Library."

Irene taught junior high social studies and language arts for most of her teaching career. She was a charter member of the Alpha Alpha Chapter of Delta Kappa Gamma, a teachers' society, serving as treasurer, vice-president and president. She was perhaps best known by her students as the Horse Club sponsor.

Irene enjoyed trail riding with her horses which she boarded in Lee's Summit. Morris joined in the fun and bought an American Saddlebred show horse. They passed on their love of horses to their son, Jeffrey Jon, who worked at Blue Ridge Stables in Raytown as a student and became a veterinarian. The horses were moved to the farm in Marshall when they retired.

Morris, a respected leader in Missouri education circles, has always been active in professional organizations. He helped to organize the Jackson County Elementary Principals' Association and served as president in 1956-57; he was president of the Missouri Elementary Principals' Association in 1973-74. He is also a past president of the Lee's Summit Teachers' Association and the Saline County Retired Teachers' Association. At present, he is chairman of the Missouri Retired Teachers' Association Retirement Planning Committee. The Forrest Jones Insurance Company of Kansas City is publishing a book written by Morris on retirement planning for teachers, *Show Me Financial Freedom: A Financial and Retirement Planning Handbook*.

Morris has served on the Board of Trustees at First United Methodist Church, and he was a founding member of the Marshall Public Schools Education Foundation. He and Irene were involved in the Adult Literacy Program after moving to Marshall.

Their retirement has been marked with sadness. In 1999 at age 36, their only son was killed in an accident with a horse, leaving their grandchildren, John W. Shikles and Katherine Shikles, fatherless. They speak warmly of their daughter-in-law, Nancy, who has recently remarried. They have been devoted to John and Katie and have taken them on several trips.

"We have been to every amusement park plus Washington, D.C. and other popular kid destinations." The Shikles talk about their son's accident without bitterness.

"Everything in life is a risk; Jeff made his own decisions, and he lived the way he wanted to live," said Irene, "I believe in a Higher Power who helps us cope with the bad times."

"God calls some people home earlier than others," said Morris.

Another challenge has been the loss of Irene's vision in the last five or six years in an unusual complication of Grave's disease. Six operations have helped some; with her right eye, she can read parts of the paper and some recipes and can see to get around the house. Morris has had some health problems in the past three years. Yet, together they display an indomitable spirit in the face of problems and seem content in their country home filled with reminders of things they enjoy.

It Takes Some Adjusting

Ann Spenser   February 2006

"It must be very hard to be blind and deaf," I said to Ann Spenser.

"It takes some adjusting," she responded. I was filled with a sense of awe as I thought about what life must be like for this lady in a wheelchair at Big Bend Retreat in Slater, Missouri. Ann could only hear what I said to her when I spoke loudly about six inches from her best ear. Her daughter, Mary Schumaker, said that her mother can still recognize her when she visits; the macular degeneration has left her with the ability to see only general shapes.

Ann Gaines Spenser was born in Slater in 1907 to Harry Gaines and Mary Duggins Gaines, a family that valued education. A brother died as an infant; the four Gaines children had to board in town in order to finish high school. Her sisters were teachers, and a brother was a civil engineer.

Ann attended nursing school at Washington University and Barnes Hospital in St. Louis. Her mother's brother, Dr. M.C. Duggins, a medical doctor in Slater for many years, may have inspired her interest in the medical field.

Ann married Joe Spenser in 1937, in Slater. When her daughter, Mary, was a child, Joe was injured in a farm accident, breaking a hip; and he was never able to return to his job on the railroad. Ann became the primary breadwinner for the family. After working as a private duty nurse at Fitzgibbon Hospital, she became a school nurse for Marshall Public Schools in 1950, retiring in 1973. The Spensers later moved to Marshall; Joe died in 1964.

In Slater, Ann played bridge and was a member of Eastern Star and the Vivian Lessley Study Club. She belonged to Slater Methodist Church from her earliest years, transferring her membership to First United Methodist Church when she moved to Marshall.   At times, her daughter and three granddaughters attended church with her.

Her granddaughter, Lisa Duvall, remembers good times with Ann as their backyards joined each other.   "Grandma never wasted a thing, she was a saver!   She watched her money carefully, but she liked to wear nice clothes."

Ann, a resident of Big Bend Retreat since 1999, was featured as "Resident of the Month" in their newsletter and in the January 18, 2007, *Slater News Rustler*.   When she was interviewed, Ann said that her favorite television programs used to be *Mash* and *All in the Family*.

Reading and listening to music were two things she especially enjoyed.   Losing her sight certainly has taken "some adjusting;" her family describes her as sweet-tempered even as she has dealt with losses and deteriorating health.

"Mother has never been a person to complain," Mary said. "She was easy-going, and she just took life as it came."

The First String Team

Kitty Sue Spradley   February 2006

Kitty Sue Spradley's daughter remembers a mother who danced in the kitchen to the radio and played "Kitten on the Keys" on the piano. Kitty Sue, born in 1913, now resides at Big Bend Retreat in Slater, Missouri; she sometimes has difficulty remembering details from her past. However, she does recall walking to Eastwood School with her two big sisters, Frances Elizabeth and Mary Eleanor. When it was snowy, her mother, Annie Burgess Thompson, wrapped her in blankets, and the sisters pulled her to school on a sled.

For many years, the Thompson family did not have a car so they walked everywhere. When Kitty Sue had vacations from high school, she drove her father, Charles Taylor Thompson, on his routes to sell china. Mr. Thompson never learned to drive and depended on his daughters to do the driving. Usually he took the passenger train to the towns in Missouri and Kansas which were his sales territory.

Kitty Sue graduated from Marshall High School in 1931. She says with pride, "I was a member of the National Honor Society, but I was never as serious a student as my sisters. I liked to have a good time!" Kitty Sue graduated from Missouri Valley College; her senior year, she was chosen as May Queen.

According to stories Kitty Sue told her daughter, Beth Spradley Yorke, the Thompson family was hit hard by the Depression in the thirties as were most families. Frances taught at Marshall High School, and Kitty Sue taught fourth grade at Malta Bend to help with the family finances. For two years, she taught in Excelsior Springs; she was very homesick living away from family during that period.

Everette Spradley from Slater, Missouri, was a friend of a cousin; when he and Kitty Sue were married, they moved to Jefferson City where he worked as a salesman for a flour company. The Spradleys later moved to Kansas City, and Everette was a salesman for Wilson Packing Company. They adopted a daughter, Eleanor Elizabeth, in December 1941.

Shortly after Pearl Harbor, Everette volunteered for the Navy. As he was in his thirties, he was considered old; but he became a training officer at Great Lakes Navel Training Academy. Kitty Sue and the baby moved to Great Lakes, but a diphtheria outbreak caused them to return to Marshall to her family home.

During the war, Kitty Sue taught at the Blosser Home for Children and substituted at Eastwood School. She saved rationing stamps to have enough gas to pick Everette up at the train in Carrollton when he could come home on leave.

For a brief time after the war, they lived in Kansas City, but Everette wanted to be in business for himself. He bought a small Vess Cola bottling plant in Coffeeville, Kansas, and the Spradley family lived in a boarding house. When unions tried to force Everette to carry beer on his soft drink trucks, he refused and sold the plant instead.

Moving to Trenton, Missouri, Everette owned and operated a Davis Paint Store until he had several heart attacks and was forced to give up retail. The Spradleys returned to Marshall; and he became an insurance broker and later, a real estate agent.

Everette served on the Board of Trustees of First United Methodist Church, and was on the Marshall School Board for several terms. Even though they lived in several communities, Kitty Sue had never moved her membership from her home church. She was active in a church circle; the Methodist Church was always an integral part of their lives.

Beth Spradley remembers her mother as a reserved person who had a surprising sense of humor. Kitty Sue loved puns; for example, while preparing fresh garden green beans one day, she said she was "on the first string team." Kitty Sue and her sisters were brought up to be "ladies"—well-dressed, dignified, and refined, and she has always been a lady.

Kitty Sue Spradley - May Queen
Missouri Valley College, 1935.

Taking Care of People

Katie Stockman   September 2006

Katie Stockman says she was the "boy" in her family of two girls. "Daddy milked the cows in the morning, and I milked them in the evening. I drove a team of mules to roll the field to level it before planting, and I drove the planter too. My sister, Mary Maude, did the inside work, but I loved being outdoors. I would swing out on vines over Salt Fork Creek which ran alongside our farm. Later when we got the Farmall tractor, my mother had a fit when I pulled the disk and the cultivator in the fields. One of my aunts said she felt bad because I wasn't raised like a proper girl!"

Kathryn Lee "Katie" Clyde was born in 1924 to Joseph R. and Bernice Blackburn Clyde on a farm near Malta Bend, Missouri. Her grandparents, John Clyde and Maud Gibbons Clyde gave a strip of their land for the construction of Highway 65, thus the curve in the road became known as "Clyde's Corner." The Clyde family ancestry goes back well over 100 years in Saline County.

The bus for Malta Bend School picked Katie up on the road one quarter mile from her house. A highlight of her grade school years was the engagement and marriage of the fifth and sixth grade teacher, Miss Ellen McRoberts, to Katie's Uncle Aubrey Clyde. In high school, Katie loved outdoor sports as well as basketball and baseball.

Katie describes a thriving Malta Bend...three groceries, a drug store, a restaurant with apartments above it, fabric store, movie theater, barber shop, bank and a Chevrolet dealer with a garage for repairs. "There was a jail, but I think they just put drunks in it to sleep it off. My grandfather, John Blackburn, ran a hardware store; he repaired and oiled harnesses for horses and mules in addition to selling nails and tools. He and my grandmother, Rachel Catherine Peters Blackburn, lived upstairs above the store."

Katie's mother taught Sunday School at Saline Presbyterian Church. Every other Sunday Reverend Crockett came from Sweet Springs to preach. In high school, she and her sister sang duets every Sunday until Katie balked at performing when she was a senior in high school.

"Every Sunday after church we went to a different relative's house for dinner, we all brought food and there were probably 30 or 35 aunts, uncles, and cousins."

After high school, Katie went to St. Joseph's Hospital School of Nursing on Linwood Boulevard in Kansas City. The Sisters of St. Joseph ran the hospital with the help of student nurses.

"We went on the floor at 7:00 a.m.—gave baths to four or five patients before 9:00 a.m. then attended classes until 3:00 p.m. After class, we went back to work on the floor until 7:00 p.m." she said. Mary Maude came to St. Joseph's the next year and roomed with Katie.

After finishing six months as "probies", the students were eligible to join the Nurse Cadet Corps, receiving $30 a month with the understanding that they were to go straight into the military after graduation. It was possible for the Cadets to work in an army hospital the last six months of school.

"We had a gray military uniform and a gray overcoat with epaulets on the shoulder. We always wore our Cadet Corps uniforms if we went to a movie because then we got the cheaper rate given to servicemen!" The war ended by the time Katie graduated so she did not have military experience.

After she finished nursing school, she worked with Dr. William Stewart, an orthopedic surgeon in Columbia for a short time; and then in 1946, she began her long career at Fitzgibbon Hospital, living at first in the nurses' residence across the street on South Brunswick.

Katie was married in 1946 to Francis Joseph Stockman with whom she had gone to Malta Bend High School. Francis, known as "Squeak" ever since his voice changed, was a sergeant in World War II. He was in Hawaii, Australia, and the Philippines during his three years of service. Squeak was custodian at Malta Bend High School for over 30 years before retiring.

After taking off some time when her children were born, Katie worked at Fitzgibbon Hospital continuously for 30 years. She was Director of Nurses intermittently for 15 years.

During her nursing career at Fitzgibbon, she worked in the operating room, the labor and delivery rooms, x-ray, medical surgical floors, the laboratory, the supply room and the emergency room.

"When I was Director of Nurses, I never bawled anybody out. They just looked at my face and knew they had better get busy. Sometimes nurses would disappear like a covey of quail when a doctor got demanding. I just stood my ground and stated my opinion. Even as a child, I always said exactly what I thought and went about my business. Some of the doctors would say, 'If Katie stomps her feet, you better get out of her way!'"

Katie regrets that registered nurses no longer wear a cap; nurses formerly wore with pride the unique cap representing their particular school of nursing. "When you are a patient in the hospital, you do not know who is in charge. Sometimes it seems to me nurses are taking care of a computer these days, not the patient. Everything has gotten too technical, in my opinion."

The three Stockman children were raised in Malta Bend United Methodist Church. Years later, Katie transferred to First United Methodist Church in Marshall. She is a faithful usher at the 8:15 a.m. service, often arriving at 7:30 a.m. to get organized.

It is not easy to get Katie down. She is a two-time cancer survivor; the last episode was 12 years ago. "I figure the dear Lord had something to do with my recovery."

Squeak has been housebound for the past two years, and had to give up the hunting and fishing which he loved. But Katie has adjusted her life and keeps going. "People have always depended on me," she said. Independent, straightforward and plainspoken, Katie continues to look after people.

Methodist Since the Cradle Roll
Betty Stone   November, 2006

"We owe Aunt Betty Chilcott so much...the kind of person she was...the fun she brought to our family," Betty Stone said as she served me tea and cookies in Aunt Betty's rose-covered breakfast dishes. Betty Fisher Chilcott was the the sister of Betty Stone's mother, Ethyl Susan Elizabeth Fisher Jackson, part of the Casebolt-Fisher-Wheeler clan which moved to Miami, Missouri from Virginia. Their ancestor, John Ferrill, was a pioneer at the first outpost in Missouri, Cooper's Fort, and helped to plot a town called Greenville, later renamed "Miami" for the Indian tribe.

Betty Chilcott, for whom Betty Parkhurst Jackson Stone was named, lived in Columbia where her husband, Claude, ran the Campus Barbershop. The Chilcotts often came home to Miami for the weekend. As a child, Betty looked forward to their visits as they were fun-loving, full of stories and jokes, and took her around with them to visit relatives. Betty would spend a week in the summer visiting her aunt and uncle.

Betty speaks of Miami where she was born in 1929. "Everything depended on the Missouri River; and Miami, historically, was the center of education in Saline County. There was a music academy which taught violin and presented concerts, a ladies seminary and an academy preparing young men for higher education and for going into the military. The town had a carriage shop and a mill.

"My grandfather, George Neal Jackson, Sr., bought out a cousin who was a greengrocer in Miami as well as buying the livery stable. He was a commissioned agent for the Chicago Livestock Market; he bought farms as an investment. My father, G.N. Jackson, Jr., studied mechanical engineering at the University of Missouri at Columbia, and he ran a garage in Miami."

The youngest of three, Betty was told that she walked at seven months and has been in everyone's path ever since. "From childhood, I have looked up to my sister, Jane*; she was the pretty one with genteel manners. I knew what the appropriate behavior should be, but I did not always perform," she laughs. Betty describes herself as an independent person who does not like to be told what to do.

Membership in 4-H was an important part of her growing-up years. Betty was a state winner for her demonstration of canning and freezing foods and was chosen as a Missouri delegate to the 25th National 4-H Club Congress in Chicago, Illinois, in 1948.

"I went around with the county extension agent to demonstrate how to freeze foods. Some homes didn't have indoor plumbing or electricity, and it was hard to give demonstrations under those circumstances." Electricity and plumbing were on the way for farm homes; however, and learning these new skills was part of rural progress.

Betty went through the eighth grade at Miami School. Her mother and Mrs. Arlene Hisle began a hot lunch program at the school before the government sponsored lunch programs became widespread. "In the summertime, our 4-H leader, Mrs. Charlie Peterman who was our cousin Josie, arranged to have us can tomatoes and green beans for the school lunch program."

"We had a nice life," Betty said. "We had a big garden and plenty of food. Dad played ball with us in the evenings. I loved to roller-skate and play with a hoop and paddle." On Sundays, the Jackson family went to Miami Methodist Church. Betty was entered on the "Cradle Roll", a Methodist since birth. "Grandma, Harriet Virginia Parkhurst Jackson, was a 'hard-shell Methodist' strictly following the John Wesley traditions. She faithfully read *The Christian Herald* for news of the church and missions. I remember having a nickel tied in the corner of my cloth handkerchief for Sunday School and going to vacation Bible School in the summer.

"Education was very important in our family; and from an early age, I wanted to go to the University of Missouri in Columbia. Since Miami High School was not accredited, we paid tuition; and my father took four of us to Fairville, Missouri, to catch the Marshall High School bus.

"I drove to Fairville starting when I was 15 years old. I played in the band and stayed with friends in town when I needed to stay for after-school events." In high school, Betty was assistant editor of the school newspaper, *The Mar-Saline*, and she knew that she wanted to major in journalism.

The University of Missouri at Columbia was quite a place for an 18-year-old girl from Miami, Missouri. "Veterans, married with families, were coming to get degrees on the GI bill. Young people like me were competing in classes with serious students who had experienced life and death. The University had purchased buildings that had been used as officers' quarters, converting them to temporary dormitories.

"There were seven of us who lived in our unit; Mary Hogge Burge and Roberta Schmidt Edwards from Saline County were among our group. We became great friends, and visited in each other's homes. On Sundays we would go to each other's churches, and I learned more about Episcopalians and Lutherans."

Carrying heavy books and her suitcase, she would get on the Greyhound bus in Columbia and disembark at Slater, Missouri, where her sister, Jane, was teaching home economics, and they would travel to Miami for the weekend together. "There was always family at some place or another," Betty said.

After graduating with a bachelor of science in journalism, Betty worked in Kansas City at jobs that led to work on the editorial staff of *TV Guide*. Promotions took her to Miami, Florida, and Atlanta, Georgia. A brief marriage did not work out. She was headed to New York City to work on a new publication when she received the news that her mother was gravely ill.

"There were no nursing homes in the early sixties; my sister was busy with her family. It seemed natural that I should be the one to move in with my parents and take over their care." After her mother died, she continued to stay with her elderly father.

"It was a complete metamorphosis," Betty said. "I was so far past living in small towns." Never the less, she was committed to staying with her aging parents. "I became active in church, in the Miami Eastern Star chapter and in Beta Sigma Phi sorority." She went back to school for an education degree and began a new career as a teacher. Her last job before retiring was as a remedial math and reading teacher for the Blue Hills Homes Corporation out of Kansas City. She drove a 32-foot long mobile classroom calling at parochial schools in the central Missouri area for 13 years.

In 1975, Betty moved to Marshall, and joined First United Methodist Church, and she became a member of Circle 5 and the United Methodist Women. Betty is inspired by music and she thinks that the hymn, "Are You Able?" "really puts it to you—are you strong enough?"

Betty was part of the church staff as Parish Visitor for six years. When the Sewing Circle disbanded and designated their remaining funds for a stained glass window over the New Life Center entrance, Betty created the dove with the olive branch design.

"At one point in my life, it seemed that I was losing everyone that I loved," Betty said. "I thought there must be something that I wasn't catching onto. In my Grandfather Jackson's library, he had many old books that he used in teaching the Men's Sunday School class at Miami Methodist Church. I went through them and I was led from one thing to another. In a series called, *The Spiritual Man* by Watchman Nee, I gained insight into understanding that we all carry a part of God within, we have to come to know what that part is."

Betty recited the following Scripture by memory. "Words to live by," she said.

Trust in the Lord with all thine heart; and lean not unto thine own understanding. In all thy ways acknowledge Him, and He shall direct thy paths. Proverbs 3:5 -6 KJV

*Jane Stonner, Betty's sister, is featured in the next chapter.

Experienced President of United Methodist Women
Jane Stonner   March 2006

In Columbia, I visited with Jane Stonner at a lovely retirement center called Tiger Place. Jane moved quite recently from Marshall to be near her daughters, Susan Crepeau and Leigh Lingwall. Walking with her tiger-striped cane, Jane gave me a tour of her apartment in which she had her own things.

The pleasant living quarters reflect her distinctive taste. I stopped to admire the Japanese robe that she purchased when her daughter, Leigh, lived in Japan. The *Upper Room* devotional magazine lies on the table beside her Bible, and it is Jane's routine to read a chapter each day in addition to the devotional.

Jane Jackson Stonner was born in 1921 to George Neal Jackson and Susan Elizabeth Fisher Jackson in Miami, Missouri, where her father ran a garage. Mr. Jackson had attended the University of Missouri studying mechanical engineering but dropped out to go to Alaska to the gold fields. He worked in a mine and drove a dog team for supplies. "No gold!" Jane laughed—he returned to Miami, Missouri.

When I asked her what she did for fun as a child, she said, "I read constantly, I can remember reading *Gone with the Wind* with a flashlight in my bed late at night." Her father was a great reader, and sometimes he read books that he felt were not appropriate for her. "As sure as dad told me I could not read something, I was sure to sneak it away to read!" she said.

Two drug stores, two groceries, one with tables and chairs for a café, a hotel and a post office made it unnecessary for folks in Miami to drive to Marshall for supplies. The Missouri River came right up to the bluff before it changed its course. "Showboats would come down the river and stop to put on shows," she said, "I was too young to go to the shows, but I remember going with Mother down to see the boats.

When the railroad went to Marshall, the town of Miami just withered away. People used to drive cattle across the river when it was frozen to load on the train at Miami Station, across from Miami to the north.

"My grandmother, Virginia Jane Fisher, was very dear to me. I spent every day with her before I went to school. Sometimes Aunt Betty Chilcott would come to take me on her big old horse, and sometimes I was taken in the car by our trusted hired hand, Sterlie Carter. There was no kindergarten at that time so I spent my early learning years with my grandmother."

Jane went to twelve years of school in Miami "on the coldest hill you ever saw." The school had outdoor toilets and an outdoor basketball court. Jane played basketball. "We had a good team. The games were at night; and with no electric lights, the families would turn their cars toward the court and turn their lights on." Miami played teams from Glasgow, Malta Bend, Nelson, Gilliam and Napton.

After graduating from Miami High School, Jane went to Central Missouri State Teachers College for two years. "There were three things I did not want to do: I did not want to be a teacher, I did not want to marry a farmer, and when I took the Civil Service examination for clerical work during World War II, I did not want to go to Washington D.C."

Jane did very well on the examination, however; and in 1944, she was offered a job in Washington D.C. Legions of young women went to the Capitol to do the paperwork associated with the war. For four years, her job was writing letters in the Department of the Army. As traveling was quite expensive, she was only able to return to Missouri once. I asked her if she got homesick during that time. "As long as I have a book to read, I am OK!" she smiled.

279

In later years, she went back to college in Warrensburg and finished a degree in home economics with a minor in science. For a short time after the war, she taught home economics in Slater, Missouri.

Completing the three things she had pledged that she would not do, Jane married Roy Stonner, a farmer with property in northern Saline County, and they settled in Miami. Jane was back again at Miami Methodist Church where she had gone since she was a child.

Jane remembers teaching pre-school children in Sunday School at the Miami church when she was still in high school. The Sunday School room was a curtained off corner of the main floor. Other Sunday School classes were downstairs in the basement. She was always active in United Methodist Women. Jane and another member took turns being president as the group was very small.

After Roy died in 1983, Jane moved to Marshall and joined First United Methodist Church. Twice she was president of United Methodist Women, and she worked in the sewing group that made quilts for the needy. Jane has a sister, Betty*, also a member of First United Methodist Church.

A fond memory is when the women's group made hard candy every Christmas and sold it to make money for missions. Pat Keener led the volunteers in this popular project; early in the Christmas season they met in the church kitchen with supplies, cooking colored sugar candy in sheets, and then snipping it into little pieces with a scissors while it was hot. Shaken with powdered sugar, the candy resembled pieces of broken colored glass.

In 1941, Jane was seriously injured in a car-train accident. She feels that she could easily have been killed. It was a snowy night, and she and a friend were driving to Marshall in a Model A Ford belonging to the grandmother of her friend. At the time, there was no signal at the railroad track on Highway 41 and no seat belts in cars.

The car slid into the side of the train, and Jane was thrown through the windshield; her body rolled down an incline, stopping just inches from water that was five feet deep. Jane feels her life was spared in this incident. She was hospitalized at Fitzgibbon hospital with sandbags around her to keep her immobile while her body recovered. "If the Lord had not been there, I would have died." Jane has felt God's continuing presence in her life.

*Jane's sister, Betty Stone, tells her story in the preceding interview.

Respect Every Living Person

Delford Thompson   February 2006

Hard work, responsibility and good citizenship are words that describe Delford Thompson who was born in Chillicothe, Missouri in 1941, the seventh in a family of ten children; one died in infancy. "Nobody worked as hard as my dad, he was a 'jack of all trades,'" Delford said.

The Glen Thompson family had a grocery and restaurant as well as a 70-acre farm with 60 head of dairy cows. The boys milked cows before school and in the evening and delivered milk to customers until pasteurization became required.

Their home, warmed with oil heaters, did not have indoor plumbing until the 1950s, and water was heated on the stove for baths. Mary Ann Thompson, Delford's mother, was always cooking and preserving food from their large garden.

Delford started school in Oak Grove, a two room school two miles across the field from their house. He remembers playing in the sandbox while the teacher taught the older kids. They played softball in the afternoons against other small schools. Later the school merged with the Chillicothe School District, and Delford graduated from Chillicothe High School.

The whole family would get in the back of Mr. Thompson's enclosed truck on Saturday night and go to the movies. They could see a double feature for 15 cents each. To make money in the summer, they would throw hay bales which weighed about 70 pounds apiece from the field to the truck and then up into sweltering hot haylofts; they were paid a half cent a bale for their work.

Delford's first church experience was in the Baptist church in Chillicothe. He remembers good times in Royal Ambassadors, a group for boys. Later they joined the Methodist church, and he had fond memories of Methodist Youth Fellowship when

Pat and Don Keener were the sponsors of the youth group. Delford said it took a lot of patience on the Keeners' part. He recalls one outing when the kids threw one of the boys into a farm stock tank as a prank.

Delford was able to go to college because the football coach at Chillicothe High School, Larry Hayes, recommended him to Coach Volney Ashford at Missouri Valley College. As student manager of the football team, he had student loans, did the team laundry and took care of the football field.

During basketball season, he was student manager for Coach Grover Redford. Grover and Jean Redford became like second parents to him.

Delford's career moved from teaching elementary education in Marshall, to running college bookstores, to operating a lawn and garden store and finally to being Saline County Collector for 24 years. "The people of Saline County were very good to me," he said.

Delford held many positions of responsibility in First United Methodist Church; the Thompson daughters were active in Sunday School. He was coach for years in Little League baseball; he is a long-time member of the Kiwanis service club.

When Parkinson's disease slowed Delford down, doctors suggested that he stop driving a car. The story is told that he drove his riding lawn mower two miles to Jean Redford's home to mow her yard, stopping at the Dairy Queen on the way for a treat.

At the time of this interview, February 2006, Delford is living at Big Bend Retreat in Slater. His wife, Carol Cohea Thompson, takes him to their home to spend time when she is not working as a nurse at the Marshall Habilitation Center. Delford speaks highly of her efforts to help him.

Coping with his symptoms is difficult and living in a nursing home has been a challenge. Delford's advice to a younger generation is to respect every living person, regardless of age or ability. Delford has lived this philosophy.

The Military Life

Pearl and Earl Underwood   February 2006

Earl and Pearl Underwood, residents of Big Bend Retreat in Slater, Missouri, are from South Dakota. As Earl puts it, "We are Presbyterian all the way."

One son, Earl, Jr., is a Presbyterian minister. At the present time, they are associate members of First United Methodist Church. Or perhaps you would call them "captive" members since their daughter, Jeanne Simonton, sees that they get out of the rest home to come to First United Methodist Church events. Both are confined to wheelchairs. Earl uses oxygen; Pearl has had Parkinson's disease for 20 years. Jeanne and her husband, George Topel, make an extraordinary effort to see that the Underwoods regularly have a change of scenery, even though it is Methodist scenery.

Earl was born in Kansas, but moved to Rapid City, South Dakota, at age three with his parents, Olive Worthington and John Underwood. Pearl Kukuk and her parents, Minnie and John Kukuk, lived a block from Earl's family. Pearl and Earl were five years old when they met, they went to the same schools, and to the same Presbyterian church where Pearl's mother was their Sunday School teacher.

During the depression, Earl remembers that candy bars were four or five cents each, but nickels were hard to come by. For Christmas money, they would hunt for cardboard boxes in alleys. Bakeries would pay five cents a box. Earl and his three sisters raised rabbits and sold them to make extra money.

Earl and Pearl dated in high school. Sometimes he would pay for the 14-cent movie tickets; but Pearl babysat, and sometimes she would have 75 cents to pay for their date. They went to church camp together. In high school, hayrides were a special treat with a wagon pulled by a team of horses out to the country where the kids gathered around a bonfire.

Earl and Pearl went to the Junior-Senior Prom together. "It is a wonder she ever married me," Earl said. "One of my buddies came up to me and said, 'The fish are biting.' I asked her to get her father to take her home!"

It was not one of Pearl's good days on the Friday of my visit. She napped most of the time that I was there. Occasionally she said something, and Earl would say, "What's that, Mother Dear?" but her words were unintelligible. The two share a room at the rest home; respect and affection is evident.

In 1939 at age eighteen, Earl enlisted in the army. He was in a battalion of military police during WWII. His group became responsible for the security of General George F. Patton in the European Theatre of Operations. In his 30 years of military service, the Underwoods moved 53 times. Pearl kept track of the number of moves; she had to be flexible as she raised two boys and two girls during their army career.

At the end of World War II, Earl was commissioned as a Second Lieutenant and worked in military intelligence.

"Does that mean you were a spy?" I asked. He explained that military intelligence is a broad field. Earl's battalion was headed for Japan by ship when the atomic bomb was dropped. The ship turned around, and headed back to the States.

After the war, he was assigned to the Philippines to hunt in the hills for remaining Japanese troops. The army took trinkets to trade with natives in order to get information about hiding Japanese.

Pearl and their two little boys accompanied him, and they lived in a bamboo hut. He recalls that she had to bake their bread. The flour had weevils and was sprayed with a chemical to kill the weevils before it could be used. Earl wonders if ingesting chemicals could have caused Pearl's Parkinson's disease in later life.

Major Underwood commanded a battalion in both the Korean and the Vietnamese wars. He recalls that during the Korean War there were many hospitalizations for frozen feet and reactions to the cold. Pearl worked as a volunteer with the men in the military hospital at Vallejo, California, where those afflicted were brought for treatment.

Later Earl's specialty became finance and budgets, and he graduated from the Command and General Staff College in Fort Leavenworth, Kansas.

Pearl was always busy with volunteer work. She worked with the younger women who had certain responsibilities in their role as officers' wives. Protocol required that they dress and behave appropriately; for example, always wearing hats and gloves. Pearl taught cake decorating classes among her many other activities.

In 1954, Earl was part of a staff of 20 that accompanied 30 or 40 scientists to the island of Enawetok, 2000 miles from Hawaii. He was present for the explosion of the first hydrogen bomb. It was set off at 3:00 a.m., 75 miles away from the three and one half mile wide island. "It looked like the moon was coming up, the flash of the bomb, then it got as bright as day. You could have read a newspaper by the light. After two minutes, the light dimmed until it became like moonlight again."

The scientists and staff went to have coffee and breakfast; 30 minutes later the shock hit the island. "It felt like an earthquake." No one really knew what the bomb would be like. Shortly afterward, a pact was made with Russia not to explode a hydrogen bomb again. Both countries then began underground testing. "It was terrifying to think of the potential for destruction," Earl said.

After military retirement, Earl and Pearl moved to Black Hills, South Dakota, and Earl took a position with First National Bank, now Wells Fargo. When he retired from the bank, they did not give him a gold watch. They gave him ten shares of bank stock. Far better than a gold watch, as they have multiplied to 144 shares over the years.

Until three years ago, Earl did all the cooking, housekeeping and taking care of Pearl as her health declined. Then he suddenly had a heart attack, gall bladder trouble and kidney failure at the same time. He was not expected to live.

His children all came to be with them; Earl overcame the worst of the problems, but his health was impaired to the point that it was necessary for him and Pearl to have nursing care around the clock. They moved to be near Jeanne in Marshall.

Earl speaks with affection of the staff at Big Bend, but living in a rest home is something like being in a prison. "You can never walk out of here," he said.

Still in the midst of hardship and losses, one gets a sense of the same young man who was awarded the Certificate of Merit framed and hanging on the wall of their room—awarded for exemplary service and noting his "unfailing good nature..." and signed General George F. Patton.

The Teacher From Elmwood

Bertha Mae Van Dyke   March 2006

Bertha Mae and I visited in the cozy sitting room of her home on East Eastwood on a dreary winter day. "I am 94," she said, "but I don't have an ache or a pain. I feel the same as I always have—I just move a little slower!"

Born Bertha Mae Carmean, the only child of Harry B. Carmean and Nora Heyenbrock Carmean, Bertha Mae's home was on a farm near Elmwood, Missouri. Elmwood boasted two general stores, one of which sold yard goods, a blacksmith shop and half a dozen houses.

Bertha Mae's grandparents, Millard Fillmore Carmean and Ida Mae Robison Carmean, lived in one of those houses, and she loved to spend time at their house. Three or four times a year the Carmeans would go to visit cousins who lived in Kansas City, a drive which took all day; and the family spent the night.

Her family was never strictly one denomination or another; but they went to the Elmwood Methodist church, one and one half miles from their farm. People in the Lutheran or Evangelical and Reformed churches in Blackburn had services in German. Bertha Mae's many memories of the Elmwood church include ice cream socials outside in the warm summer weather and basket dinners at noon on special occasions.

The minister lived in Sweet Springs; when there was a dinner at noon, there would be preaching again in the afternoon. She remembers Children's Day and Christmas programs when the kids were all dressed up and eagerly participated in the services. Her grandfather was Sunday School Superintendent for years. The Grange, an organization of area farmers, often met in an upstairs room at the church.

A big event each year was the fall Lord's Acre Sale. Each family was requested to donate the proceeds from one acre

289

of their farm. Church members also brought eggs, canned goods, jelly, preserves and fresh produce to sell for the benefit of the church budget.

After grade school in Elmwood, Bertha Mae went to Blackburn High School, four and one-half miles away. Bertha Mae rode her horse in the spring and fall and kept it in the barn provided by the school for students' horses. During the winter months, her parents did not want her to ride in bad weather, and she boarded in town with the family of her good friend, Frances Lou Maddox, who lived in Blackburn.

After high school, Bertha Mae and Frances went to William Jewell College in Liberty for a year and a summer. Mr. and Mrs. Carmean wanted Bertha Mae to finish four years at William Jewell, but Frances Lou planned to teach school, and Bertha Mae thought she would like to teach also.

Her first job in teaching was at Elmwood where she had gone through the first eight grades. "The students did their assignments on slate blackboards that lined three walls of the one room schoolhouse."

Later, Bertha Mae taught at Sunnyside School, south of Shackelford, for a total of eight years staying with a family near the school. She remembers teaching Castle, Hutcherson, and Schilb children. With an eight-month school year, the students were free in April to help with spring planting.

To complete her teaching degree, she would go to Central Missouri State Teachers College in Warrensburg in the summer, rooming with Frances. The school in Shackelford would sometimes have a Catholic summer school session because the community could not afford a year-round parochial school.

Bertha Mae met Leonard Van Dyke at a wedding reception for Bill and Betty Murrell in the big brick house at 741 East Eastwood, the present home of Paul and Kim Thompson. She had attended the reception with someone else but got acquainted with Leonard at the party.

"The young people danced to a Victrola in the downstairs parlor," Bertha Mae remembers. Bertha Mae and Leonard were married for almost 61 years before his death

Bertha Mae sees her son, Bob, and her daughter, Jane Huff, almost every day, and she feels greatly blessed. "A lot of things in life are just not in our hands; prayer helps you accept what you cannot change." Bertha Mae's favorite hymn is "It is Well with My Soul," and she seems to reflect a sense of peace in her life.

> *When peace, like a river, attendeth my way,*
> *When sorrows like sea billows roll;*
> *Whatever my lot, Thou has taught me to say,*
> *It is well, it is well, with my soul.*
> *Horatio Spafford*

License Plate: LTCBVH
Barbara Van Horn   December 2006

Barbara Van Horn warned me not to focus too heavily on the sadness of her youth. "I have really had a very good life," she said. Barbara, born in Vermont in 1924, lost her father when she was five years old; David Purdy, died from tuberculosis when he was only 29.

Three years later, her mother, Helen Piatt Purdy, died from cancer. Barbara moved to Bayonne, New Jersey, directly across from Staten Island, New York, to live with her maternal grandparents, Emma Somerset Piatt and Samuel Piatt.

When she was 12, her grandparents died and she moved to Westfield, New Jersey, to live with family friends, Roy and Lucy Sutherland. "I knew no one in that town, but the Sutherlands were very good to me. I joined Girl Scouts, made neighborhood friends and adjusted to the new situation."

When Pearl Harbor was bombed on December 7, 1941, Barbara was a senior in high school, and war colored life on the East Coast. "There were black-outs; windows had to be covered so that the enemy could not see lights from the ocean. There were shortages of everything imaginable."

It was patriotic to write to servicemen overseas, and all the girls had correspondents who looked forward to letters from the U.S.A. "I wrote to six or seven servicemen, sometimes ten page letters. A girl friend of mine was trying to find someone to write to James Roland Van Horn, so I started sending letters to him as well."

Barbara went to Berkeley Secretarial School in East Orange, New Jersey, keeping up with her letter writing while she studied. Most of her classmates wanted to get jobs in the fashion industry in New York City, but Barbara took a job in the office of a factory making electric motors. She walked to work and lived at the Y.W.C.A., very much like a college dormitory with a housemother to watch over the girls.

Roland Van Horn had grown up in Plainfield, New Jersey, about a half-mile from her home, but Barbara had never met him. He was stationed with a quartermaster unit in the Pacific near the Philippines.

The sun and sand caused him to have temporary blindness, and he was transferred back to the States. In 1944, he and Barbara were married at Trinity Dutch Reformed Church in Plainfield.

"Coupons were necessary to buy goods. I had to choose how to use my coupons, and I saved them to get a going away dress. I had white satin cloth slippers to go with my wedding gown—leather was almost impossible to get.

"While Roland was in the service, we moved in with his parents, Elizabeth and John Van Horn. They treated me like one of their own, and I had brothers and sisters at last because Roland had two brothers and three sisters."

After the war, Roland went to work for Ford Motor Company. "We bought our first house with a mortgage for $9999. I could hardly sleep at night—it seemed like such an enormous amount of money to have to pay off!"

After the birth of her children, Barbara continued her career. She was board secretary and business manager for Green Brook Township public schools for 12 years. When a new building was to be constructed, she was the person who went to Wall Street to purchase school bonds; she arranged for the contractors and made decisions about flooring and interior details.

Barbara worked for another school district for 11 years and then decided to make a career change, going back to school to refresh her skills. She found that the younger students were being taught a different method of Gregg shorthand, but she was faster using ways she had learned previously.

Typing 65 words a minute without errors helped her get a job with Dun and Bradstreet, an establishment which researches and offers credit ratings on businesses. "It was all strictly confidential, and we were pledged to secrecy about our work," she said.

She and Roland were building a new home and acting as their own contractors when he was diagnosed with Parkinson's disease at age 40. At first his symptoms did not interfere with his life, but increasingly she began to have to take him to doctor's appointments, and supervise his care. From time to time, he needed short-term nursing home care.

Her husband's health continued to deteriorate, and their youngest son, Doug, helped Barbara with decisions and arrangements. In 1966, Roland had brain surgery that took the shaking away for a while; he was able to return to work, but eventually he could no longer drive, and he had to give up his job.

In 1984, the Van Horns moved to Missouri to be near their son, David, who had settled in Marshall after going to school at Central Methodist College in Fayette, Missouri Valley College, and St. Paul's School of Theology in Kansas City.

"It was a more relaxed pace than living in cities with all the traffic, less rushing, pushing through crowds; I have loved it here," she said. Her daughter-in-law, Marlene, grew up in Miami, Missouri, and Barbara has been included in the large family of Leola and Frederick Cooper, Marlene's parents.

Influenced by her grandmother, Emma Piatt, who was the Sunday School Superintendent at Burgen Point Methodist Church in New Jersey, Barbara is a Methodist at heart. She is quite ecumenical, however, as she was part of the Dutch Reformed Church as a youth and has supported churches of several different denominations.

294

In spite of her metropolitan city origins, she has always been a member of smaller congregations. Barbara retains her membership and continues support of Mount Hore United Methodist Church in Warren, New Jersey, in addition to First United Methodist Church in Marshall. She is a member of United Methodist Women and Circle 5; she feels the congregation has been warm and friendly to her for more than 20 years.

For 13 years, Barbara has been Finance Officer in the local Civil Air Patrol, an auxiliary of the Air Force and a United Way agency. The organization attracts young boys and girls, beginning in the sixth grade, to study about flying.

"We meet weekly at the airport on Saturday mornings, learn cardiopulmonary resuscitation (C.P.R.) and take part in rescue operations. The cadets wear uniforms, conduct flag ceremonies and take tests for promotions. Some of our best students have become pilots. Civil Air Patrol has been a big part of my life—I am now a Lieutenant Colonel and my car license plate says 'LTCBVH!"

Barbara has always helped other people, and she continues by delivering Meals on Wheels to the housebound and by volunteering at Fitzgibbon Hospital. Thinking of others has been a way of life for her.

Last year she had a stroke and could not speak or write for a couple of months, but with time, things improved. "At times I can't think of the right word, and I need to read out loud sometimes to understand the content, but I am much better now. I can't always trust my right leg, and I have a walker handy when I need it," she said.

"You seem to have been a strong person in the face of difficulties." I commented to her.

"What else would you do?" she responded. "I guess I am basically optimistic. I do not think I have ever been seriously depressed. As a young child, I realized that I was all alone, and I said to God, 'You gotta take care of me.'"

World War II Navy Nurse
Winnie Warnock   September 2006

Winnie Warnock was born in 1919 in rural Alabama, 100 miles south of Montgomery, almost in Florida. Her parents, Mamie Lee Willis Clark and Audie Clark, had two families of children according to Winnie, "There were three of us and then, 11 years later, three more. When I would come home from nursing school, my little brother would say, 'Who is that girl? Is she my sister?'"

Winnie remembers peanut-shelling parties on Saturday nights. Corn, cotton and peanuts were their major crops; neighbors would gather to shell the peanut crop for use as seeds. Every weekend during the harvest, people gathered at a different home to work while the children played outdoors and had a great time together. She remembers playing "Spin the Bottle." "You would go for a walk with the person; none of this kissing business because your father was watching!"

Her mother made her own peanut butter by roasting and grinding the nuts, adding oil and a little sugar and salt. The jars were sealed with paraffin. Green peanuts were boiled in salt water for a tasty snack.

"During the Depression, people in the country in Alabama just did not have flour. We took our corn to a grist mill down on the creek, and we made cornbread from the cornmeal," Winnie recalls. "My mother preserved and canned produce from the garden, and we raised our own meat."

Winnie walked one half mile to Rhodes School for her first two or three grades. When the school closed, she went to grade school and high school in Kinston, Alabama, a very small town. She enjoyed participating in Future Homemakers of America (F.H.A) with projects in sewing, cooking and home decorating.

"We lived many miles from a church when I was a child, and we did not have transportation. My grandfather, William Joseph Willis, was a Baptist minister; and on Saturdays, he would stop by our house with his horse and buggy on his way to the church some distance away. He stayed all night there, and he would stop at our house again on Sunday afternoons when he returned."

An uncle who was a Methodist minister was a great influence in Winnie's younger years. Reverend J.R. Helms, a very kind man, moved to different churches as is the custom with Methodist ministers; and Winnie often spent summers at his home as a teenager. She helped take care of her Aunt Ida, his wife, who was not well. Perhaps this experience caused her to think about becoming a nurse.

Winnie went to Baptist Hospital Nursing School in Birmingham, Alabama. "Discipline in the dormitory was very strict. We had to be in at 10:00 p.m. every night, even on weekends. My roommate slipped out one night down the fire escape to meet a doctor, and she was kicked out of school. We wore beautiful blue uniforms with a white apron, white hose and white shoes. We were so proud of our starched nursing caps!"

After graduation in 1944, she joined the Navy Nurse Corps. "All my friends were going, so I did, too," she said. "At first when I arrived in Norfolk, Virginia, we stayed in a huge room with bunk beds for about 50 nurses. The lights never went off because people worked different shifts and were constantly coming and going. It was hard to sleep!

"Soon we were assigned to a room for two with a shared bathroom down the hall. I learned to march and to salute, but mostly I worked in a huge hospital for the war injured. Nurses rotated two-week shifts between medical, surgical, orthopedic and maternity units. There were soldiers in body casts who were very uncomfortable as there was no air conditioning. We gave medications and saw that the doctors' orders were carried out. Navy corpsmen gave the personal care to the injured men."

"Wasn't it depressing work?" I asked.

"You were so busy and there was so much going on that you didn't have time to get depressed. Then, too, we always had fun. A movie was shown every day on the base and on Saturday nights dances were held—big name bands came to entertain the injured troops, and the Marine and Navy bands played as well. Once Red Skelton, the famous comedian, visited the unit when I was at work.

"The big ships would come into port; the captain would call the nurses' residence, and say they would like a certain number of guests for dinner. I remember being on the Alabama, the Enterprise, the Missouri and the Ticonderoga. They would send a jeep to pick us up and take us out to the boat.

"We would sit at the Captain's table with the finest crystal, silver and china you have ever seen. The sailors were just so glad to have female company. In a couple of months, they would be back in port again, and they would have the name of a nurse to call for a date."

Later Winnie was transferred to Camp Shoemaker, California, east of San Francisco. "It was a long, hot trip with no air-conditioning; for several days we ate and slept on the train. Out in the desert, you would burn up in the daytime, and freeze at night!

"The nurses did everything—from working in a maternity ward for dependent wives to counting linens to working on a locked ward, the brig, for sailors who had broken the rules or had gone Absent Without Leave (AWOL) but were sick.

"I especially remember the polio ward where we used the Sister Kenney method of wrapping affected limbs with hot wool blankets—wringing out the hot water and changing them frequently – and the heat of the desert was intense. Some never walked again as the result of polio."

After she was discharged in 1944, Winnie went to work at Chicago Lying-In Hospital in labor and delivery, post-partum and newborn units. "It was a learning experience. We had the most up-to-date equipment of that time. Mothers stayed in the hospital for seven days, and fathers were not allowed in the hospital at all; they didn't see the baby until discharge."

A friend who graduated from the University of Kansas brought Winnie to Kansas City to work at Trinity Lutheran Hospital on the maternity ward. In Kansas City, she met her husband, Harry F. Warnock, Jr., on a blind date. Harry, a WW II veteran, worked for Meinrath Food Brokerage, a wholesale food supply company.

Married in 1948, Harry and Winnie were active members of Asbury United Methodist church. "Harry was a wonderful man, a devoted Methodist and he taught children's classes at Asbury," she said. "We lived in Prairie Village, Kansas, and raised two daughters there, Martha Meyer of Gilliam, Missouri, and Nancy Fletcher of Jackson, Mississippi.

"I did not work for 17 years because I was busy with my children," Winnie said. "Then one day in 1968 I heard on the radio that Avila College was offering refresher courses for nurses. I went back to school and learned new procedures and medicines and went to work on a medical-surgical unit at Research Medical Center.

"Harry bought a car for me to get to work as we only owned one car. I think the good Lord spoke to me and said, 'Get up and get going!'" In 1976, Harry died unexpectedly, and Winnie was left a widow. Having her work was a lifesaver for her.

After living in Prairie Village for 42 years, Winnie moved to Marshall in 2000 to be near her daughter, Martha, who comes to see her once a week before she goes to work as a nurse at Fitzgibbon Hospital.

"I really like living in Marshall. First United Methodist Church has been important to me in adjusting to a new place. I attend the Keystone Sunday School Class, and I help get the church newsletter into the mail. I am in a Bible Study group; I don't think I know enough about the Bible, and I always want to learn more."

One aspect of living in Marshall that has been especially important to Winnie is the Optimist Club. Sally Sherwood invited her to the 7:00 a.m. Saturday morning breakfast meetings; Winnie enjoys working in the club's concession stands which raise money for community youth activities.

"Since I got my cataracts fixed, I can drive at night again, and I work at the Friday night baseball games," she said. Recently the Optimists gave her an award for "Outstanding Service to Children and Youth."

As we visited at her round oak table drinking coffee served in her antique blue willow china cups, Winnie reminds me that the annual Cornhusking Contest is coming up this weekend; she is actively involved in the community. She likes to play pitch in a card group at the Senior Center.

"I am greatly blessed with good health. If I sit at home, I sit alone. It is important for me to be with other people."

Work is a Blessing

Margaret Waters   November 2006

Several months ago Margaret Waters went through an aggressive chemotherapy regimen to treat cancer, a physically and mentally debilitating experience. She spoke of how much she had appreciated the support of the church congregation. "Every day three or four cards filled with good wishes would arrive in the mail, and it would lift my spirits. I keep them all in a basket and read them over and over; I will probably keep them forever because they have meant so much to me."

Margaret is very appreciative of her family who took her to appointments, and rallied around her. "My daughter, Dona McInteer Hahn, made countless trips to the doctor with me." Her son, Mike McInteer, who lives with his family in Canada, was able to take her to the last one of her chemotherapy treatments. Margaret, now cancer-free, says, "Family, friends and church all help you get through illness."

Work has always been an integral part of Margaret's life; at present she keeps books for her son, Ed McInteer, and works two mornings a week in the Central Missouri Title Office. Her early memories are of pulling weeds and working in gardens when she lived on a farm in rural Saline County.

Otho Copeland Sutton lost his first wife in 1920 due to the flu epidemic; he was left with three children. In 1925, he married Linnie Lee Whetzel; Margaret is the younger of their two surviving children. Mr. Sutton died when Margaret was six years old.

The Sutton children rode in a pony cart or on a five-gaited mare to the one room Orearville School. On Sundays, they attended Shiloh Methodist Church on Highway 41. "I remember Reverend Tom Harris, who was retired, sitting right in front because he was hard of hearing."

302

In 1945, the family moved to Marshall so that her mother could go to work at the Page Creamery. Margaret went to Marshall High School and worked as an assistant in the school office. At age 13, she started selling popcorn for Leo Hayob at the old Mary Lou Theatre on North Street, one of three theaters in Marshall at the time.

Margaret received 15 cents an hour, all the popcorn she could eat and unlimited movie viewing, mostly Westerns. She remembers "clickers" used to record how many people attended the show. "I don't know why they kept track of the numbers; maybe the cost of the movies to the theater was related to how many people came."

When the new Mary Lou theatre opened on North Jefferson street, the present site of the Wood and Huston drive-through facility, Margaret sold tickets. "We did about anything there was to be done at the theatre building—I recall once the insulation on the roof got wet, and Leo had us up there turning the insulation over to dry out," she remembers.

"It was a beautiful auditorium with murals painted on the side walls, illuminated with black lights. An artist did a collage of Saline County in bright colors—Missouri Valley College football players, an Arrow Rock scene, and other local sights."

Margaret worked at the theater while she went to Missouri Valley College for a year and a half, but the $200 semester fees were too much and she had to quit school. By this time, her mother had gone to work at the Marshall State School, working with clients.

"My mother worked very hard. When we lived on the farm, she made our dresses from feed sacks. She had been a teacher in Virginia before she was married. When she was in her sixties, she took classes at Valley so she could return to teaching. She was a cook and teacher at Orearville School before she retired. I can still hear her voice late at night saying, 'Thank you, Lord, for the bed.'"

When Margaret was divorced and the mother of three young children, her mother was a great help to her as well as were her sister, Sue Sutton Cromley of Sedalia, and her half-brother, Lowell Sutton, and his wife Bertha. Margaret worked as a bookkeeper for the Missouri Farmers Association Feed Division, then as a supervisor of inventory for Hales and Hunter, Red Comb Pioneer Feed Mill.

"I believe that work is a blessing God gives to us. I feel sorry for people who cannot work." Margaret said. "I was with the *Democrat-News* briefly, but when George Waters offered me $2.50 an hour, $100 a week, to keep books for Red Cross Pharmacy, I could not refuse because I needed the money, and that salary was a small fortune for me at the time."

George's father, Grover Waters, had owned Red Cross Pharmacy along with pharmacists Celsus Booth and Don Vandergrift. George returned to the states from the Pacific in World War II suffering from phosphorous burns from a bomb. When his father died, he moved to Marshall to work in the business.

On Thanksgiving Day, 1956, Reverend Arnold Prater married George and Margaret in First United Methodist Church. In 1968, Red Cross Pharmacy was sold to Steve and David Hartwig, and the Waters opened Gibson's, a full service department store...clothing, hardware, pharmacy and grocery. Margaret progressed into management as well as book-keeping.

Margaret was the first woman to serve on the Marshall Chamber of Commerce board. She was also the first woman elected as a director and as an officer, Vice-president in 1976.

In the seventies, George was diagnosed with multiple sclerosis; his health deteriorated, and it became necessary for him to use a wheelchair. "The Veterans Administration paid for his care—a great blessing because eventually he had to go to the nursing home in Columbia. He lived in the nursing home for nine years; he received excellent care with registered nurses and all the therapy that he needed."

After Gibson's closed in 1984, Margaret became office manager for Odell Avenue Medical Clinic. She supervised the transition of the group of nine doctors and almost 50 employees into new offices built near Fitzgibbon Hospital and re-named Missouri Valley Physicians.

"I am proud of our church," Margaret said, "At one time it was strait-laced and 'picky'; if anyone came to church dressed differently, people would stare. Now they are accepting of all kinds of people. Prayer time during the Sunday service is such a spiritual experience—when the microphone is passed around, and people speak of their joys and concerns, you can feel the presence of God right there."

Margaret feels a good sense of humor is essential in getting through life's trying times. "You have to laugh at yourself," she said. "Also I try to forgive everyone. I do not dwell on past hurts. If you carry bad times with you, you only hurt yourself. I don't remember the bad times in my life—I give it to God, and He takes care of it."

Farming and Music
Jane and Nelson Weber   May 2006

Music is the common tie that brought Nelson Weber and Jane Shaw together. Born in 1938, they were in the same high school class and in Marshall High School band; Nelson played saxophone, and Jane played clarinet.

Harold Lickey had taught instrumental music at Eastwood School and started Jane on the clarinet. She remembers walking to the home of Ruth Storts for piano lessons. Nelson took piano lessons from Sister Mary Elizabeth who gave lessons to countless children in Marshall for several decades; she is remembered by some for using a ruler on the wrists when a wrong note was played.

At the Robert Leigh one room school near Nelson's home on Highway 41, a teacher named Lois Joyce taught music and had a little band. Nelson learned to play a baritone horn. The pupils had an hour at noon when they played baseball and "Annie Over," a game in which a ball was tossed over the schoolhouse roof. If the team on the other side caught the ball, they ran around and tagged members of the other team who joined their side.

If they did not catch the ball, they threw it back. No winners, just fun throwing, chasing and running! In the winter, they played "Fox and Goose," a form of tag in a big circle with a safe area in the center. Snowball fights were another popular activity.

Nelson remembers community square dances with fiddlers in the little school house with all the desks pushed against the wall. Music was part of his family life as well; his mother, Helen Louise Farmer Weber, and his father, Louis George Weber, played piano and saxophone in a neighborhood band.

Nelson believes Robert Leigh School was named for Robert Leigh Brown, a local landowner who arranged for the building of Mount Carmel Methodist Church and two large country homes on Highway 41, one the present home of Tom and Anna Dyer. The Browns probably donated the land for the neighborhood schoolhouse.

In 1951, schools in the Miami area were reorganized. More than 14 or 15 one room schools combined to form a new district. Among them were Robert Leigh, Herring, Fairville, Steel and Sunnyside as well as the town of Miami. Nelson recalls his father was on the school board that planned the reorganization; the planning required meetings until midnight two or three times a week for months.

"Everyone wanted the new building to be in their old district, and feelings were heated. It is a wonder there weren't some barn burnings; people were really mad!" Nelson said. He was in the first eighth grade class to graduate from the new Miami School on Highway 41 with 25 students in his class.

"There were no girls in Mount Carmel Methodist Church when I grew up. Mr. George Lorimer was a Sunday School teacher with six of us boys in the class. He put up with a lot. He often talked about 'the Pauline epistles'. As a kid, I always wondered who Pauline was because I had never read about her in the Bible," Nelson said.

Mount Carmel was an active congregation; they decided to jack up the building, and church members dug a basement by hand. "When it was finished, we thought we had the world by the tail—a kitchen in the basement!" An Easter breakfast cooked by I.G. Dyer became a popular annual event.

Even though Nelson's eighth grade class was large compared to Robert Leigh school, he was unprepared for the size of Marshall High School. "I was never so lost in all my life. It seemed to be a huge complex." Band and Future Farmers of America were important parts of his high school years.

Marching 15 miles in the American Royal Parade in Kansas City with the national F.F.A. band stands out in his memory.

Outside of school hours, a small band practiced at Mercy Academy playing for dances at the Catholic high school and Missouri Valley College. Performers, in addition to Nelson on his saxophone, were Wade and Ronnie Blum, Marvin Lickey, Norman Frazee, James Brown, Bob James and Jim Stone.

Jane was born in 1938 in Miami, Missouri, where her dad, Clarence George Shaw, had a barbershop. Before she started to school, Clarence and his wife, Jewell Harriet Simmons Shaw, moved to Marshall where he joined the Wells and Nicely Barbershop on the square, 52 East Arrow, presently Larry's Barber Shop. The slogan painted on the window read: "It pays to look Well and dress Nicely."

When Jane was eight or nine years old, she contracted polio, the dread disease of the forties and fifties. Hospitalizations at St. Luke's in Kansas City including surgery have blocked out many of her childhood memories. She recalls quarantine in a room with bars at the window and no visits with family because of contagion. Jane wore a brace on her right leg, and she was happy to be able to walk again but discouraged with the slight limp that remained.

Richard Kemm, the high school vocal music teacher, encouraged his students to sing solos and perform in ensembles. In high school, Jane had a lead part in the operetta, *The Fortuneteller*, playing the little gypsy. She said, "Mr. Kemm was a big influence in my life. He really encouraged you if he knew that you liked to sing."

Jane worked hard at her music lessons. Her brother, Jerry, was a gifted musician with perfect pitch. "I know he found it frustrating to hear me hit the wrong notes!" she said. Her earliest experience with First United Methodist Church was walking across the sanctuary to play the grand piano at Mrs. Storts' piano recitals. "I was filled with fear!" she said.

The Shaw family were members of First Baptist Church which has played an important role in Jane's life. Richard Kemm was the choir director for the congregation; music was an integral part of the church community. Jane remembers revivals and many loving Sunday School teachers.

After their marriage in 1959, Nelson and Jane were active together in First Baptist Church; Nelson taught the young married couples' class; their son and daughter grew up in the congregation. Jane, a soloist and accompanist, encouraged youth in music. She said, "Many young people learned to be musicians and several went on to become church organists."

Jane became a skilled organist when majoring in music education at Missouri Valley College. Dr. Claude Ficthorn, choir director at First United Methodist Church, taught organ and encouraged Jane to become organist at the Episcopal Church. His wife, Marguerite Ficthorn, was organist at First Baptist.

The Ficthorns, who were neighbors of the Shaws on Arrow Street, left detailed instructions for the organist at their funerals. Many years later, Jane played on both occasions. Mrs. Fichthorn had requested, "The Battle Hymn of the Republic" to close her service, saying, "Open up the stops and don't hold anything back!"

Nelson cannot remember when he was not a part of the farming operation on Highway 41. Long before he started school, he was in the fields when the Weber brothers, Adolph, George and Jake, farmed a section of land together.

Grandpa Jake put Nelson on his lap and taught him to drive a tractor while raking hay. Playing in straw stacks, Nelson watched the men throw bundles of wheat and oats into the Case threshing machine that ran from a flat belt 50 to 60 feet away from the tractor.

Nelson has an early memory of sitting on an old Wallace tractor with steel lug wheels playing with the hand clutch and pretending to steer while his father was cranking the engine in front. "Suddenly the motor started and the tractor lurched forward in gear! I thought I'd get my hide whipped off over that." By age eight or nine, he was driving a small Ford tractor by himself.

After the threshing machine years came a new improved Massey-Harris combine pulled by the Wallace tractor; it could cut standing grain and thresh it in one continuous operation. The age of farming with big machinery had begun.

"Every farm household used to be a self-sustaining unit—you didn't need to go to town except for salt, sugar, flour and a few supplies. I wish we could return to those days before the use of chemicals and specialization in two or three crops." After taking all the accounting classes offered by Missouri Valley College, Nelson went into the farming business with his father.

Jane, as a young wife, found moving to the country a change from living three or four blocks from the Marshall Square in the center of town. "Suddenly I could see forever—the sun, the landscape, approaching weather. I got used to cooking a big noon meal and to the irregular schedules of planting and harvesting," she said. Jane loves gardening; in recent years, she has done the farm bookkeeping.

In 1973, after meeting people at a local Lay Witness Mission, Nelson and Jane's spiritual lives took a turn-around, and they helped to establish Cornerstone, a non-denominational church in Chillicothe. Singing together and providing leadership, Nelson became an elder, and Jane, the pianist.

In 1999, First United Methodist Church approached Jane to be choir director, a position she held for five years. Equally comfortable with classical and contemporary music, she sometimes plays with "Testify", the praise band. Nelson teaches an adult Sunday School class. The two continue to sing together for special events and in the Chancel Choir.

Religious music composed by Bill Gaither has special appeal to Nelson and Jane. "He Touched Me," "The New Twenty-third Psalm" and "Fill My Cup" are favorites.

Psalm 91 is meaningful to both of them. Jane speaks of "meditating the Word" when times are difficult—putting your own voice into Scripture readings such as "Lord, I am walking through a valley." or "I will rejoice and be glad in this day." Nelson and Jane Weber encourage each other spiritually, and they strive to help others catch a vision of faith.

No Vacations
Muriel and Ed Weinreich   December 2006

The Weinreich house sits high on a hill overlooking farmland near Highway 41 four miles north of Marshall. Ed Weinreich said, "This house was built by my grandparents, Mary Elvina Plourde Weinreich and William Weinreich, in 1915. My parents, Arthur and Anna Watkins Weinreich, lived in a house across the highway from here, and I was born there in 1920.

"Our family came to Saline County from St. Louis 128 years ago; they purchased this farmland from the Sappingtons. All the Southerners who lived in these parts at the time pronounced our family name 'Wainwright', but the correct German pronunciation is 'Wine-rike'."

Ed continues with the history of his farm, "The Santa Fe Trail runs through the woods here, and you can still see the wagon ruts. From our driveway to the Wildcat Road is part of the original trail. We found a dug-out clay pit in the woods that early settlers had used to make bricks for building."

As young boys, Ed and his brother would hunt rabbits in the winter, dress them, pack them in a box and mail them to St. Louis to an aunt who paid them 15 cents apiece and sold them for 25 cents. "The cold weather kept them refrigerated until they got there," he said.

"I remember getting paid for carrying water to the threshing machine crew. Also when I was a kid, I would throw the wheat shocks onto the threshing machine belt that led to the separator to get the grain out."

"Don't ask him what he did for fun; he only knows about work," interjected his wife Muriel, an attractive lady with a droll sense of humor.

"Those were poor times," Ed said, "We just did everything we could to get by. I didn't finish high school because there was so much work at the farm; the thirties were hard years. I did not get any pay for the time I put in working on my dad's farm. We always had enough to eat because we raised our own food, but there was not anything extra.

"My grandmother had a huge garden; they told me she had sticks in the garden to hang lanterns on so that she could work before dawn and after the sun went down."

"I used to have a large garden and canned and preserved food," said Muriel. "Last season it was just a small square plot. Next year, I may only have a flower pot."

Muriel met Ed at a dance; and after they were married, she moved with Ed to a nearby house with her two daughters from a previous marriage, Virgie and Vickie. Muriel and Ed have two sons, Eddie and John, who continue the farming operation.

"I have been contented living in the country. I learned to drive in the field, just going back and forth. Driving made me much more independent," Muriel said.

"Next month we will have been married for 50 years," said Ed.

"If we make it that long," added Muriel.

Ed went to Robert Leigh School; the one room building still exists, but it is now used as a barn. "I was the janitor at $8 a month, but money became scarce and they lowered my salary to $6.40 a month. I kept the woodstove going, mopped and put oil on the floors to keep them from rotting."

Ed's dad was lucky enough to be able to purchase a 1925 Model T Ford for $500. "It had roll-up Eisenglass windows," Ed said. "Before that, we went everywhere in a horse and buggy. We went to Mount Carmel Methodist Church in our surrey with side curtains to keep the weather out."

The Weinreich family started going to First United Methodist Church when Ed was nine years old. The education building wing was just a big hole in the ground at that time, and his Sunday School class met in the room under the sanctuary.

Many changes have taken place in farming since Ed's youth. "Once I shucked 128 bushels by hand in one day. I weighed the corn at the elevator at Stanhope at the railroad station. My dad would drive the hogs to Stanhope and then get on the train with them to St. Louis. That is how he met my mother. She lived next door to my dad's parents in St. Louis."

"I used to enjoy riding my 1949 Harley Davidson motorcycle," Ed remembers. "I would take it to St. Louis to see my relatives and ride all over the city."

Years later, on a trip to St. Louis, he discovered workers were razing the cemetery where his great-grandparents were buried to turn it into a parking lot. Ed got his truck, rescued the tomb-stones and brought them back to the Weinreich home.

Ed said he has always been mechanically inclined. Although they started out farming with horses, Ed quickly took to using tractors. He liked tractor-pulling contests. In 1959, sponsored by the local Ford dealer, he won the Missouri state Two Row Ford Mounted Cornpicking Contest in Higginsville, Missouri, and went on to win the national contest in Straung, Indiana—a $500 prize.

"It was a lot of money for the times." said Ed, "but that tractor was nothing compared to the combine the boys use on the farm now—it has a 30-foot head and when they turn it in the field, it makes a round the size of a football field.

"I have worked on the farm my entire life," Ed said.

"Never a vacation," said Muriel.

"Too much work to be done," he responded.

Muriel Strohkirch Perkins was born in 1935 in Alton, Illinois, to Jeanette Lynch Strohkirch and Scott Phillip Strochkirch. Her family lived in an ethnic neighborhood of Mexican, Greek and

Italian families; she has fond memories of playing cards around the dining room table of an Italian grandmother.

"There were always six to eight kids and 'Nonna,' and we played rummy for pennies. We could buy a deck of cards for five cents. The ragman would give you five cents for rags, so we all had our cards to play.

"My grandchildren today go for the card deck the first thing when they come to visit." Muriel's family moved several times, and she went to school in Slater, Missouri. She attended the Catholic church with cousins as a child.

Muriel loved Mount Carmel Methodist Church, and she regrets the gradual deterioration of the building since it closed more than a decade ago. She and Ed would alternate Sundays attending Mount Carmel and the Methodist Church in Marshall. She has been active in the Lamplighter Class and in United Methodist Women.

For 17 years, Muriel sewed samples for display in Betty Sue Odell Simonson's business, one-of-a-kind patterns for clothing.

"How did you learn to sew?" I asked.

"I still don't know how," she said modestly. "Sometimes things just don't turn out the way you would like for them to." She credits Betty Sue for helping to improve her skills.

Muriel was a forty-year member of the Fairville Extension Club when it disbanded. She is a member of several organizations in Marshall, and she is presently learning to play duplicate bridge. Muriel often takes community classes, and she enjoys taking trips with tour groups. "I would love to learn something new every day."

"We have been blessed. We haven't had really hard times." Muriel said.

Ed, whose hearing impairment keeps him from joining into conversations easily, said, "I guess I am an optimistic person, I have just always thought things would work out somehow."

As I leave the Weinreich home, fall leaves are swirling around the two reclaimed tombstones in the fencerow by their long driveway. . .

William A. Weinreich   Vater   9 Marz 1826   5 April 1906
Anna M. Weinreich   Mutter   8 Juli 1826   24 Juli 1881

Writing as a Second Career
Peggy Wickizer October 2006

The Amish Story by Peggy Wickizer continues to be available for sale in Jamesport, Missouri. Tourists to the area seem to appreciate the information and stories in her book about the Amish community. Peggy, a member of Marshall Writers Guild, was a feature writer for 20 years for the *Chillicothe Constitution Tribune*.

"I met many interesting people," she said, "and I learned to use the computer. We would put the typed computer disk into a huge printer, four-foot by three-foot and 36 inches wide, and it would shoot out the paper in columns. Then I would write the headlines."

Newspaper work was a second career for Peggy. Her husband, Robert was postmaster at Lock Springs, Missouri, and Peggy served as assistant postmaster. She retired from the job when he retired as she was his leave replacement, and it had been impossible to take vacations. She took a folder of her writing to the newspaper and was hired as feature writer.

"I have always liked writing. For my thirtieth birthday, my husband bought me a Royal portable typewriter because he knew I loved to write." Peggy showed me a copy of an article she wrote for the November 11, 1973, edition of the *Constitution Tribune* about her own experiences, "World War II: A Bride's View."

Peggy Broaddous was married to Robert Wickizer in April 1942, and he was drafted in December of 1942. She remembers he was sent initially to Mineral Wells, Texas, and she did not see him for three months. Finally, she took the 16-hour trip by train and bus to Texas to find that Robert had only a six-hour pass.

"After Mineral Wells, he went to West Point in New York, became a specialist in the M-1 rifle and stayed there until the war was over. Housing for wives was scarce so I stayed in Missouri with my parents, Bessie Helen Phillips Broaddous and Dee Porter Broaddous. I made nineteen 36-hour trips on the train from Kansas City to New York!

"My mother worked in a defense plant testing radio crystals for airplanes. After Baby Michael was born, I would meet her at the bus stop and hand her the baby, and I would go to work the next shift to earn enough money for the train trip to New York. Eventually Robert found living quarters for us 20 miles from the base. The allotment for a spouse was $80 a month and rent was $40. He came home on an overnight pass every fourth night. When he went out on training sessions in tents for a month, the baby and I would return to Kansas City."

Life was considerably more peaceful after the war when Robert was appointed Postmaster at Lock Springs, Missouri, a town of 85 people halfway between Jamesport and Chillicothe, Missouri. The Wickizers moved to Robert's family farm located about two miles from Lock Springs.

Peggy, born in 1922, lived in downtown Chillicothe as a child in an apartment above her father's shoe repair shop. She was educated in Chillicothe Public Schools. She recalls playing the flute in high school band and orchestra, taking bus trips to special performance events and marching in the American Royal parade. Peggy attended Chillicothe United Methodist Church and was a member of the Epworth League, a youth organization.

After graduating from high school she worked as a secretary in the business office of Chillicothe Business College before joining two girl friends in Kansas City where she was a bookkeeper in a downtown shop that installed thermostats.

No car was necessary because she could walk to work. Her future husband lived in the same apartment building as one of her friends. After attending the University of Missouri in

Columbia for a year, Robert Wickizer worked for Montgomery Ward in Kansas City.

Peggy remembers the beginning of the war that brought such major changes to their lives. Newsboys selling papers on street corners called out the headlines, "Pearl Harbor Has Been Bombed!"

Following their post-war move to Lock Springs, Peggy was quite active in the Lock Springs United Methodist Church; she served as treasurer of the congregation. Music continued to be a special interest, and she became a soloist, singing at funerals. She remembers singing "Crossing the Bar," a traditional funeral hymn using the poem written by Alfred, Lord Tennyson. The words are very meaningful to Peggy.

Sunset and evening star,
And one clear call for me!
And may there be no moaning of the bar
When I put out to sea.
-Music by Charles Hubert Hastings Parry

Peggy's life took a dramatic change in 1994 when Robert died after a long battle with cancer; they had been married for 52 years. Peggy managed alone on the farm for several years. She had lived on the farm for 45 years when she and one of the farm cats, Stubby, moved to Marshall in 2001. Stubby seems to enjoy life in town, taking a post by the window to watch neighborhood activities from a comfortable chair.

Peggy was ready for the change because mowing the one-acre lawn and general upkeep had become a burden. Sadly, the twelve remaining Methodists at Lock Springs decided to close the church after she left.

Being a part of First United Methodist Church in Marshall has helped Peggy with the transition. "The people welcomed me with open arms. I felt at home immediately." She participates in the Keystone Sunday School Class and in United Methodist Women.

On the day I visited Peggy, her cozy bungalow on Eastwood was filled with the aroma of baking ham. She and her daughter, Becky Porter, were planning to take food to a family friend and help her with a garage sale.

In one corner of the dining room, Peggy has an office area with her computer. She continues to write regularly; reading biographies is one of her interests. Evidence of her active mind is the thoughtful letters that she sometimes writes to the editor of the local paper about community matters.

Although Peggy has health problems and walks with a cane, she continues to think beyond herself; she is involved with the world around her.

Special Friends with a Caring Spirit
Donna and Eddie Zahn   November 2006

Ed Zahn says he was drafted in 1960, "at the end of a gun," and he learned to cook on a coal stove at cook school in Fort Leonard Wood, Missouri. He became First Cook for the Little John Missile outfit at Fort Sill, Oklahoma; the Fort Sill unit was one of two in the Army which conducted training for Little John Missle units in other countries. Military cooks worked 24 hours on and 24 hours off, cooking food for 140 to 160 men and baking pies, cakes and cookies from scratch.

Several years after his military discharge, Ed was "Cook of the Week" in the *Marshall Democrat News*. He is quoted as saying, "The government figured they had about $8000 invested in each man's training. Cleanliness was strict. We cut up GI soap and boiled it in a ten-gallon pot with cut-up lemons. I remember we had red tile floor with grout in-between the tiles, and when it was scrubbed, it was spotless."

For many years, Ed cooked for the Methodist Men's Club at First United Methodist Church, and he originated the annual "Souper Bowl Sunday" in January to raise money for utilities for needy persons in the community.

Ed was born in 1937 to Audrey Henley Zahn and Virgil Zahn who lived on a farm on the northwest edge of the Marshall city limits. He was named for his grandfather, Edward Zahn, an interesting individual who at the turn of the century decided to make an around-the-world trip.

Carrying his bicycle, he took a train to San Francisco, caught a steamship to Australia, bicycled across the continent and completed the journey in the other direction—India, Egypt, Europe and back to New York City. Ed possesses a journal kept by his grandfather of his trip.

Engaged to John Ella Waters of Corder, Missouri, the senior Edward Zahn purchased land in Saline County to be nearer to his future bride. He was a farmer with vision, and he organized the Farm Bureau in Saline County and in the state of Missouri. Mr. Zahn invented a movable fence to keep his sheep in the pasture. He speculated that one day nitrogen would be taken from the air to make fertilizer; anhydrous ammonia is just such a process.

Ed Zahn, the younger, purchased adjoining property to his grandfather's original land and farmed for 40 years. About farming, he said, "It is a good life; you are close to nature, and farming is rewarding."

"Did you find it frustrating to be dependent on the weather conditions?" I asked.

"You take the cards that are dealt to you," Ed said. "God's in control."

In 1991, Ed rented out his farm and became a member of the staff at Campbell-Lewis Funeral Home. Now retired, he works part-time occasionally for the funeral home.

Ed attended Northwest Grade School. He remembers Ed "Smittie" Smith, the school custodian who kept the coal-fired furnaces going. Miss Lena Moore, Miss Kate Koch and Miss Harmon Rectenwalde were favorite teachers. Ed's mother, Audrey Zahn, helped to get the hot lunch program started in the Marshall Public Schools.

At Marshall High School, Ed was a member of F.F.A. Wood and Huston Bank owned a farm which they let F.F.A. members plant and harvest. With the profits from the farm, the boys and their teacher, Ray McClure, took trips every summer.

"We took a school bus and coolers with food; and every night we camped and cooked. We went to Detroit, Canada, and Niagara Falls on one trip; our plans to go to New York City changed when one of our group, R.E. Weinreich, had to have an emergency appendectomy. On another trip, we traveled to Arkansas; Biloxi, Mississippi; and New Orleans."

Ed met his wife, the slim and stylish Donna Igo, when he stopped by John Deere Implement Agency one day for a coffee break. Donna was bookkeeper and accountant for Deems Equipment dealership on Highway 41 adjacent to the home of Ed's parents. Donna lived in Napton, Missouri; she said the population was "72 people counting dogs and cats."

Donna was born in 1943 at the old Putnam Hospital on Yerby Street in Marshall, now an apartment building. Napton was the center of life for the Igo family when Donna grew up. At Napton Grade School, she was in a class with three other children.

Her parents took Donna and her brother to Zoar Baptist Church regularly. Donna's mother, Emily Elaine Staub Igo, taught Sunday School and Vacation Bible School; her father, Samuel Dennis Igo, was Sunday School Superintendent and also taught Sunday School. Donna remembers two week long summer revivals with singing and preaching.

In 4-H, Donna took woodworking and built a lawn chair under the leadership of J. Logan Buntin, a well-known, local craftsman who is remembered for ice-skating when possible, from Napton to Nelson on Salt Fork Creek until he was 90 years old. Mrs. Myrl Buntin, his wife, gave Donna piano lessons in the seventh and eighth grades.

Donna rode the school bus to Marshall High School, taking secretarial and bookkeeping classes in Cooperative Education taught by J.D. Nichols. She remembers taking Driver's Education from Coach W.H. Lyons; when she was a student helper in School Superintendent Armin Bueker's office, she helped to count the lunch money. In her senior year, she was chosen Cooperative Education Queen.

Following high school, Donna took a bookkeeping course in Kansas City, worked briefly at Rose and Buckner clothing store and then began a 44-year career with Deems Farm Equipment where she is currently employed.

"The job has changed several times. I started out keeping books by hand then it changed to key punch data processing on a big adding machine. Next, we used Texas Instrument equipment, and information was typed into a cassette player.

"I flipped a switch at the end of the day, and the information went to Kansas City where the order was filled and the inventory was kept up; a printout of the day's business was returned to us. The next phase was having an in-house computer for our records.

"But the biggest changes have been in the size of equipment. Eddie bought a John Deere 60 two-cylinder tractor in the 1950's for $2000. Now a big John Deere tractor sells for $200,000!"

After their marriage, Donna joined First United Methodist Church. She and Eddie were Methodist Youth Fellowship sponsors. "We convinced the church that it was all right to have a dance for teenagers in the basement—that was a first!" she said. Donna has been Chairman of the Council of Ministries and Superintendent of the Sunday School.

At present, Ed is Chairman of the Administrative Board; he served as district lay leader as well as on the Conference Episcopacy Committee. Ed remembers the investment his family has made in the church in the past. "My dad was Sunday School Superintendent for 25 years, and my mother taught Sunday School for years.

"My mother and my Aunt Ruth Zahn were very active in United Methodist Women. Aunt Zelma and Uncle Volney Ashford were key figures in the church. Uncle Volney would bring the Missouri Valley College football team to church when he was the coach. The team took turns visiting other churches on Sundays as well."

Donna has played piano duets with the organ at the late morning church service for 35 years; one of her favorite piano numbers is "Because He Lives." Ed recalls the music at revivals when Reverend George Dent, Pasadena, Texas, would come to sing; "He Touched Me" was Ed's personal favorite.

Ed and Donna were special friends to Mary Sheetz Riley who asked them to help her with her personal affairs as she got older. They took her to appointments with the doctor and assisted her when she had surgery and health problems. Mary and Ed had a jovial relationship; she always called him "Buddy Boy." The Zahns helped her with the closing of her house and the transition of moving to Mar-Saline Manor.

Ed and Donna demonstrate a caring spirit in the community. Donna feels she is indebted to her family for the foundation for life and values they instilled in her.

Ed is a practical man who believes that you "get out of life just what you put into it." With his unusual sense of humor, he appreciates a quote from the late Bill Vaughn in his "Starbeams" column in the *Kansas City Star*, "Remember the thirteenth beatitude: 'Blessed is the man who expecteth nothing, for he shall not be disappointed.'"

A Soul That Sings

Mary Anna Zimmerman   May 2006

Mary Anna Zimmerman remembers dragging a sled behind her on snowy days when she walked one and one-half miles to Salt Branch School just so they could slide at recess and during the noon hour.

Mary and Kitty Swisher lived on the road that led to school, and Mary Anna made a regular stop at the home of these ladies to eat cookies and visit. On Sunday afternoons, she and her friends, Joanne Merchant Brown and Mary Elizabeth Lewis Mackler rode horseback for miles along country roads.

Was this as much fun as she makes it sound? Or is it that joy just shines through Mary Anna? She tells me about all the good things she enjoys at Big Bend Retreat in Slater where she is confined because of hip and knee problems which have slowed her down.

Mary Anna was born to Florence Estelle Morrow Prugh and Fred Prugh on Watermill Road in rural Saline County. Morrow Street in Marshall was named for her great grandfather. Mary Anna has lived all her life in the same general area east of Marshall. She misses her beagle dog and her flock of chickens on the Zimmerman farm. She was keeping up with feeding and gathering eggs by using a John Deere Gator to ride from her back door to the hen house until she began to have increasing problems getting around.

Mary Anna went to Shiloh Methodist Church as a child. She could cut through the fields straight back to the church on Highway 41 directly behind the Prugh farm.

"I loved that church. During the week sometimes, I would go over and hunt for morel mushrooms behind the building. It was a big congregation; they had wonderful ice cream socials outside in the summer time. My mother went with me when I turned 16 and I could drive."

Mary Anna chose to go to Napton High School; she could have gone to Marshall, but she wanted to play basketball. They played on outdoor courts against Miami, Malta Bend, Blackwater and Nelson; Napton High School was unique in having a gym large enough for a basketball court.

After she graduated from high school, she stayed at home and helped her parents on the farm. "I have always been a big talker, and I walked all over the place to visit neighbors," she said.

Mary Anna was dating Elmer Zimmerman who also lived in the neighborhood; he was one of a family of five children whose names all began with "E"—Elsie, Elmer, Earl, Elwood, and Ethyl. It was a long courtship because he had no money or car. He lived with the Will Mallman family, and he worked as a hired hand for seven years at a dollar a day.

Mary Anna remembers many good times. "There were square dances in barns; Hardeman School owned a wood platform which people borrowed to have dances out on their lawns. Mary Elizabeth's big brothers, John Hall and Leonard Lewis, always saw that she and I had a ride to events. Brownie French along with others played the fiddle and the guitar, and the dances had live music."

Before they were married in 1947, Elmer saved enough money to buy a combine, planning to make money doing harvesting for other farmers. Then he went to Sedalia and bought a used Allis Chalmers tractor that he drove home in cold weather. To this day, he is fascinated with antique farm equipment; he owns a steam engine.

Elmer joined Mary Anna at Shiloh Methodist Church. He was treasurer of the church board until it closed in 1984. Shiloh members decided to raze the church instead of letting it tumble down in disrepair.

"I was Methodist until they burned my church down, Honey," she said, "Then we joined Cumberland Presbyterian because we wanted to be part of a smaller congregation."

Elmer is a member of the Board of Trustees at Cumberland Presbyterian Church. The Zimmermans especially enjoy their pastor, Reverend Randy Shannon, as he has family connections to the old Shiloh congregation; his great-aunt, Miss Edith Eddy, and his mother, Dora Alice Arni Shannon, were members at Shiloh.

At 85, Elmer does not waste much time; he works regularly as a carpenter. For 57 years, he has been community leader for Clay Center 4-H Club. Elmer has served on the Saline County Fair Board for decades, and he is a longtime member of the National Corn Shucking Association and the Saline County Antique Machinery Club.

Elmer visits Mary Anna as often as he can at Big Bend; they will soon celebrate their sixtieth wedding anniversary. Mary Anna is a ray of sunshine as she chats with rest home employees and other residents. Her love of the out-of-doors is reflected in her favorite hymn, "How Great Thou Art." Mary Anna is an individual whose "soul sings."

Then sings my soul, my Savior God to thee;
How great Thou art, how great Thou art!
Carl Boberg

Assorted Memories

Memories from New Mexico
Mary Hains Jones in a letter to Carol Raynor

I understand that you are doing a book on the "olden days" at the Methodist Church. First United Methodist Church was a very important factor in our family when I was growing up. My mother arranged flowers from her garden for church services and was very active in the Philathea Sunday School Class.

For several years, the Philathea Class published a cookbook. In the 1925 cookbook, I counted a membership of 90 women; my mother, Edna Lawless Hains, was president of the class that year. A.R. James, who lived in the brick house to the west by First Baptist Church, was the class teacher.

The cookbook contained poems and household hints at the beginning of each section. "A good dinner sharpens the wit, while it softens the heart." Some of the household hints appear quaint in today's world. "To remove blackberry stains from hands, do not use soap, but wet hands and hold over lighted matches. For burns, use lime water and sweet oil, well-mixed in equal parts, put in a bottle and shake well, apply when needed."

Mother was born November 18, 1889, and died April 17, 1987. Because she was always cooking something for church, my husband and I designated funds for new kitchen cabinets in her memory. My father, Rosier Hains, worked until he was 80 as owner and editor of the *Marshall Democrat News*. Of course, my cousin Kathryn Lawless Bagnell was "Mrs. Kitchen Director" for many years!

My family lived in Marshall for five years when my husband, Ralph Homer Jones, was a physician in the medical practice of Dr. James Reid and Dr. Richard Kennedy. I met Ralph when we were in kindergarten at Eastwood School.

We were married in First United Methodist Church on September 3, 1944. The temperature was 103 degrees and the candles leaned from the heat! Our minister was Reverend Willis L. Perryman, and Bishop Ivan Lee Holt happened to be in town that day so he conducted part of the ceremony. My new husband complained because he had to pay two preachers!

Docia Trigg Cooney
By Marvin N. Wilhite

The following information is taken from articles in the January 20 and January 27, 2005, editions of *Slater Main Street News*, "You've Come a Long Way, Baby," and is used with permission of *Slater Main Street News*.

Women such as Docia Trigg Cooney who resided in Saline County, Missouri, most of her life, worked with national leaders such as Lucretia Mott, Elizabeth Cady Stanton and Susan B. Anthony to achieve the right to vote.

Docia lived to see her hard work become reality, but the others did not. Cady Stanton died in 1902, seventeen years before Congress passed a Woman's Suffrage Constitutional Amendment by a narrow margin in 1919. Susan B. Anthony died in 1906, fourteen years before the amendment was ratified by the States in August, 1920.

Docia A. Trigg Cooney was born April 20, 1850, according to one source. Marvin N. Wilhite, historian for the Saline County Historical Society, says that other sources suggest she was born in 1856 (census records). Her age is not important; who she was and what she accomplished is what matters. All women living today owe a great deal, not just to Docia, but to all those who fought for the rights of women.

Docia Trigg was the daughter of John A. Trigg and Amanda Harette Harvey. She was born on the old Trigg homestead southeast of Marshall, Missouri, near what is now known as the town of Nelson.

John Trigg was born in 1815, in Virginia, but as a small child he moved with his parents to Tennessee, then to Alabama and finally to Chariton County, Missouri, and resided not far from the town of Glasgow. His parents made sure that he received a thorough education that he later provided for his own children as exemplified by the education Docia received.

Unfortunately, it is not possible to find out the details of Docia's early education because all the public school records of Saline County were destroyed in 1864 in the Civil War. But Docia did attend the historic Young Ladies Seminary located in Arrow Rock, Missouri, and later, the Boston Conservatory of Music in Boston, Massachusetts.

One can speculate that it was in Boston that Docia first came into contact with the Women's Suffrage Movement; although, some have suggested a later date—when Susan B. Anthony journeyed to Pittsburg, Kansas.

Docia married James Cooney in Marshall, Missouri, on December 21, 1882. James A. Cooney was born in Ireland, August 26, 1848; at the age of six, he traveled to the United States with his parents who settled in Troy, New York. He lost both of his parents two years later. Little is known about his childhood except that he worked on a farm and received an education by his own efforts, going to school and teaching at the same time. For a short time, he was a student at the Knoxville Academy in Knoxville, Illinois, and later attended the State University in Columbia, Missouri, now the University of Missouri.

During the years 1873 to 1875, Mr. Cooney was the high school principal at Sturgeon, Missouri. It was in Sturgeon that he met, married and lost his first wife after a brief marriage of only four months. After this tragic event, Cooney moved to Marshall, Missouri, and soon afterward was admitted to the bar. From that time forward, he was prominently connected with the legal and political interests of Saline County and central Missouri.

Cooney was a partner for a number of years in the law practice of L.W. Scott. From 1876 to 1880, he was Justice of Peace for the township of Marshall, and in 1880, was elected Probate Judge of Saline County. In 1882, he was elected Prosecuting Attorney and re-elected in 1884. In 1886, Judge Cooney was elected to Congress from the Seventh District and was re-elected in 1896 and 1900. He served out his term and retired in the spring of 1903.

The Honorable James A. Cooney died November 16, 1904, in his home at 528 East Eastwood after a brief bout with pneumonia.

During Judge Cooney's term in Congress in 1896, Mrs. Cooney had made contact with Susan B. Anthony. The gathering represented in the photograph on the following page represents the first Women's Suffrage meeting held in Marshall and Saline County between the years of 1890 and 1895. The poster on the Susan B. Anthony Balcony reflects information associated with voting, so this is a political meeting.

Mr. and Mrs. James Cooney are sitting on the far right on the balcony. Originally, it was thought that the Susan B. Anthony Balcony was named because Ms. Anthony was in the picture. However later research found that structures were given the name "Susan B. Anthony Balcony" because she spoke from this kind of balcony to dispense the message that women should be allowed to vote.

The balcony was erected in the Cooney's spacious back lawn around one of the grand old maple trees where Marshall groups met and held picnics and parties; the discussion would eventually turn to politics or subjects dealing with a civic movement, especially the right of women to vote. Docia was a woman who was intensely interested in these matters.

Docia Cooney died September 8, 1941, almost 37 years after the death of her husband. The legacy she left deserves our consideration because she has been described as one of Marshall's widely known citizens. The photograph is "like footprints on the page of time" enforcing the concept that "we cannot know or understand where we are going unless we know or understand where we have been."

The first Women's Suffrage meeting held in Marshall and
Saline County between the years of 1890 and 1895 at the
home of Docia Cooney. Dorothy Carter and her sisters
performed on this balcony in the early 1900s.
(see "Eastwood Memories")

In An Ivy League of Her Own

Elsie Galatas

On the first day of March, Paul Galatas pulled his chair close to his mother and posed a simple question: "Mother, is there any one area in your life that has left you unfulfilled?"

Elsie Galatas thought for a moment. By and large, her years of Christian service and making ends meet as a Methodist minister's wife had been filled with contentment. But there was a gnawing piece of unfinished business, something she rarely mentioned. Her greatest regret, she told her son, was that she never received a degree for her graduate work at Yale.

Paul, of Liberty, had known what her answer would be. He smiled and handed her a typed letter. It said that finally, as the result of Paul's prodding, Yale officials had combed through old records and determined that she did indeed earn her graduate degree in 1928—72 years ago.

Elsie sat stunned, then said, "Oh, my."

Six weeks later, just four days after she turned 102 years old, the dean of the Yale University Divinity School presented her with a master's in religion, a framed document written in Latin.

"I was deeply impressed with her," Dean Richard J. Wood said. "I would love to be that sharp at 102." He had traveled from the East Coast to Higginsville, Missouri, where Elsie lives at the Meyer Care Center, part of John Knox Village East.

In the center's activity room more than 100 people showered elsie with cards, flowers and good wishes. Wood emphasized to the crowd that Yale was granting Elsie an earned degree, not an honorary degree.

"It's a remarkable distinction," he said. "The university awards honorary degrees very sparingly, and in some ways it's more important and more significant that she received an earned degree. There's a big difference."

At Yale, administrators were intrigued with this unusual case of a brilliant scholar who completed her course work and master's thesis but left in 1928 without a degree because of an unjust, unfortunate twist of fate. Her story caught the attention of Linda Koch Lorimer, vice president and secretary of Yale University, who did the detective work to find Elsie's old records.

"I was so impressed by her story and how pioneering she had been," Lorimer said. "To think, when she was growing up, it was quite unusual for women to go to college, much less pursue higher education and to come east to school."

At the care center where Elsie lives, the degree now hangs on her wall, not far from her own iris paintings. She has struggled in recent years with a hip replacement, pneumonia, a broken hip and shoulder and a profound loss of hearing. So receiving the degree has been a great boost, a renewal of sorts.

It's given her family reason to pull old scrapbooks from her closet, to pore over photos of Yale professors in their three-piece suits, looking beyond reproach. It's given her reason to pull out her shiny Corona manual typewriter, still in her closet, the one she used to type her master's thesis. She can call up details of those years in an instant—names, dates, places—even though it all happened in the 1920s. A lifetime ago.

Elsie Jeffers Galatas was born in another century, April 11, 1898, around the time horseless carriages were being developed. No one had heard of ice-cream cones, the Wright brothers or world war. Her father, Charles Jeffers, was a school superintendent and later bought real estate, and she remembers that her mother, Fannie Jeffers, was a kindhearted woman who had taught school.

From the beginning, Elsie was an exceptional student. She committed classical poetry to memory, poetry that she would use the rest of her life. "She taught many of those poems to me over the kitchen sink," said her daughter, Ellen Schroeder of Kearney, Nebraska.

Elsie graduated from high school in 1915, graduated with honors from Missouri Wesleyan College in Cameron in 1919, then taught high school language classes. But, she said matter-of-factly, "I wanted to give my life to Christian service."

So she enrolled in the Kansas City National Training School for Christian Workers. After two years she had earned the titles of "home missionary" and "deaconess," a woman trained for pastoral work. Old photos show her and her deaconess friends dressed in the required outfits: dark, drop-waist dresses with white frilly collars.

She was happily occupied as a deaconess working with a church in Philadelphia when she was recommended for a full scholarship for graduate work at Yale, an astounding offer. She arrived at Yale in 1925, only five years after women had earned the right to vote.

"They admitted women fairly grudgingly," Wood said, because the attitude then was that women should feel lucky to be there.

She did well in her two years of course work. But when it was time to work on her master's thesis, her proposals were rejected. Instead she was directed to work on a faculty member's project, analyzing a book and preparing it for use in Sunday Schools.

Paul the Dauntless, Elsie said now without hesitation, "by Basil Matthews."

After a year of work, she presented her thesis, but her adviser surprised her by saying the material needed to be tested in Sunday Schools. Because of the time and expense involved, that would have been nearly impossible for her.

There was another factor: Elsie had met a young man at Yale, a certain Clinton Galatas, who had graduated and become a Methodist minister. "He was waiting for me to marry him," Elsie said.

And so she left Yale for Missouri in 1928, three years of work behind her, no degree in hand. Perhaps it was not a case of terrible abuse, Wood said, but it was certainly unjust.

Ultimately there was no way to reconstruct what happened. Elsie's Yale records were available, but the thesis could not be found, and of course, the professors were long gone.

But Linda Lorimer took a different direction. She searched for transcripts from Elsie's work at the Kansas City National Training School for Christian Workers, which no longer exists. Lorimer's assistant found the records stored in Tennessee. Those transcripts and Elsie's Yale records were measured against the Divinity School's current standards for awarding degrees, and the faculty and Yale trustees agreed that Elsie had more than met the requirements.

"It was quite pleasing to me that we could honor and recognize a pioneer in the study of religious education by a woman early in the century," Lorimer said. "It was quite pleasing to take a little extra effort to honor someone who was a trailblazer."

If Elsie was a trailblazer, she never let on. Her friends and family remember her as "very caring," thrifty," "so loving," "always busy" and "extremely intelligent." They remember the banana bread she brought when she visited, the grapes she grew in her backyard, the way she helped divide a special fern. They remember Elsie and her husband hunting for antiques and how she could name all the birds that visited her yard.

What they don't remember is much mention of her remarkable education. "I knew she had some kind of religious training," one friend said.

If there had been a Yale script on how to live a Christian life of service, it might look like Elsie's years after leaving the university.

She took on a traditional role at her husband's side, raising their two children and caring for people in the Missouri congregations he led. She became an educator in her own right, establishing church school programs and assisting with many conferences and youth programs.

Her daughter, Ellen, remembers Elsie as a loving, hands-on mother who learned to stretch a small income during the Depression with great "financial discipline." Food came from the garden, and raising chickens, canning vegetables and making grape jelly were part of the yearly ritual.

"One of the big favorites was mint jelly," Paul said. Both Paul and Ellen say their mother had a disdain for pretense or anything extravagant. Earrings, for example.

Although restraint was the rule, Paul and Ellen remember the rare splurge. A set of encyclopedias, for example, or the car travels around the United States on a shoestring budget, a sack of peanut butter and tomato sandwiches in hand. There was the new red bicycle Paul got when he was about 12. "I can remember the look on my mother's face," he said.

Ellen had piano, vocal and speech lessons while growing up, and when she went off to college, her mother said she must have a new wardrobe. "She spent more on those clothes than she had spent on her own clothing for years and years," Ellen said. "I still almost cry when I think about that."

In later years Elsie was quite active in community organizations such as PEO and the American Association of University Women. She also pursued her passions in life—button collecting, stamp collecting and growing wildflowers.

Elsie and Galatas served churches in four Missouri towns, and he was also superintendent for a Methodist district. When his health declined, they moved to John Knox Village East. He died in 1987 at the age of 89.

Until last year, Elsie had her own apartment and did much of her own cooking. Now she lives in the assisted living area and continues a life of discipline. She reads the newspaper each day. At mealtime she uses her walker to make her way to the dining room, and while the residents wait, she asks if they've heard about the latest news.

She's quite careful about what she eats, careful to get plenty of fruits and vegetables and to drink plenty of fluids, said Jeanie Adkins, director of the center.

Her daughter has enrolled her in a Harvard study that is looking at the genetics of longevity, the reason centenarians live so long. But to those who know her, this is no mystery. "She is a strong person," said Lucy Murphy, a former neighbor in Chillicothe, Missouri. "Obviously you don't live to be 102 unless you're a strong person."

Note: Dr. Clinton B. Galatas and his wife, Elsie, were in the ministry at First United Methodist Church in Marshall from 1934 to 1936 and from 1949 to 1963.